INTERNATIONAL SERIES OF MONOGRAPHS IN
PURE AND APPLIED BIOLOGY

Division: **MODERN TRENDS IN PHYSIOLOGICAL SCIENCES**

GENERAL EDITORS: P. ALEXANDER and Z. M. BACQ

VOLUME 16

UNSATURATED FATTY ACIDS IN ATHEROSCLEROSIS

SECOND EDITION

UNSATURATED FATTY ACIDS
IN ATHEROSCLEROSIS

SECOND EDITION

BY

J. ENSELME

*Professeur à la Faculté de Mixte de Médecine
et de Pharmacie de Lyon
France*

TRANSLATED BY

R. D. PLUMMER

PERGAMON PRESS

OXFORD · LONDON · EDINBURGH · NEW YORK
TORONTO · SYDNEY · PARIS · BRAUNSCHWEIG

Pergamon Press Ltd., Headington Hill Hall, Oxford
4 & 5 Fitzroy Square, London W.1
Pergamon Press (Scotland) Ltd., 2 & 3 Teviot Place, Edinburgh 1
Pergamon Press Inc., Maxwell House, Fairview Park, Elmsford, New York 10523
Pergamon of Canada Ltd., 207 Queen's Quay West, Toronto 1
Pergamon Press (Aust.) Pty. Ltd., 19a Boundary Street, Rushcutters Bay,
N.S.W. 2011, Australia
Pergamon Press S.A.R.L., 24 rue des Écoles, Paris 5^e
Vieweg & Sohn GmbH, Burgplatz 1, Braunschweig

First edition 1962
Second edition 1969

Library of Congress Catalog Card No. 69-17317 H

PRINTED IN GREAT BRITAIN BY THOMAS NELSON (PRINTERS) LTD., LONDON AND EDINBURGH
08 013060 7

Contents

Preface

THE increasing number of catastrophes caused by thrombosis in the arteries of the brain, the lower limbs and, most frequent of all, the coronaries worries the lay public and fascinates the doctor. It is a question which claims the attention of biologists and especially biochemists since observations from animal experiments should throw light on the pathological mechanism of these accidents and indicate the possibility of preventive treatment.

At autopsy two features may be apparent. At the site of the thrombosis, the wall may show a lesion which appears to be the primary cause of the coagulation. Most often this lesion is due to a condition still poorly defined: atherosclerosis. It is this condition that the biochemist is able to investigate freely, and this will be the field of our study and the subject of this book. More rarely the lesion does not appear to be primary but secondary to a previous obstruction. In some cases hardly any mural lesions are seen. In these two circumstances the abnormal coagulation depends on an irregularity of the blood which it is up to the haematologist to define. We will not consider this since it is outside our field.

Study of the original arterial lesion, the atherosclerotic lesion, raises a physico-chemical or chemical problem which must be solved and this will be discussed at some length. As this abnormality may belong to one of the regions of biochemistry as yet incompletely described we will investigate various compounds which make up our bodies.

All the various metabolic problems need to be considered, which obliges us to extend the field of our investigations in this second edition. Some chapters have therefore been added. The chapters which made up the first edition have sometimes been extensively revised in the light of knowledge since acquired.

Introduction

SEVERAL quite distinct points will be examined:

I. Definitions

We will concern ourselves first with establishing some definitions of words which we shall use. Definitions often vary from one author to another so that the meaning we adopt needs to be clearly understood to facilitate the reading of this book.[1]

A. *Definition of Atheroma*

This word already used by Greek authors tends to be defined from the work of Haller in 1735.[2] It concerns the plaques or nodules containing viscous material. Turndull in 1915 gives it the following definition: "Atheroma is a degeneration which affects, and is almost confined to, the intima. It is found in both the elastic and the muscular arteries, but is more common in the large elastic. The degeneration is characterized by the accumulation of debris, which is at first fatty and is later frequently impregnated by calcium. Intimal fibrosis is merely a modification of atheroma."

B. *Definition of Arteriosclerosis*

This word which literally means hardening of the arteries was proposed in 1829 by Lobstein[3] of Strasbourg, in the following terms:

> This illness consists of an increase in the thickness and hardness of the arterial walls without ossification. This thickening is usually very considerable, so that if the walls of the artery are half a line thick in their natural state then in this illness they become a line and a half and even two lines. Examination of the internal surface of the artery shows it to be uneven and knobbly similar to the external surface of bones affected by osteosclerosis. Its constituent knobs are separated from one another by an immense number of furrows which do not have any regular arrangement and render the internal surface of the arterial tube uneven. Independently of this arrangement the artery shows also a change in its colour, this is pale yellow, alternating with red-brown.

C. *Definition of Atherosclerosis*

In 1904 Marchand[4] of Leipzig at the congress of Wiesbaden proposed the term atherosclerosis (literally: soft hardening, which is contradictory) quite close to the previous definition but implying some differences and particularly those indicated by Aschoff who remarked that the conception of Marchand indicates the presence of calcification in the media. This term has been widely

1

used but everyone understands it in his own way, we will adopt the definition given in 1958 by the O.M.S. "It comprises a variable lesion in the intima of the arteries, consisting of focal accumulations of lipids, complex glucides and calcium deposits. The whole is accompanied by changes in the media." It is with this meaning that we shall use the word. Wherever possible we indicate the intensity of those changes which are only present in advanced cases.

The O.M.S. definition also includes blood deposits, but these would appear to indicate a complication.

II. Experimental Forms in Animals

In animals some lesions have been produced which more or less resemble the spontaneous lesions of atherosclerosis. It is necessary to take into account the fact that certain animals such as the chicken present some spontaneous lesions like man, which does not make it easy to differentiate between the pathological and the induced lesion.

The animals used are mainly: the rabbit, which has practically no spontaneous lesions; more rarely the chicken, which has frequent spontaneous lesions; and most rarely the dog, which needs to have its thyroid wholly or partly inactivated by surgery or antithyroid drugs. Exceptionally, because of the practical difficulties, monkeys are used.

The products administered to obtain lesions of the atherosclerotic type are quite varied. In 1909 Ignatowski administered meat extract enriched with egg yolk and milk and obtained plaques in the aortic intima. In 1911 and 1912 Stukkey[5] stressed the very important role of milk and Chalatow showed that a cholesterol deposition occurred easily recognized by the birefringent droplets of cholesterol esters deposited in the liver of the rabbit. In 1912 and 1914 Anitschkow in collaboration with Chalatow[6] administered cholesterol as a suspension in sunflower oil to rabbits and obtained deposition of cholesterol in the intima of the aorta. The cholesterol deposits grew larger, occasionally inducing degenerative lesions in the intima.

Synthetic diets have also been used since then, one example of this is the diet of Wigand (see Table I).

These diets allow the introduction of products one wishes to test for atherosclerogenic properties; it is in this way that the action of the saturated fatty acids has been discovered.

The results are relatively easy to appreciate at post mortem examination. Histological examination can be carried out but the section taken may be outside the region of the plaques. A large number of sections would be necessary for each plaque which renders this kind of examination very costly and rather delicate. It is preferable to use only direct observation of the aorta,

TABLE I. COMPOSITION OF EXPERIMENTAL SEMI-SYNTHETIC DIET

	Weight %	Calories %	Salt mixture	mg/100 g
Casein, pure				
(0·21 % of the lipids)	25·26	34·4	$CaCO_3$	12·62
Saccharose	5·51	7·5	K_2HPO_3	7·58
Glucose	6·73	9·2	Na_2HPO_4	6·14
Corn starch	16·83	22·9	$Ca_3(PO_4)_2$	11·78
(0·03 % of lipids)			NaCl	
Fat	8·42	26	$MgSO_4$ Sicc.	2·78
Cellulose	18·94		$FeSO_4$ Sicc.	0·21
(0 : 0·8 % of lipids)			$MnSO_4(4 H_2O)$	0·35
Salt mixture	4·89		KI	0·03
Choline chloride	0·25		$ZnCO_3$	0·02
Inositol	0·34		$CuSO_4$ (5 H_2O)	0·02
Ascorbic acid	0·42			
Amino-benzoic acid	0·21			
Potassium acetate	2·10			
Magnesium oxide	0·42			
Talc	3·37			
Colloidal silicic acid	6·31			
Other vitamins	mg/100 g			
A (palmitate)	0·59			
a-Tocopherol acetate	1·96			
D_2	0·004			
K (menadione sodium sulphate)	0·2			
Aneurine hydrochloride	1·59			
Pyridoxine hydrochloride	1·59			
Riboflavin	1·59			
Nicotinic acid	19·63			
Calcium pantothenate	3·93			
Folic acid	0·59			
Biotin	0·059			
B_{12}	0·004			

reserving the possibility of preparing sections for the more definite plaques or the more doubtful ones. The preparation of sections is required after the initial deposits are formed in depth so as to be certain about the tissue reactions which characterize atherosclerosis. The examination is carried out generally on the aorta and the coronaries. Another method of study is the *in vitro* system. To acetyl coenzyme A are added the energy-rich intermediates and compounds necessary for cholesterol synthesis as well as the essential enzymes. Since very low amounts are involved one generally uses radio-active materials and measures the change in radio-activity of the test compounds.

In man any direct examination is impossible so one uses on the one hand clinical signs and on the other hand chemical changes in the blood. The changes most often studied are the serum cholesterol level, the Burnstein reaction, the level of glycerides and the serum Nbt. The same estimations can also be done on animals.

Finally, notice that infarcts cause disturbances in the normal distribution of serum lipids. Deegan and Hayward[7] estimate that the return to normal takes place about the fourth week after the infarction. Treatment with anticoagulants does not affect this phenomenon.

III. Outline of the General Plan

The normal biochemistry is given in a definite order from the outset by a general plan which considers successively the carbohydrates, lipids, proteins and mineral compounds. This order justifies itself entirely by the increasing difficulty of the subjects dealt with in terms of the complexity of the molecular structure. In short, this presentation is at the same time logical and didactic. Let us note, however, that we know more and more about complex molecules (glycoproteins, lipoproteins, etc.), whose constitution includes the previous categories. This presentation may appear at times to be rather artificial but it is still kept because it constitutes an excellent basis for instruction. These facts are known to our readers, also we do not believe we are obliged to follow blindly the classic order. We will give priority to the substances which appear to play an important role in the genesis, development or treatment of atherosclerosis. While keeping the classical divisions of the compounds, which is indispensible, we will present them in an order which is based on their pathogenic or therapeutic role. Therefore each chapter of the pathological biochemistry must have the most suitable classification.

References

1. ENSELME, J., HENRY, C. and PERRIN, A., Les examens chimiques actuellement utilés pour l'étude d'un sujet athéroscléreux. In *Actualités Cardiovasculaire*, 1 vol. Masson, 1965.
2. HALLER, A., *Opuscula Pathologica*, Bousquet, Lausanne, 1735.
3. LOBSTEIN, J. G. C. F. M., *Traité d'Anatomie Pathologique*, Levrault, Paris, 1829.
4. MARCHAND, F., Über Arteriosklerose (Atherosklerose). *Verhandl. Kongr. Inn. Med.*, 1904, **21**, 23.
5. STUKKEY, N. W., Über die Veränderungen der Kaninschen Aorta bei der Fätterung mit verschiedenen Fettsorten. *Zbl. Allg. Path. Anat.*, 1912, **23**, 910.
6. ANITSCHKOW, N. and CHALATOW, S., Über experimentelle Cholesterinsteatose und ihre Bedeutung für die Entstehung einiger pathologischer Prozesse. *Zbl. Allg. Path. Anat.*, 1913, **24**, 1.
7. DEEGAN, T. and HAYWARD, P. J., Modifications des lipides sériques à la suite d'un infarctus du myocarde. *J. Atheroscler. Res.*, 1965, **5**, 267.

CHAPTER 1

Cholesterol
(Δ^5–3β–ol–cholestane)

I. General Chemistry

Cholesterol has been known since the end of the eighteenth century and the study of its formula and reactions continued throughout the nineteenth century (see Table II and formula).

The alcohol group in position C_3 can be esterified by various acids such as the fatty acids (oleic, palmitic, etc.), so that two forms of cholesterol are possible, one free and the other esterified. In addition it contains four rings, a side chain and a double bond.

Cholesterol is synthesized from acetyl coenzyme A (CH_3COC_4A). This compound is known today to arise from many precursors and is the meeting-point of the metabolism of lipids, carbohydrates and the carbon skeleton of the proteins. It therefore has a central metabolic role. Its catabolism follows various pathways which can be complete in themselves or related to each other. On the one hand, it carries out the synthesis of fatty acids, ketone bodies and cholesterol. The balance of these different possibilities is not always perfect and alteration results in various diseases. On the other hand, it is normally oxidized in the Krebs cycle to give water and carbon dioxide; this is the usual form of its catabolism. It therefore appears as the very centre of biochemistry but changes in its metabolism can cause disease. These changes are most often due to abnormalities of the enzymes when the energy-rich intermediates that carry out these reactions can increase the formation of compounds such as cholesterol or the ketonic acids already mentioned.

A decrease or increase of these compounds is then produced which results in diseases of which atherosclerosis is perhaps the most common. Its study may not reveal the whole of the pathology of this disease but it will be none the less one of our principal preoccupations. The pathological problem of cholesterol has been dealt with only during the last 25 years. It is therefore a matter of relatively recent ideas and liable consequently to some revision.

II. Historical Table

TABLE II. CHOLESTEROL (Δ^5–3β–ol–cholestane)

Date	Author	Discovery	Anatomical origin
1769	Poultier de la Salle		Gallstones
1789	de Fourcroy	Repeated this finding	
1816	Chevreul	Name=cholesterine	
		(*chole*=bile)	
		(*steros*=solid)	
1824	Chevreul		Bile
1838	Müller		Cholesteatoma
1838	Lecanu		Blood
1843	Vogel		Atheroma
1846	Gobley		Egg yolk
1909	Rosenheim and Tebb		Adrenals

Date	Author	Constitution
1853	Berthelot	An alcohol. Gave the name cholester*ol*
1904	Diels and Abderhalden	A secondary alcohol
1932	Windaus	
	Diels and Wieland	Actual formula discovered

Date	Author	Detection and measurement (principal methods)
1872	Salkowski	Colour reaction with sulphuric acid in chloroform solution
1885	Liebermann	Colour reaction with acetic anhydride in chloroform solution
1889	Burchard	Improved the previous method
1909	Tschugaeff and Gasteff	Colour reaction with acetyl chloride and acetic acid
1909 1910	Windaus	Gravimetric method with digitonoside
1934	Schoenheimer and Sperry	Combined the two methods of Liebermann and Windaus
1950	Sperry and Webb	Improved the previous method

III. The Cholesterol of Normal and Pathological Aortas

A. *Distribution of Cholesterol in the Vascular Wall in Man*

Windaus[30] estimated cholesterol in two normal and two atheromatous aortas. He dried the wall, extracted it with ether and precipitated cholesterol with digitonoside. The results are given as percentages of fresh weight of aorta. The complete aorta is used in this case.

(1) Normal aortas (% of wet tissue):

free cholesterol	0·119–0·103
bound cholesterol	0·047–0·032
total cholesterol	0·166–0·135

The first aorta contained about 75 per cent of water, which made the percentages for dry weight as follows (% of dry tissue):

free cholesterol	0·476
bound cholesterol	0·188
total cholesterol	0·664

(2) Atheromatous aortas (% of wet tissue):

free cholesterol	0·741–0·678
bound cholesterol	1·053–0·792
total cholesterol	1·794–1·460

The higher values calculated for dry weight are (% of dry tissue):

free cholesterol	2·964
bound cholesterol	4·212
total cholesterol	7·176

(3) There was thus 6 and 7 times more free cholesterol, 26 and 20 times more bound cholesterol and 6·6 and 10·8 times more total cholesterol in the atheromatous aorta.

(4) The first normal aorta gave the following percentages for the cholesterols in the ether extract:

8·71 per cent of free cholesterol, 3·46 per cent of bound cholesterol and 12·1 per cent total cholesterol. (Values for complete aortic wall.)

The corresponding values for the first atheromatous aorta were:

17·7 per cent of free cholesterol, 42·3 per cent of bound cholesterol and 60 per cent total cholesterol.

Schonheimer[26] studied the aorta as a whole. He split off an internal fraction (intima + a part of the media) with a finger and studied this separately. He dried it, extracted it with ether and then effected digitonoside precipitation as before. As the author does not indicate the weights of aortas employed, it is impossible to give percentages for the various forms of cholesterol in the ether extract. The estimations were made by digitonoside precipitation. An example is given in Table III.

TABLE III

% ether extract	Free cholesterol	Esterified cholesterol	Total cholesterol
Nine normal aortas	26·8	9·54	36·31
Two slightly affected aortas: subjects 30 and 35 years old	28·09	25·36	53·45
Aorta of woman, 70 years old, dying from coronary disease	22·55	35·20	57·75

The figures for normal aortas appear particularly high when compared with the preceding figures, but here they relate to the surface and parts of the intima.

In 1940 Weinhouse and Hirsch[28] published two tables. These authors studied human aortas after separating (a) the media and (b) the intima with the lesions. They consider that their examination of the media shows the effect of ageing. Their results are given in Table IV.

In the media total lipids, all forms of cholesterol increased with age.

In the intima total lipids, free cholesterol and esterified cholesterol increased as the gravity of the condition increased.

Table V lists the findings in atherosclerosis.

Table VI was constructed from these results.

Morrison et al.[19] studied the coronary arteries. They compared the values for subjects who had died from coronary involvement and subjects dying from other conditions. Their results are given in Table VII.

TABLE IV*

Age (years)	Water (% fresh weight)	Total lipids (% dry weight)	Cholesterol (% dry weight)			Phospholipids (% dry weight)			Galactosides
			Free	Esterified	Total	Ether-soluble	Ether-insoluble	Total	
0–40	68·4	6·42	1·05	1·24	1·78	2·13	0·22	2·21	0·59
41–60	71·8	8·31	1·36	1·44	2·23	1·25	1·53	2·7	1·09 (media)
61–84	70·3	10·57	1·87	3·3	3·84	1·29	1·59	2·91	0·95

* For practical reasons we are also giving the values of lipids other than cholesterol. We shall comment on these in subsequent chapters.

TABLE V

	Water (% fresh substance)	Total lipids (% dry tissue)	Cholesterol			Phospholipids		
			Free	Esterified	Total	Ether-soluble	Ether-insoluble	Total
Intima	71·6	14·4	14·2	28·6	42·8	13·7	6·4	20·1
Fatty plaques	67·5	25·9	16·2	38·5	54·7	10·8	8·2	19·0
Fibrous plaques	66·5	27·2	18·1	47·5	65·6	5·9	9·0	14·9
Calcified tissue	38·6	12·8	21·9	47·2	69·1	3·9	9·3	13·2
Atheromatous ulcer	60·8	36·0	27·2	42·1	69·3	5·8	10·2	16·0

Percentage of total lipids

TABLE VI

Changes with	Total lipids	Cholesterol		Phospholipids		Totals
		Free	Esterified	Ether-soluble	Ether-insoluble	
Age	increased	increased	increased	reduced	increased	increased
Atherosclerosis	increased	increased	increased	reduced	increased	reduced

TABLE VII

	Average age	Coronary cholesterol (% dry tissue)	Extent of lesions
Coronary subjects	64	2·04	3·5
Non-coronary subjects	62	0·5	1·5

In terms of dry weight, the atherosclerotics had four times more cholesterol in their coronary arteries than the other subjects.

Luddy et al.[16] separated the different groups of fats on silicic acid and obtained the following distribution in percentages of total lipids in an atherosclerotic plaque.

Sterols	39	Phospholipids	13·5
Sterol esters	28	Free fatty acids	traces
Glycerides	19		

This analysis resembles the preceding ones.

Smith[27] gives various analyses in which he distinguishes the intima from the media, giving the quantities as percentages of fresh tissue (see Tables VIII and IX). These results are not very significant.

TABLE VIII

	From 25 to 59 years (% fresh tissue)			From 60 to 85 years (% fresh tissue)		
	Total lipids	Cholesterol	Phospholipids	Total lipids	Cholesterol	Phospholipids
Normal	1	0·52	0·29			
	2·04		1·4			
Slight atherosclerosis	2·84	0·32–1·08	0·65			
Moderate atherosclerosis	0·97	0·367	0·32	2·12	1·037	0·38
	1·4	0·54	0·40			
Severe atherosclerosis				1·55	0·69	0·37
Fresh atheromatous tissue	1·68	0·66	0·33			
Average ages	1·29	0·47	0·39	2·04	0·86	0·41

TABLE IX

	Total lipids (% fresh tissue)	Cholesterol (% total lipids)	Phospholipids (% total lipids)	Sphingomyelins (% phospholipids)	Lecithins (% phospholipids)
Normal:					
intima	1·63	40·2	23·9	48·0	40·7
media	1·33	35·9	42·1	61·3	25·8
Slight atherosclerosis:					
intima	4·98	40·0	16·7	49·8	39·6
media	2·6	32·4	21·8	56·9	29·6
Fibrous plaque:					
intima	5·1	53·3	16·2	51·1	39·0
media	2·8	53·3	18·8	55·4	32·0
Graded:					
intima	8·48	42·4	14·0	55·0	30·5
media	4·81	41·2	14·5	60·1	31·0
Fatty	6·4	45·2	13·6	68·8	21·2
Dry	4·6	44·0	9·1	81·5	15·4
Pulp	18·0	55·0	17·1	60·0	33·0
Two cases	11·8	54·8	14·4	70·4	17·0

There are increases in total lipids and total cholesterol.

The results of Böttcher et al.[6] for the aorta are given in Table X. The table shows that cholesterol alone was increased.

TABLE X. STUDY OF AORTAS

Stages of the disease	Evolutionary stages			
	0	I	II	III
Percentage of dry tissue:				
Lipids	3·0	4·2	9·8	12·0
Percentage of lipids:				
Free cholesterol	8·0	12·7	16·3	19·3
Esterified cholesterol	5·6	12·3	30·2	33·8
Phospholipids	61·3	58·4	42·3	38·0
Triglycerides	16·8	12·9	10·0	9·7
Fatty acids	8·5	4·2	1·4	1·0

B. *Lipids in the Aorta of Rabbits given an Atherosclerogenic Diet*

Interest lies in following the chemical evolution occurring in the deposits as they develop. The difficulty is to obtain a homogeneous series as, even under the same conditions, deposits vary enormously from one subject to another.

Weinhouse and Hirsch[28] used 12 rabbits which were given a diet containing 1 g cholesterol daily. The animals were killed at varying intervals and various organs were examined.

The lipid contents are shown in Table XII, which is taken from the author's paper. All forms of lipids increased but the increases were very irregular as the examination involved a fresh animal on each occasion.

The results of Day et al. for the aorta are given in Table XI; the values (mg) indicate a progressive increase of lesions in rabbits receiving 0·75 g cholesterol for eight weeks.

TABLE XI

Lesions	0	I	II	III	IV	V
Cholesterol (mg)	2·2	4·0	6·6	7·4	11·0	15·0
Phospholipids (mg)	1·6	2·8	2·4	3·5	1·8	6·7

TABLE XII. EVOLUTION OF AORTIC LIPIDS IN A RABBIT SUBJECTED TO AN ATHEROSCLEROGENIC DIET

Sex	Duration (days)	Free cholesterol*	Esterified cholesterol*	Total cholesterol*	Phospho-lipids*	Neutral fats*	Total lipids*
	Initial	0·19	0·06	0·22	1·01	4·25	5·51
F.	16	0·19	0·00	0·19	1·22	3·11	4·53
M.	75	0·47	0·87	0·99	1·16	8·58	11·1
F.	83	0·92	3·81	3·18	1·39	4·63	10·8
F.	92	0·7	1·12	1·36	1·9	2·1	5·82
M.	97	1·84	6·79	5·86	2·91	3·92	15·5
F.	106	2·76	5·72	6·15	2·76	1·77	13·0
F.	125	1·06	2·52	2·56	1·81	7·56	13·0
F.	144	1·77	1·55	2·69	2·19	10·1	15·6
M.	155	2·11	4·87	5·0	2·52	8·09	17·6
M.	159	0·93	2·16	2·21	1·5	6·96	11·5
F.	186	2·64	1·36	3·45	2·72	12·0	18·7
M.	260	3·22	1·76	4·27	3·26	3·26	11·5

* Percentage of fresh tissue.

Hirsch *et al.*[15] obtained the results given in Table XIII for the composition of the arterial tissue of the rabbit.

TABLE XIII

	Intima	Primary plaques	Media
Free cholesterol	14·2	16·2	17·3
Esterified cholesterol	38·6	38·5	16·7
Phospholipids	20·1	19·0	34·1
Neutral fats	27·1	26·3	31·9

Figures are percentages of total lipids.

Stormby gives a description of the morbid anatomy of the atheromatous lesions in the aorta and coronaries and in the visceral lesions induced by a semi-synthetic diet containing walnut oil, reduced coconut oil or glycerol trilaurate. The visceral lesions are typical of an accumulation of cholesterol.

C. *Conclusions*

These related ideas about the chemical constitution of normal or atherosclerotic arteries provide us with information which may be useful in a consideration of the pathogenic mechanism. We can in fact check their authenticity.

(a) *Quantitative presence of cholesterol in the lesion.* The cholesterol in the media increases progressively in the lesion produced experimentally by an abnormal supply of cholesterol. According to the most recent investigations we have quoted, the quantity of cholesterol in the media appears quite definitely to increase with the severity of the lesion.

In spontaneous atherosclerosis the cholesterol is definitely increased both as a percentage of the weight of the aorta and as a percentage of the total lipids. This increase is very variable but always very high, and sometimes considerable in both forms of cholesterol. Such an increase supports the view that cholesterol plays a pathogenic role.

(b) *Effect of administration of cholesterol.* Examination of Tables IX–XIII will show that these increases are progressive and that they begin very early, which is a second argument in favour of the pathogenic role of cholesterol.

The fact that experimental overloading of an animal organism, which is otherwise healthy, with cholesterol leads to the development of anatomical and histological aortic lesions similar to those in the spontaneous disease does not constitute absolute proof of their identity of origin. The quantities of cholesterol administered to animals in experiments are considerable. 1 g cholesterol given to a rabbit weighing 2 kg corresponds to a daily supply of 35 g cholesterol for a man weighing 70 kg. This dose is almost 40 times more than the quantity contained in the normal food of man, a fact which implies definite unphysiological action. Conclusions cannot be formed from conditions which are so abnormal, even though account is taken of the fact that the aim is to create in 2 months lesions which take several years to develop in man.

The effect of these large quantities would appear to be that deposits of excess cholesterol coat the healthy aorta and create local zones of asphyxia from which the lesions start.

(c) Of the two forms of cholesterol, it is the esterified form which is most often increased in spontaneous atherosclerosis.

IV. Cholesterol in Plasma and Serum

The cholesterol of the serum arises from dietary cholesterol and also from that which is synthesized in the body. Various products of digestion are involved in this synthesis but mainly the saturated fatty acids. In the following pages we shall see evidence of both these transformations.

A. *Normal Value of Serum Cholesterol*

It is very difficult to decide on a normal value for serum cholesterol. There is a wide variation from one normal person to another, which is due to a number of factors such as heredity or nutrition, which should be considered when evaluating results reported by the laboratory.

In France, Cottet gives a very wide range:

values less than 0·2 g/100 ml normal,
values between 0·2 and 0·3 g/100 ml doubtful,
values greater than 0·3 g/100 ml probably pathological.

In the United States these values would be considered low as we shall see in one of the following chapters.

There are two forms of cholesterol, the free form (0·35 to 0·09 g/100 ml) and the esterified form which constitutes a steroid.

B. *Foods which affect the Serum Cholesterol Level by contributing*
    Preformed Cholesterol or those Compounds which are converted
    into Cholesterol in the Liver

This question will be the subject of the following chapters.

V. Origin of Mural Cholesterol

The cholesterol found in the arterial wall which is healthy or affected by plaques of atherosclerosis can have various origins. The primary or secondary role of cholesterol depends on these origins which are not mutually exclusive. They can easily be complementary. It is expedient then to define what is the principal cause.

Furthermore, other compounds play a role in the constitution of these lesions. There is nothing to prove that cholesterol is the sole cause of the change in the wall but this last point can only be considered at the end of this work. By then we will have reviewed all the substances which can cause the lesion. We will return then in a later chapter to this discussion and only see here how at one point of the artery the production of cholesterol can take place.

First Ribbert[24] in 1904 and then Aschoff[1] in 1906 stated that the lipid elements found in the atherosclerotic plaque were brought by the plasma which infiltrated into the inner part of the vessel wall as far as the lumen.

A. *Comparison of the Values of the Same Lipid in the Serum and*
    in the Vessels of the Same Subject

If this theory is correct there should be a certain state of equilibrium established for each of these substances between the fraction brought by the plasma and the fraction deposited in the artery.

Molecules travel at speeds which vary with their spatial properties, their shape and size, or again with their electrical properties—charge and polar fractions exposed on their surfaces.

Equilibrium, if it does occur, will require a certain time for its establishment; during this period which, as we have said, varies for different substances, the values of these substances in the serum but more particularly in the vessel wall are continually changing. When equilibrium is finally established, these values will remain constant. They are not then necessarily equal. This conception of equilibrium between the blood stream and the aortic wall would be suspect if a substance varied in the same proportions in the two media.

Such concordant relationships have in fact been observed. They are, however, only very roughly approximate, the imperfect correspondence observed being not unexpectedly indicative of the multiplicity of factors involved.

In 1950 Morrison et al.[19] studied fourteen coronary arteries from subjects dying of non-vascular conditions and eleven arteries from subjects dying of coronary involvement. Some degree of parallelism was established in a general way between the values of the blood cholesterol in these subjects before death and the values for the cholesterol in their aortas, but there were evident anomalies. The mean values given in Table XIV illustrate these facts.

TABLE XIV

Cause of death	Age (years)	Serum cholesterol (mg/100 ml)	Coronary cholesterol (mg/g tissue)	Degree of atheroma
Coronary arteries of subjects dying from causes other than coronary	62	186	5·1	1·5
Coronary arteries of subjects dying from coronary conditions	64	303	20·4	3·5

It will be noted that the blood cholesterol was doubled and the coronary deposit of cholesterol increased four times.

Piccinelli et al.[23] were able to make parallel investigations on non-atheromatous and atheromatous subjects before and after their deaths. They compared the respective figures. The increases seen in the atheromatous serum, compared with normal serum, were repeated in the aorta in respect of glycerides, steroids or phosphatides. On the other hand, when the esterification index of the β-sterols was increased in the plasma, it was reduced in the aorta. No exact correlation could, however, be established between these variations.

The overloading of cholesterol does not necessarily imply a deposit in a lesion. It is then that a second question is raised.

B. *Comparison of the Biochemical State of the Plasma and the Histological State of the Aorta*

Some authors have estimated not the deposited lipids but only those carried by the plasma, and have compared these chemical values with the results of histological examinations.

Firstbrook,[12] Berthaux et al.[4] and Paterson et al.[22] failed to find any consistent relationship between the histological state of the arterial wall and increase of blood cholesterol. In the rabbit Day and Wilkinson[11] (1958) observed more definite relationships.

Against this type of investigation can be set the experimental work of MacMillan et al.[17] These authors gave an atherosclerogenic diet containing cholesterol to rabbits for 3 months, then withdrew the supply of cholesterol and killed the animals at various times over a period of 6 months. There was histological regression in the aortic lesions which was not proportional to the changes in the cholesterol content of the aortas.

Distinction must evidently be made between the rabbit, an animal which was healthy initially, in which the only atherosclerogenic factor ingested is cholesterol and which, in consequence, is very definitely the responsible factor, and man, who presents lesions in which the factors are multiple and disturb a relationship which can then be only very approximate.

In 1964 Moore and Williams[18] confirmed that in the rabbit there is no relation between the amount of plasma cholesterol and the degree of atherosclerosis in the aorta.

When a deposit is formed this is preceded by disintegration of the elastic layer caused by accumulation of lipids and cholesterol in and around this layer (Friedman, 1963[13]).

In addition it must be observed (Christensen, 1964[8]) that the rate of transfer of cholesterol from the intima-media is 6 times greater than the rate of accumulation of cholesterol during the feeding of cholesterol to the cockerel.

C. *Foods Rich in Cholesterol*

(a) *Eggs*. The sterols of egg have been fairly well studied. A typical egg yolk contains $0 \cdot 25$–$0 \cdot 30$ g sterol.

These sterols are cholesterol, Δ^7 cholesterol (3 mg for one egg yolk); a sterol with two conjugated bonds, $\Delta^{5,24}$ cholestadienol and its isomers.

(b) *Crustacea*. The feeding of shrimps to rabbits raises the serum cholesterol and increases the lesions. It is known moreover that crustacea contain large quantities of cholesterol (Connor, W. E. et al., 1963[9]).

(c) The percentage of cholesterol varies from one animal to another but taking a value greater than 1 per cent as high, one still finds large quantities of cholesterol in the liver and adrenals. In the latter case cholesterol is distributed in an irregular manner in the surrounding fat which it is advisable to exclude from the diet of people suffering from atherosclerosis.

D. In vitro *Biosynthesis of the Cholesterol of Arterial Deposits*

Several experiments indicate that the arterial wall can synthesize cholesterol.

(1) In 1949 Chernick et al.[7] showed that, in three hours, the rat aorta could, starting with ^{14}C-labelled acetate, effect the synthesis of extremely small quantities of fatty acids. In the same way ^{32}P could be incorporated in phospholipids.

(2) Using sections of aorta from normal animals—rabbits and fowls—and ^{14}C-labelled acetate, Siperstein et al.[25] showed that these aortas formed cholesterol at a rate which was a quarter that of renal tissue. Acetates were oxidized to CO_2. They concluded that there was endogenous anabolism in the aorta. It may be added that in this experiment cholesterol was not determined by precipitation with digitonoside.

(3) In the experiments of Azarnoff[2] a first precipitation was effected with digitonoside and the cholesterol was then purified by combination with dibromide.

This author showed that labelled acetate was incorporated in a substance which was precipitated by digitonoside but could not be recovered from the product of purification by combination with dibromide.

The exacting chemical demands of this double purification would appear to indicate that, *in vitro*, the coronary arteries and aorta of man and the aortas of the dog and the rat cannot incorporate ^{14}C-labelled acetate in the cholesterol (the human aorta was used 8 hours after death).

On the other hand, the aortas of the rabbit, hen and guinea pig can effect this synthesis.

(4) After perfusing the aorta of the calf, Nelson[20] found the ^{14}C of the perfused acetate in the free cholesterol and the free fatty acids of the wall at a level five to eight times higher than in the cholesterol esters.

It can be concluded that these authors, although they have not settled the question absolutely, have, however, shown that the aortic wall can probably synthesize cholesterol.

VI. Sequence of Absorption and Fixation of Arterial Deposits

Beaumont et al.[3] in 1963 carried out an investigation of the cholesterol content of rabbits given a diet designed to produce atherosclerosis.

(1) During the period of treatment the following observations were made. (a) Cholesterol increases most in the blood, then in the sclerotic, liver, achilles tendon, adrenals, spleen, cornea and least of all in the stomach. (b) This increase is rapid in the blood, liver, spleen but slower in the aorta sclerotic, tendon and cornea, due to an initial delay followed by a quicker rise.

(2) After returning to a normal diet the following facts were noted. (a) The cholesterol content falls rapidly in the blood, liver and the spleen, but more

slowly in the sclerotic, tendon, cornea and adrenals. (b) Cholesterol does not decrease and even appears to increase in the aorta.

(1) These results show that of the thirteen organs and tissues studied, only the sclerotic, tendon, cornea and to a lesser degree the adrenals behave similarly to the aorta. This similarity can be explained by the presence of the same connective tissue in these organs.

(2) The aorta is distinguished to a certain extent from all other organs studied because it is the only one in which the amount of cholesterol did not fall and even appeared to increase. This fact suggests the stimulation of a structure or function peculiar to the artery.

Newman and Zilversmit in 1962,[21] by using a diet containing ^{14}C cholesterol, showed that the plasma cholesterol is the principal source of the cholesterol in the atheromatous aorta and that the accumulation of cholesterol in the atherosclerotic lesion is a dynamic not a static process. With respect to plasma ^{14}C, the rate at which the free cholesterol penetrates the intima is much greater than that of the esterified cholesterol.

In 1963 Gasdorth et al.[14] showed that the cholesterol pool turnover is increased by the introduction of a diet rich in lipids.

In 1964 Whereat[29] observed some modifications of the Krebs cycle enzymes in rabbits subjected to an atherosclerogenic diet. The oxygen consumption in the intima increased, as did fatty acid synthesis and was at a maximum in advanced lesions.

References

1. ASCHOFF, L., Ein Beitrag zur Myelinfrage. *Verhandl. Deutsch. Pathol.-Ges.*, 1907, **10**, 166–70.
2. AZARNOFF, D. L., Species differences in cholesterol biosynthesis by arterial tissue. *Proc. Soc. Exp. Biol.*, 1958, **98**, 680–3.
3. BEAUMONT, J. L., GROSGOGEAT, Y., RICHARD, J. L. and CLAUDE, J. R., La teneur en cholesterol de l'aorte et d'autres organes chez le lapin nourri avec du cholestérol. *J. Atheroscler. Res.*, 1963, **3**, 210.
4. BERTHAUX, BECK and VIGNALOU, Cholestérolémie et lésions artérielles chez le vieillard. *Presse Med.*, 1959, **67**, 2108.
5. BLANKENHORN, D. H. and CHIN, T. W., A micro determination of β-cholestanol in atheromatous lesions employing gas liquid chromatography. *Fed. Proc.*, 1962, **21**, 97.
6. BÖTTCHER, C. J. F. and WOODFORD, F. P., Fatty-acid distribution in lipids of the aortic wall. *Lancet*, 1960, **1**, 1378–83.
7. CHERNICK, S., SRERE, P. A. and CHAIKOFF, I. L., Metabolism of arterial tissue. II. Lipide syntheses: the formation *in vitro* of fatty acids and phospholipides by rat artery with ^{14}C and ^{32}P as indicators. *J. Biol. Chem.*, 1949, **179**, 113–18.
8. CHRISTENSEN, S., Le transfer de cholestérol marqué à travers la surface de l'intima aortique chez le cochet normal et celui nourri avec du cholestérol. *J. Atheroscler. Res.*, 1964, **4**, 151.

9. CONNOR, W. E., ROHVEDDER, J. J. and HOAD, J. C., Production of hypercholesterolemia and atherosclerosis by a diet rich in shellfish. *J. Nutrit.*, 1963, **79**, 443–50.

10. DAY, A. J. and WILKINSON, G. K., Severity of atherosclerosis in rabbits in relation to serum lipids and to aorta cholesterol content. *Austral. J. Exp. Biol.*, 1956, **34**, 423–32.

11. DAY, A. J. and WILKINSON, G. K., Gravité de l'athérosclérose chez les lapins par rapport au contenu du sérum en lipides et de l'aorte en cholestérol. *Exc. Med. Card. Dis.*, 1958, **2**, S.18, 235.

12. FIRSTBROOK, J. B., Newer knowledge of atherosclerosis. *Brit. Med. J.*, 1951, **2**, 133.

FRIEDMAN, M. and BYERS, S. O., Endothelial permeability in atherosclerosis. *Arch. Pathol.*, 1963, **76**, 99–105.

13. FRIEDMAN, M., Spontaneous atherosclerosis and experimental thromboatherosclerosis. *Arch. Pathol.*, 1963, **76**, 571–7.

14. GASDORTH, H. R., JUERGENS, J. L., ORVIS, A. L. and OWEN, C. A., Jr., Rate of disappearance of cholesterol—^{14}C from the bloodstream of dogs. *Proc. Soc. Biol.*, 1963, **112**, 191–4.

15. HIRSCH, E. F. and NAILOR, R., Atherosclerosis. IV. The relation of the composition of the blood lipids to atherosclerosis in experimental hyperlipemia. *A.M.A. Arch. of Pathology*, 1956, **61**, 469–87.

16. LUDDY, F. E., BARFORD, R. A., RIEMENSCHNEIDER, R. Q. and EVANS, J. D., La composition en acides gras des composants lipidiques du plasma humain et des athéromes. *J. Biol. Chem.*, 1958, **232**, 843–52, and *Path. et Biol.*, 1959, **7**, 478.

17. MACMILLAN, G. C., SILVER, M. D. and WEIGENSBERG, B. I., Elaidinized olive oil and cholesterol atherosclerosis. *Arch. Path.*, 1963, **76**, 106–12.

18. MOORE, J. H. and WILLIAMS, D. L., The effect of diet on the level of plasma cholesterol and the degree of atheromatous degeneration in the rabbit. *Brit. J. Nutrit.*, 1964, **18**, no. 2, 253–73.

19. MORRISON, L. M. and JOHNSON, K. D., Cholesterol content of coronary arteries and blood in acute coronary artery thrombosis. *Amer. Heart J.*, 1950, **39**, 31.

20. NELSON, W. R., Comparative incorporation of ^{14}C from labelled acetate into free cholesterol, fatty acids and esterified cholesterol and fatty acids in the calf aorta. *Circulation*, 1959, **20**, 988.

21. NEWMAN, H. A. I. and ZILVERSMIT, D. B., Quantitative aspects of cholesterol flux in rabbit atheromatous lesions. *J. Biol. Chem.*, U.S.A., 1962, **237** (7), 2078–84.

22. PATERSON, J. C., DYER, L. and ARMSTRONG, E. C., Serum cholesterol levels in human atherosclerosis. *Canad. Med. Ass. J.*, 1960, **82**, 6–11.

23. PICCINELLI, O. and MOROSINI, F., La Composition lipidique de la plaque athéromateuse. *Arch. Sci. Med.*, 1960, **109**, 168–79.

24. RIBBERT, H. H., Über die Genese der arteriosklerotischen Veränderungen der Intima. *Verhandl. Deutsch. Pathol. Ges.*, 1904, **8**, 168–77.

25. SIPERSTEIN, M. D., CHAIKOFF, I. L. and CHERNICK, S. S., Significance of endogenous cholesterol in arteriosclerosis: synthesis in arterial tissue. *Science*, 1951, **113** (1), 747–9.

26. SCHONHEIMER, R., Zur Chemie der gesunden und der arteriosclerotischen Aorta. *Ztschrft. Physiol. Chem.*, 1926, **160**, 61–76.

27. SMITH, E. B., Intimal and medial lipids in human aorta. *Lancet*, 1960, 799–803.

28. WEINHOUSE, S. and HIRSCH, E. F., Atherosclerosis. II. The lipids of the serum and tissues in experimental atherosclerosis of rabbits. *Arch. of Path.*, 1940, **30**, 856–67.

29. WHEREAT, A. F., Biosynthèse lipidique dans l'intima aortique provenant de lapins normaux et de lapins nourris avec du cholestérol. *J. Atheroscler. Res.*, 1964, **4**, 272.

30. WINDAUS, A., Über den Gehalt normaler und atheromatöser Aorten an Cholesterin und cholesterinen askin. *Z. Physiol. Chem.*, 1910, **67**, 174–6.

CHAPTER 2

The Fatty Acids

I. History of the Role of Fatty Acids in Hypercholesterolaemia and the Production of Plaques

Research workers were agreed on the fact that cholesterolaemia can be increased by the ingestion of cholesterol and fats, when Kinsell *et al.*[6] at the Institute for Medical Research, Oakland, California drew attention to the fact that certain vegetable fats reduce cholesterolaemia in man: "It would appear that the ingestion of synthetic diets containing a large amount of vegetable fats consistently result in an impressive fall in the level of serum cholesterol and phospholipids." The observation although correct is not true for some solid vegetable fats such as those from the coconut.

In 1955 Bronte-Stewart, Keys and Brock[3] of Cape Town reported on the effect of race, but in their paper the following significant passage occurs on the subject of foods of animal origin: "Two consistent and paralleled trends emerge:

an increase of the mean total cholesterol in the serum and particularly of the lipoprotein fraction;
an increase in the consumption of fat, particularly '*animal fat*'."

We make here the same reservations as before for the distinction between lipids of animal and vegetable origin, they write:

Animal fats and hydrogenated animal fat behaved differently from vegetable, and marine fish and mammal oils. The most likely common difference between these fats and oils is the proportion of saturated and unsaturated fatty acids in the fats and oils concerned.
Sunflower-seed oil and a highly unsaturated fatty acid from pilchard oil have, in the persons studied, consistently depressed the serum-cholesterol levels when fed alone, with a supplement of cholesterol or with one of animal fat. . . .
Certain discrepancies in the dietary-fat theory of the aetiology of coronary heart-disease may be explained by variations in the nature of the fatty-acid composition of the fats concerned.

Malmros of Lund[8-10] at the Stockholm Congress in September 1954 made the two following points:

The diet in Italy differs in one important respect from U.S.A. and Sweden, namely in the consumption of fat. According to the data available in Italy as a whole, fat represents some 20 per cent of the caloric supply. In Naples, the fat consumption is probably less. The corresponding figure for U.S.A. is 40 per cent. According to Swedish statistics for the year 1953, fat represents 37·5 per cent of the caloric supply.

In addition:

> Of particular interest in this respect is the cholesterol content of the lipoprotein fraction. The values noted for the Swedish material were higher than those found for the normal population in Naples. This may help to explain why myocardial infarction is by no means so common in Italy as in Sweden.

Malmros and Wigand thus started to consider the possible role of saturated lipids and since 1955 they have used a number of diets. This work led them to divide lipids into three groups.

Reduced fats from butter and coconut do not cause any lowering of serum cholesterol; olive oil, colza oil and refined whale oil act slightly after 3 weeks. Saffron oil, sunflower oil and above all maize oil clearly reduce the serum cholesterol.

In 1956 Sinclair[11] of Magdalen College, Oxford, suggested that the absence of essential fatty acids (linoleic, arachidonic acid) constitutes a most important factor in atherosclerosis. In fact he later extended his idea to the other fatty acids: "We cannot necessarily equate the lowering with essential fatty acid activity, because there might be polyunsaturated fatty acids (e.g. of the $[CH_2=CH(CH_2)]_9COOH$ class) which lower the serum cholesterol, but unlike acids of the linoleic classes do not permit growth in rats on a fat free diet."

He later added the transisomers and conjugated isomers which cause elevation of the blood cholesterol and induce atheroma. In 1956 he wrote:

> Cholesterol becomes esterified with abnormal or unusually saturated fatty acids, and these abnormal esters are less readily disposed of and so cause atheroma.
> Phospholipids (such as phosphatidyl ethanolamine) contain abnormal or unusually saturated fatty acids, and these abnormal phospholipids being less readily disposed of, are retained in plasma and increase the coagulability of blood thereby contributing to coronary and cerebral thrombosis.
> The similar deficiency of normal phospholipids (or the presence of abnormal phospholipids) in the nervous system causes defective structure including demyelination, which causes disseminated sclerosis and possibly mental disease.

Ancel Keys[5] in 1956 drew attention to the fact that the role of the fatty acids was suspected for a long time and that, apart from their nature, the quantity ingested by the patient must be noted. Only a reduction in quantity could reduce cholesterolaemia in any important way. He also expressed fears about the changes undergone by some fats during industrial processing.

We come to 1957 when Ahrens[1] of the Rockefeller Institute did some experiments on men. His results confirmed that some vegetable lipids lower cholesterolaemia and phospholipidaemia. Meanwhile the author searched for the cause. Some reduction of the fat supressed the effect and he concluded: "Experimental data lead to the presumptive conclusion that unsaturated fat in the diet causes depression in the levels of cholesterol and phospholipids." Meanwhile there was nothing to prove absolutely that the hypercholesterolaemia was the cause of atherosclerosis. Furthermore, the experiments were too few in number. He suggested: "Radical changes in dietary habits are not recommended to the general public at this time. However, patients with existing or threatening atherosclerosis may be justifiably advised to eat higher proportions of unsaturated fats."

Since then experiments have been multiplied and we will consider them in the course of each chapter.

II. General Chemistry

Although these are accepted by all, we summarize their meaning here.

A. *The Ethylenic Bond*

In a chain of atoms, e.g. carbon atoms, the latter are generally connected with one another by bonds termed covalent. These bonds, which have a high energy value, are effected by the sharing of electrons from one or other atom or, most frequently, from both atoms. A group of two bonding electrons which thus attach two carbons to one another is termed a doublet.

If the atoms (in our example carbon atoms) are joined together by a single pair of electrons the chain is said to be saturated. The bond is termed mono-covalent. It is shown by a single line which arbitrarily represents the two electrons. Example, ethane:

$$\begin{array}{ccc} & H & H \\ & | & | \\ H- & C- & C-H \\ & | & | \\ & H & H \end{array}$$

If, however, the linkage between two atoms is formed by two pairs (four electrons) there is said to be a double bond. Ethylene affords the simplest example of these double bonds, and they are still known as ethylenic bonds. Example, ethylene:

$$\begin{array}{ccc} H & H \\ | & | \\ C & = C \quad \text{or} \quad CH_2 = CH_2 \\ | & | \\ H & H \end{array}$$

This double bond is shown by two lines each arbitrarily representing a pair of electrons. The atom chain is then said to be unsaturated. A chain which has one such bond is said to be mono-ethylenic and one containing several, poly-ethylenic. Thus we have:

monovalent bonds (two electrons) (—) and
ethylenic bonds (four electrons) (=).

Two of the four electrons are particularly mobile. Being readily available,
they tend to fix atoms which come into contact with them and to incorporate
them in the molecule. This is the case, for example, with iodine. The quantity
of iodine fixed by a molecule will indicate the importance of the ethylenic
bonds in this molecule and is termed the iodine index.

In the case of hydrogen, the unsaturated chain will take it up in the
presence of a catalyst and will become saturated.

Oxygen is introduced in the same way; the result is an unstable substance
or even immediate rupture at the ethylenic bond.

Ethylenic bonds may occupy various positions in the atom chain. When
there is regular alternation of simple and double bonds, there is said to be a
system of conjugated double bonds. Example:

$$-CH=CH-CH=CH-CH=CH-$$

The arrangement is different in the fatty acids with which we are concerned:

$$-CH_2-CH=CH-CH_2-CH=CH-CH_2-$$

In analysis one tries to change the natural arrangement to one with
conjugated chains which are more easily detected and can be estimated
spectrophotometrically.

B. *The Fatty Acids*

Fatty acids are organic acids with at least four atoms of carbon.

The ethylenic fatty acids are those whose molecules contain one (mono-
ethylenic acid), two (di-ethylenic acid), three (tri-ethylenic) and so on,
ethylenic bonds. Those with several ethylenic bonds are termed poly-
ethylenic (or poly-ethenic).

The chemical and physical characteristics of ethylenic fatty acids differ
from those of saturated acids. Thus the fluidity of a poly-ethylenic acid
increases with the number of double bonds it contains. Poly-ethylenic fatty
acids are constituents of the most fluid oils, and oleic acid, a mono-
ethylenic acid, is the main constituent of a less fluid oil, olive oil. Saturated
fatty acids enter into the composition of fats which are solid at laboratory
temperature.

The metabolism of ethylenic acids in the living organism is also very
different from that of saturated acids. A fatty acid is said to be indispensable
to an animal when it must necessarily be introduced in the animal's diet to
ensure normal functioning of its cells because the organism is unable to
synthesize it, or to synthesize it in adequate quantity.

A fatty acid is said to be essential when it plays an important part at cell level, whether it is obtained from indispensable foods or is entirely synthesized *de novo* by the organism (Le Breton and Ferret).

C. List and Formulae of the Fatty Acids most important in Connection with this Subject

Saturated acids:

Butyric acid	(tetranoic acid)	$CH_3 \cdot (CH_2)_2 \cdot COOH$
Myristic acid	(tetradecanoic acid)	$CH_3 \cdot (CH_2)_{12} \cdot COOH$
Palmitic acid	(hexadecanoic acid)	$CH_3 \cdot (CH_2)_{14} \cdot COOH$
Stearic acid	(octadecanoic acid)	$CH_3 \cdot (CH_2)_{16} \cdot COOH$
Arachidic acid	(eicosanoic acid)	$CH_3 \cdot (CH_2)_{18} \cdot COOH$
Behenic acid	(docasanoic acid)	$CH_3 \cdot (CH_2)_{20} \cdot COOH$

Unsaturated acids:

Palmitic acid   (Δ^9 hexadecanoic)

$$CH_3 \cdot (CH_2)_5 \cdot CH = CH \cdot (CH_2)_7 \cdot COOH$$

Oleic acid   (Δ^9 octadecanoic)

$$CH_3 \cdot (CH_2)_7 \cdot CH = CH \cdot (CH_2)_7 \cdot COOH$$

Linoleic acid   (Δ^{9-12} octadecadienoic)

$$CH_3 \cdot (CH_2)_4 \cdot CH = CH \cdot CH_2 \cdot CH = CH \cdot (CH_2)_7 \cdot COOH$$

Linolenic acid   ($\Delta^{9-12-15}$ octadecatrienoic)

$$CH_3 \cdot CH_2 \cdot CH = CH \cdot CH_2 \cdot CH = CH \cdot CH_2 \cdot CH = CH \cdot (CH_2)_7 \cdot COOH$$

Arachidonic acid   ($\Delta^{5-8-11-14}$ eicosatetraenoic)

$$CH_3 \cdot (CH_2)_4 \cdot CH = CH \cdot CH_2 \cdot CH = CH \cdot CH_2 \cdot CH = CH \cdot CH_2 \cdot CH =$$
$$CH \cdot (CH_2)_3 \cdot COOH$$

If the carbon atoms are counted from the carboxyl group (COOH), it will be seen that the molecule of oleic acid is perfectly symmetrical about an axis established between C-9 and C-10. To indicate the position of an ethylenic bond, the carbon atoms are numbered from the carboxyl group. The letter Δ is written and it is given as exponent the number of the weaker of the two carbons between which the bond is situated. An example is afforded by the Δ^9 in oleic acid. As the denaturation of natural fatty acids proceeds ethylenic bonds separated by a CH_2 group (non-conjugated bonds) appear between C-10 and C-18, i.e. between the ethylenic bond Δ^9 and the CH_3 group, the carbon of which is C-18. The oxidation of linoleic acid which gives the arachidonic acid, produces two ethylenic bonds between C-1 (COOH) and the Δ^9 bond, two new carbon atoms being added. Example:

Linoleic acid (C_{18})

$$CH_3 \cdot CH_2 \cdot CH_2 \cdot CH_2 \cdot CH_2 \cdot CH^{\Delta 12} = CH \cdot CH_2 \cdot CH^{\Delta 9}$$
$$= CH \cdot CH_2 \cdot CH_2 \cdot CH_2 \cdot CH_2 \cdot CH_2 \cdot CH_2 \cdot CH_2 \cdot COOH$$

Arachidonic acid (C_{20})

$$CH_3 \cdot CH_2 \cdot CH_2 \cdot CH_2 \cdot CH_2 \cdot CH^{\Delta 14} = CH \cdot CH_2 \cdot CH^{\Delta 11}$$
$$= CH \cdot CH_2 \cdot CH^{\Delta 8} = CH \cdot CH_2 \cdot CH^{\Delta 5} = CH \cdot CH_2 \cdot CH_2 \cdot CH_2 \cdot COOH$$

two additional carbons
original double bonds $\Delta 11$ and $\Delta 14$
two new double bonds $\Delta 5$ and $\Delta 8$

The acids with which we are concerned have chains consisting of two fractions, one running from the CH_3 group to the ethylenic bond at $\Delta 9$. This is a zone in which other ethylenic bonds may appear but the animal can only effect this change in very slight degree and only in the red cells; double bonds may likewise appear in the other zone, but the animal organism makes this change. We thus have:

$$CH_3 \cdot (CH_2)_7 \cdot CH = CH \cdot (CH_2)_n \cdot COOH$$

I	II
Zone of action of vegetable organisms.	Zone of action of the animal organism.

The fatty acids with ethylenic bonds in zone I are thus necessarily introduced with the food; they are indispensable fatty acids and, as they are often very useful for the normal functions of the organism, they are also often essential fatty acids. To be useful, however, they must be introduced in fairly large quantities. They cannot, therefore, be regarded as vitamins.

References

1. AHRENS, Jr., HIRCH, J., INSULL, W., TSALTAS, T., BLOMSTRAND, R. and PETERSON, M. L., Dietary control of serum lipids in relation to atherosclerosis. *J. Amer. Med. Ass.*, 1957, **164**, 1905.
2. BÖTTCHER, C. J. F., WOODFORD, F. P., TER HAAR, ROMENY, WACHTER, C. CH., BOELSMA-VAN HOUTE, E. and VAN GENT, C. M., Fatty acid distribution in lipids of the aortic wall. *Lancet*, 1960, 1378.
3. BRONTE-STEWART, B., KEYS, A. and BROCK, J. F., Serum-cholesterol, diet, and coronary heart-disease. An interracial survey in the Cape Peninsula. *Lancet*, 1955, **2**, 1103.
4. CHALVARDJIAN, A. M. and STILL, W. J. S., La composition en acides gras de tissus chez le lapin nourri avec du cholestérol. *J. Atheroscler. Res.*, 1964, **4**, 507.
5. KEYS, A., ANDERSON, J. T., ARESU, M., BIORCK, G., BROCK, J. F., BRONTE-STEWART, B., FIDANZA, F., KEYS, M. H., MALMROS, H., POPPI, A., POSTELI, T., SWAHN, B. and DEL VECCHIO, A., Physical activity and the diet in populations differing in serum cholesterol. *J. Clin. Invest.*, 1956, **35**, 1173.

6. KINSELL, L., PARTRIDGE, J., BOLING, L., MARGEN, J. and MICHAELS, G., Dietary modification of serum cholesterol and phospholipid levels. *J. Clin. Endocr.*, 1952, **12**, 909.

7. LOOMEIJER, F. J. and VAN DER VEEN, K. J., Incorporation de l'acétate (1–14C) dans des lipides divers par l'aorte du rat *in vitro*. *J. Atheroscler. Res.*, 1962, **2**, 478.

8. MALMROS, H., BIORCK, G. and SWAHN, B., Hypertension, atherosclerosis and the diet. *Proceedings of the Third International Congress of Internal Medicine*, 1954.

9. MALMROS, H. and WIGAND, G., The effect on serum-cholesterol of diets containing different fats. *Lancet*, 1957, **1**, 273.

10. MALMROS, H. and WIGAND, G., Atherosclerosis and deficiency of essential fatty acids. *Lancet*, 1959, **2**, 749.

11. SINCLAIR, H. M., Deficiency of essential fatty acids and atherosclerosis, etc. *Lancet*, 1956, **270**, 381.

12. SMITH, S. C., STROUT, R. G., DUNLOP, W. R. and SMITH, E. C., Composition en acides gras de cultures de cellules aortiques prélevées sur des pigeons white carneau et show racer. *J. Atheroscler. Res.*, 1965, **5**, 379.

13. STEIN, Y. and STEIN, O., Incorporation des acides gras dans les lipides de coupes d'aorte provenant de lapin, du chien, du rat et du babouin. *J. Atheroscler. Res.*, 1962, **2**, 400.

CHAPTER 3

The Fatty Acids of the Lipid-esters in the Aortic Wall

THE fatty acids have been estimated by gaseous chromatography, generally in the fractionation products obtained by silicic acid chromatography of a lipid extract of the aortic wall. Two types of fatty acid can be distinguished but it is still impossible to decide *a priori* whether one is more important than the other in relation to atherosclerosis. We shall follow their evolution in the various stages (I, II) of the disease.

A. *Quantitatively Important Fatty Acids*

In this category we shall place the saturated acids, palmitic and stearic, the mono-ethenoid acids, palmitioleic and oleic, and the poly-ethenoid acids, dienoic and arachidonic acids.

(1) Their proportions in the total lipids of the wall are shown in Tables XV–XIX.

TABLE XV. PERCENTAGE DISTRIBUTION

	Saturated fatty acids	Oleic	Palmito-leic	Lino-leic	Lino-lenic	Arachid-onic
Wall of aorta Wright *et al.*	25·1	35·2	—	30·7	3·0	4·6
Atheromatous plaque Wright *et al.* Tuna *et al.* Luddy *et al.*	26·2 20·5 20·46	34·2 32·5 54·4	— 5·6	30·0 22·9 16·0	2·9	5·0 7·6 5·7
Coronary arteries in atherosclerosis Wright *et al.*	21·3	42·8		27·0	3·7	4·0

It is difficult to draw any exact conclusion from these findings. The differences appear to be slight and it is impossible to speak of a constant change in any group.

29

(2) Separation of the various lipid groups gives the results listed in Tables XVI and XVII.

TABLE XVI. FATTY ACIDS ESTERIFYING CHOLESTEROL
(Percentages of the fatty acids in this category)

Fatty acids	Böttcher et al.[1]				Luddy et al. Plaque	Tuna et al. Plaque
	0	I	II	III		
Saturated	31·2	22·9	18·7	17·0	9·7	13·4
Mono-ethylenic	39·9	39·9	35·1	36·7	41·3	28·6
Linoleic	24·6	30·0	37·0	36·0	38·5	42·6
Arachidonic	2·2	2·6	5·1	4·7	9·7	6·3

TABLE XVII. FATTY ACIDS ESTERIFYING GLYCERIDES
(Percentages of the fatty acids in this category)

Fatty acids	Böttcher et al.[1]				Luddy et al. Plaque
	0	I	II	III	
Saturated	44·9	42·8	34·7	35·3	22·18
Mono-ethylenic	40·4	41·8	48·0	43·3	67·4
Linoleic	9·6	10·5	10·8	12·6	7·0
Arachidonic	2·7	2·6	2·9	3·9	2·26

TABLE XVIII. FATTY ACIDS ESTERIFYING PHOSPHOLIPIDS
(Percentages of the fatty acids in this category)

Fatty acids	Böttcher et al.[1]				Luddy et al. Plaque
	0	I	II	III	
Saturated	55·2	59·4	61·2	62·0	32·2
Mono-ethylenic	19·4	15·6	16·6	16·6	55·7
Linoleic	5·0	4·4	3·9	4·2	7·21
Arachidonic	9·9	10·1	9·4	7·4	2·57
Behenic C_{22} saturated	1·6	3·4	4·5	4·4	
Lignoceric C_{24} saturated	3·4	3·8	6·1	6·4	
Tetracosanoic C_{24} mono-ethylenic	1·2	1·5	3·3	4·7	

TABLE XIX. FREE FATTY ACIDS

Fatty acids	Böttcher et al.[1]			
	0	I	II	III
Saturated	44·9	41·5	37·9	36·9
Mono-ethylenic	28·6	27·1	28·0	29·3
Linoleic	17·6	18·7	15·7	19·2
Arachidonic	5·5	8·0	12·1	9·5

TABLE XX. SUMMARY OF EVOLUTION IN VARIOUS COMPOUNDS

Fatty acids	Steroids	Glycerides	Phospholipids	Free Fatty acids
Saturated	much reduced	reduced	little changed	reduced
Mono-ethylenic	little changed	increased	reduced	little changed
Linoleic	increased	increased	reduced	little changed
Arachidonic	increased	little changed	reduced	increased

It is difficult to see why there should be this increase in the ethylenic acids (an increase most frequently observed if the phospholipid group is excluded). It may be that the saturated fatty acids are reduced because they are converted *in situ* into cholesterol with the result that the percentage values of the others are necessarily increased. We shall return to this difficult question of interpretation later.

Zilversmit[5] established the difference in the composition of the fatty acids and lipids of the plasma and the phospholipids of the artery. But the greatest similarity in fatty acid composition is found in the triglycerides of the plasma and the intima. It may be that lipids deposited on the arterial wall undergo metabolic alterations.

Böttcher[1] described a method combining chromatography on silicic acid and differential hydrolysis which can be used to determine the fatty composition of seven phospholipid fractions, each one having its characteristic pattern of fatty acids. The compositions change in the manner of an increase in saturation with the degree of atherosclerosis. This increase is due above all to a decrease of arachidonic acid. This increase is found again in the esterified fraction of the serum and liver cholesterol of dogs suffering from atherosclerosis.

Chalvardjian et al.[2] (1964) noticed that there was a considerable increase in the oleic acid content of cholesterol esters in rabbits subjected to a diet designed to produce hypercholesterolaemia.

B. *Fatty Acids Found only in Small Quantities in the Arterial Wall*

These are fatty acids with values ranging from 1 per cent to, at most, 3 per cent.

Those with short chains appear to be slightly reduced and those with long chains increased in the intima which has been altered by atherosclerosis. According to Böttcher *et al.*, these acids are the following:

Saturated acids	C_{10}, C_{12}, C_{14}, C_{15}, C_{17}, C_{20}, C_{22}
Mono-ethenoid acids	C_{14}, C_{15}, C_{17}, C_{20}, C_{22}, C_{24}
Di-ethenoid acids	C_{20}, C_{22}
Tri-ethenoid acids	C_{18}, C_{20}, C_{22}
Tetra-ethenoid acids	C_{20}, C_{22}
Penta-ethenoid acids	C_{20}, C_{22}
Hexa-ethenoid acids	C_{22}

C. *Experiments* in vitro

Loomeijer and Van der Veen[3] showed that the isolated rat aorta is capable of incorporating acetate into the various groups of lipids.

Stein and Stein[4] studied the rat, the rabbit, the dog and the baboon. Sections of the aorta show the presence of ^{14}C linoleic acid in the arterial lipids of animals which had received the labelled acid. The greatest accumulation was in the phospholipids.

References

1. BÖTTCHER, C. J. F., WOODFORD, F. P., TER HAAR, ROMENY, WACHTER, C. CH., BOELSMA-VAN HOUTE, E. and VAN GENT, C. M., Fatty acid distribution in lipids of the aortic wall. *Lancet*, 1960, 1378–83.
2. CHALVARDJIAN, A. M. and STILL, W. J. S., La composition en acides gras de tissus chez le lapin nourri avec du cholestérol. *J. Atheroscler. Res.*, 1964, **4**, 507–16.
3. LOOMEIJER, F. J. and VAN DER VEEN, J., Incorporation de l'acétate (1–^{14}C) dans des lipides divers par l'aorte du rat *in vitro*. *J. Atheroscler. Res.*, 1962, **2**, 478.
4. STEIN, Y. and STEIN, O., Incorporation des acides gras dans les lipides de coupes d'aorte provenant de lapin, du chien, du rat et du babouin. *J. Atheroscler. Res.*, 1962, **2**, 400.
5. ZILVERSMIT, D. B., Le mécanisme du dépôt des lipides dans l'athéromatose. *Conférence, Faculté de Médecine*, Paris, 3 Nov. 1961.

CHAPTER 4

The Evolution of Ethylenic Fatty Acids in the Body

WE SHALL follow the ethylenic fatty acids in the body by dividing the process of metabolism into several periods.

I. Digestion and Absorption

Let us follow the ingested lipids step by step, paying particular attention to the ethylenic fatty acids.

(1) Frazer[14] has shown that the intestinal flora can reduce unsaturated fatty acids; this activity takes place in the large intestine; it appears to be of only slight interest to us.

(2) On reaching the intestine the lipids trigger off two secretions, biliary secretion and a pancreatic secretion which contains lipase.

(3) The biliary acids make a fine emulsion of the fats and the lipase condenses on the surface of the emulsion, which is thus very open to attack.

(4) The lipase acts on the triglycerides with the successive production of diglycerides and monoglycerides. The free fatty acids yield soaps. The whole forms a very fine emulsion which should be very easily absorbed.

The hydrolytic action of lipase should be particularly useful for the tripalmitates and trioleate; it should not be necessary for the acids with longer chains.[24] In any case, most fatty acids are absorbed in the free state.[33]

(5) In the course of absorption the process within the cell consists largely of triglyceride and phospholipid formation.[15] A considerable fraction is, therefore, found in the form of phospholipids or lipoproteins.[34] After the liberation of fatty acids by the lipase there is some exchange of fatty acids which is not yet clearly defined.[3]

The monoglycerides, diglycerides and triglycerides of long-chain fatty acids are incorporated into the neutral fats by means of a system which comprises ATP, Mg^{++} and CoA. This activity is seen particularly at the level of the duodenum.[10]

The electron microscope photograph produced by butter, which gives some spots of indefinite shape, differs from that produced by maize oil, which exhibits small spherules.[32]

(6) The triglycerides pass into the lymph.[35] Fatty acids with less than ten carbon atoms travel by the portal system.[1]

The triglycerides of the chyle appear to constitute the main mode of transport for oleic, palmitic and stearic acids in man. After the ingestion of linoleic acid only 4 per cent of the radioactivity of the lymph is found in the phospholipids, whereas with stearic acid the proportion is 20 per cent.

When the lecithins were isolated from the lymph, about 75 per cent of the ^{14}C-labelled linoleic acid was in the α-position. 80 per cent of the stearic acid was in the β-position.[4]

(7) The entire process of digestion and absorption can be summed up by the equation:

$$\frac{\text{Fats ingested} - (\text{faecal fats} - \text{metabolic fats})}{\text{Fats ingested}}$$

the values for the fats ingested and the faecal fats being taken from animals subjected to various experimental ingestions, and those for metabolic fats being taken from a group which does not receive any special supply of fats.

The absorption coefficient is high for sunflower seed oil, maize oil and pig fats; it is low for beef suet.[13] The saturated fatty acids have coefficients which diminish as the carbon chain of the acids lengthens. An ethylenic bond increases the coefficient to the same extent as the removal of six carbon atoms (oleic acid with eighteen carbon atoms has a coefficient close to that of lauric acid with twelve). The free acids have coefficients lower than the corresponding triglycerides. Triolein has the same coefficient as trilinolein.[8, 9]

When glucose, sucrose or starch was administered at the same time as olive oil, it was found that, in the rat, the quantity of oil found in the stomach five hours afterwards was increased as a result of the presence of these glucides.[27]

Disturbances of absorption have been noted in atherosclerotics.[17]

II. Transport by the Blood Stream

The absorbed fatty acids have been followed by Bragdon et al.[6] in the chylomicrons of the chyle in the rat and, later, in the chylomicrons of the blood in the rat and in man. The absorptions of olive oil which introduce particularly oleic acid gave the chylomicrons a content of oleic acid close to that of the oil. The percentages were in proportion to the totals of the lipids ingested: olive oil—67 per cent; chylomicrons of the chyle—63 per cent; chylomicrons of the blood—64 per cent. Under the same conditions absorption of maize oil introduced large quantities of linoleic acid: maize oil—57 per cent; chylomicrons of the blood—51 per cent. Coconut oil introduced large quantities of saturated acids which were found in the same way in the chylomicrons of the rat: coconut oil—95·6 per cent; chylomicrons of the lymph—86·3 per cent; blood—74 per cent. Corresponding figures for man were: coconut oil—100 per cent; chylomicrons of the blood—79 per cent.

In the same way cod liver oil introduces appreciable quantities of mono-ethenoid acids with twenty and twenty-two carbon atoms. In all these cases the chylomicrons reflect the composition of the oil in their fatty acids.

At times other than periods of absorption the different fatty acids of the serum lipids appear to maintain remarkably constant percentage values, and vary very little or not at all in the presence of atherosclerosis.

According to Holmer et al.,[19] youth favoured a high plasma content of poly-ethenoid acids except in the animal subjected to a diet containing arachis oil (10 per cent). In the latter case there was an increase of tetra-ethylenic and a reduction of di-ethylenic acids. There was also a deposit of di-ethylenic and tetra-ethylenic acids in the heart.

III. Influence of Atherosclerotic States

The findings of different authors vary somewhat, mainly because of differences in the method employed. Comparisons between normal and atherosclerotic subjects should, therefore, always be made with results published by the same author.

A. *Glycerides*

We shall use the investigations of Schrade et al.[29, 30]

	Normal	Atherosclerotic
Di-ethylenic fatty acids	11·2	10·9
Tri-ethylenic fatty acids	0·9	0·7
Tetra-ethylenic fatty acids	1·5	0·8

It is doubtful whether the disease reduced the percentage of poly-ethylenic acids. The difference is very small.

B. *Sterol Fatty Acids*

We give two analyses in Table XXI.

TABLE XXI

	Di-ethylenic	Tri-ethylenic	Tetra-ethylenic	Penta-ethylenic	Hexa-ethylenic
Björntrop et al.[2]					
Normal	42·2	2·6	6·1	2·2	1·7
Familial					
hypercholesterolaemic	37·8	2·7	5·9	2·1	1·8
Schrade et al.[29, 30]					
Normal	47·1	0·8	6·3		
Atherosclerotic	38·0	1·5	5·0		

Reduction is more sharply defined in the case of di-ethylenic and tetra-ethylenic fatty acids.

C. *Phospholipid Fatty Acids*

Schrade *et al.*[29, 30] give the values shown in Table XXII.

TABLE XXII

	Di-ethylenic	Tri-ethylenic	Tetra-ethylenic
Normal	22·2	0·7	6·6
Atherosclerotic	19·6	1·2	4·5

Here again the di-ethylenic and tetra-ethylenic fatty acids are reduced.

D. *Total Fatty Acids*

Table XXIV gives the results of two authors.

The reduction in the di-ethylenic and tetra-ethylenic acids seen in Schrade's analysis is not reproduced in that of Herdenstam.[18]

E. *The Iodine Indices of the Blood Lipids*

We give the analysis by Caren[7] in Table XXIII.

TABLE XXIII

	Glycerides	Steroids	Phospholipids
Normal	103·1	144·7	99·7
Coronary	97·0	148·0	123·0

It is hardly possible to draw any conclusion bearing on analysis of the different fatty acids from these figures. (In all the analyses the fatty acids are expressed as percentages of total lipids.)

F. *The Arachidonic Acid Content of Cholesterol Esters*

Finally, the arachidonic acid content of the cholesterol esters has been the subject of an interesting investigation by Swell *et al.*[31] They demonstrated that the species most sensitive to atherosclerosis were those in which the arachidonic acid content was lowest. The actual figures were: for the rat, 50 per cent; the dog, 17 per cent; man, 7·5 per cent; fowls, 5·2 per cent; the rabbit, 2·3 per cent; and the pig, 1·8 per cent.

TABLE XXIV

	Saturated	Mono-ethylenic	Di-ethylenic	Tri-ethylenic	Tetra-ethylenic	Penta-ethylenic	Hexa-ethylenic
Schrade[29, 30]							
Normal	46·2	26·86	19·43	4·43	3·1		
Atherosclerotic	53·5	26·11	14·67	4·11	1·58		
	55·5	25·1	13·7	3·99	1·53		
Herdenstam[18]							
Normal (males)			10·0	1·6	2·0	0·9	1·8
(females)			10·2	1·6	2·1	0·9	1·7
Coronary (males)			9·7	1·6	2·1	0·9	1·1
(females)			10·2	1·6	2·1	0·9	1·8

IV. Metabolism of Mono-ethylenic Fatty Acids

We know the course of the synthesis of saturated fatty acids, which reproduces very obviously the process of β-oxidation in reverse. The animal is capable of synthesizing very large quantities of oleic acid.[22]

A. *Analysis of Mono-ethylenic Acids*

It would appear that the anabolism of mono-ethylenic acids can occur in two ways.

(1) By desaturation of a saturated acid. Bloomfield *et al.*[5] give a schema obtained with *Saccharomyces cerevisiae*, which can perhaps be extended to man. Starting with palmitic acid there is the following series of reactions:

$$\text{Palmitic acid} \xrightarrow{\quad CoA+ATP+Mg^{++} \quad} \text{Palmityl CoA}$$

$$\text{Palmityl CoA} \xrightarrow{\quad O_2+TPN\ H \quad} \text{Oxypalmityl CoA}$$

$$\text{Oxypalmityl CoA} \longrightarrow \text{Palmitoleyl CoA}$$

$$\text{Palmitoleyl CoA} \longrightarrow \text{Palmitoleic acid} + CoA$$

Thus, the action of the thioester extends to a distance of eight carbon atoms.

(2) For several years Faverger *et al.*[11, 12] have been insisting that, within the first few minutes after an intravenous injection of ^{14}C-labelled acetate, a considerable quantity of unsaturated fatty acids appears. They are of the opinion that "saturated acids and oleic acid each have their own mode of formation".

Synthetic processes involving reduction occur in the soluble cytoplasm, which constitutes a reducing medium. The process of oxidation occurs in the mitochondria.[23]

B. *Catabolism of Mono-ethylenic Acids*

Catabolism appears to take place in two ways.

(1) By a process, the reverse of that which we have previously described, oleic acid may be converted into stearic acid and palmitoleic into palmitic acid.

(2) James *et al.*[20, 21] assume that the evolution of oleic acid proceeds in a manner parallel to that of poly-ethylenic acids, towards the formation of poly-ethylenic acids with twenty carbon atoms, the two new ethylenic bonds being situated in the chain of eleven carbon atoms between the ethylenic bond and the carboxyl group. We then have the acid:

$$CH_3 \cdot (CH_2)_7 \cdot CH = CH \cdot CH_2 \cdot CH = CH \cdot CH_2 \cdot CH = CH \cdot (CH_2)_3 \cdot COOH$$

C. *Organs Co-operating in these Conversions*

Various organs co-operate in these conversions: classically, the liver is the central organ, but Favarger [11, 12] is of the opinion that hepatic metabolism in the mouse is not particularly directed to lipid anabolism. Lonedec *et al.*[25] have, however, shown that fatty acids are grouped in the rat liver in the following way.

(1) The triglycerides are of the following type:

$$glycerol \begin{cases} \text{unsaturated acid} \\ \text{saturated acid} \\ \text{unsaturated acid} \end{cases} \text{66 per cent of unsaturated acids}$$

(2) The phosphoglycerides are of the types:

$$glycerol \begin{cases} \text{unsaturated} \\ \text{saturated} \end{cases} \text{and glycerol} \begin{cases} \text{saturated} \\ \text{unsaturated} \end{cases}$$

with 60 per cent saturated acids (particularly stearic).
Penta-ethylenic and hexa-ethylenic acids are found in sphingomyelin.

(3) The steroids contain 80 per cent unsaturated acids particularly oleic.

Synthesis appears to be more active in the brown intrascapular fat of the mouse. The fatty deposits in the connective tissue are active centres for the catabolism of fatty acids.[28] The intestine and lung synthesize an appreciable quantity of fatty acids from acetate and glucose.

The brain would appear to behave differently from the other organs. Essentially it incorporates mevalonic acid in fatty acids.[16]

V. **Metabolism of Poly-ethylenic Fatty Acids**

The poly-ethylenic fatty acids are essentially introduced in food. Their unsaturated bonds are situated between the CH_3 group and the $CH=CH \triangle 9$ bond, which is that of oleic acid. There are thus two series, that of linoleic and that of linolenic acids. Feeble synthesis of animal origin appears, however, to occur in the red cells of man.[20, 21]

Catabolism causes these acids to undergo two changes (those which we have indicated for oleic acid). These are augmented by two carbon atoms situated in the chain between the Δ^9 ethylenic bond and the carboxyl group and the appearance of two new ethylenic bonds in the same portion of the chain. The following schema of linoleic acid can be transposed to arachidonic acid.[26]

$$CH_3 \cdot (CH_2)_4 \cdot CH = CH \cdot CH_2 \cdot CH \cdot ^{\Delta 9-10}$$
$$= CH \cdot (CH_2)_7 \cdot COOH \text{ linoleic acid}$$

$$CH_3 \cdot (CH_2)_4 \cdot CH = CH \cdot CH_2 \cdot CH \cdot ^{\Delta 9-10}$$
$$= CH \cdot CH_2 \cdot CH = CH \cdot (CH_2)_4 \cdot COOH \quad \gamma\text{-linoleic acid}$$

$$CH_3 \cdot (CH_2)_4 \cdot CH = CH \cdot CH_2 \cdot CH \cdot ^{\Delta 9-10}$$
$$= CH \cdot CH_2 \cdot CH = CH \cdot (CH_2)_6 \cdot COOH$$

$$CH_3 \cdot (CH_2)_4 \cdot CH = CH \cdot CH_2 \cdot CH \cdot ^{\Delta 9-10}$$
$$= CH \cdot CH_2 \cdot CH = CH \cdot CH_2 \cdot CH = CH \cdot (CH_2)_3 \cdot COOH$$
arachidonic acid

We shall see the important part played by these acids.

References

1. BELLA, DI, Absorption intimale des triglycérides. *Minerva Med.*, 1960, **51**, 153–8.
2. BJÖRNTROP, P. and HOOD, B., Pattern of cholesterol ester fatty acids in serum in normal subjects and in patients with essential hypercholesterolemia. *Circ. Res.*, 1960, **8**, 319–23.
3. BLOMSTRAND, R., Intestinal absorption of phospholipids in the rat. *Acta Physiol. Scand.*, 1955, **34**, 1–11.
4. BLOMSTRAND, R., DAHLBACK, O. and LINDER, E., Asymmetric incorporation of linoleic acid 1-^{14}C and stearic acid 1-^{14}C inhuman lymph lecithins during fat absorption. *Proc. Soc. Exp. Biol.*, 1959, **100**, 768–71.
5. BLOOMFIELD, D. K. and BLOCH, K., The formation of Δ^9 unsaturated fatty acids. *J. Biol. Chem.*, 1960, **235**, 337–45.
6. BRAGDON, J. H. and KARMEN, A., The fatty acid composition of chylomicrons of chyle and serum following the ingestion of different oils. *J. Lipid Res.*, 1960, **1**, 167–70.
7. CAREN, R. and CORBO, L., The degree of unsaturation of plasma lipid fractions in coronary artery disease. *Amer. J. Med. Sci.*, 1958, **236**, 362–8.
8. CARROL, K. K., Digestibility of individual fatty acids in the rat. *J. Nutrit.*, 1958, **64**, 399–410.
9. CARROL, K. K. and RICHARDO, J. F., Factors affecting digestibility of fatty acids in rat. *J. Nutrit.*, 1958, **64**, 411–24.
10. DAWSON, A. M. and ISSELBACHER, K. J., The esterification of palmitate 1-^{14}C by homogenates of intestinal mucosa. *J. Clin. Invest.*, 1960, **39**, 150–60.
11. FAVARGER, P., La synthèse des graisses chez l'animal intact. *Path. Biol.*, 1958, **6**, 1021–32.
12. FAVARGER, P. and GERLACH, J., Recherches sur la synthèse des graisses à partir d'acétate: étude expérimentale critique. *Helv. Physiol. Pharmacol. Acta*, 1958, **16**, 188–200.
13. FEDDE, M. R., WAIBEL, P. E. and BURGER, R. E., Factors affecting the absorbability of certain dietary fats in the chick. *J. Nutrit.*, 1960, **70**, 447–52.
14. FRAZER, A. C., Absorption des corps gras. *Path. Biol.*, 1956, **32**, 239–50.
15. FRAZER, A. C., Fat absorption and its disorders. *Brit. Med. Bull.*, 1958, **14**, 212–20.
16. GARATTINI, J., PAOLETTI, P. and PAOLETTI, R., Lipid biosynthesis *in vivo* from acetate 1-^{14}C and 2-^{14}C and mevalonic 2-^{14}C acid. *Arch. Biochem. Biophys.*, 1959, **84**, 254–5.
17. GRANDONICO, F., SALVINI, L. and CITI, S., Etudes sur l'absorption des graisses chez l'homme dans divers états pathologiques, au moyen de l'oléine et la trioléine marquée sur l' [131]I. *Minerva Gastroenter.*, 1960, **6**, 1–5.

18. HERDENSTAM, C., Serum polyunsaturated fatty acids in coronary heart disease. *Acta Med. Scand.*, 1960, **166**, 475–86.
19. HOLMER, G., KRISTENSEN, G., SONDERGAARD, E. and DAM, H., Poly-enoic fatty acids and cholesterol in blood and liver of chicks on hydrogenated and unhydrogenated arachis oil. *Brit. J. Nutrit.*, 1959, **14**, 247–51.
20. JAMES, A. T., Essential fatty acids. *Amer. J. Clin. Nutrit.*, 1958, **6**, 650–1.
21. JAMES, A. T., LOVELOCK, J. E. and WEBB, J. P. W., The biosynthesis of fatty acids by the human red blood cell. *Essential Fatty Acids* (Ed., Sinclair), Butterworths, London, 1958, pp. 72–79.
22. KLENK, E., Über die Biogenese der C_{20} und C_{22} Polyensäuren bei den Säugetieren. *Proc. 2nd International Conference on Biochemical Problems of Lipids, Ghent*, 1955. Butterworths, London, 1956, pp. 187–92.
23. LANGDON, R. G., The biosynthesis of fatty acids in rat liver. *J. Biol. Chem.*, 1957, **226**, 615–29.
24. LIN, T. M., KARVINEN, E. and IVY, A. C., Function of pancreatic juice in fat utilization in the rat. *Amer. J. Physiol.*, 1957, **189**, 113–16.
25. LONEDEC, A. and PASCAUD, M., Nature des acides gras des divers lipides hépatiques du rat. *C.R. Acad. Sci. (Paris)*, 1958, **247**, 1408–11.
26. MEAD, J. F. and HOWTON, D. R., Interconversions of the unsaturated fatty acids. *Essential Fatty Acids* (Ed., Sinclair), Butterworths, London, 1958, pp. 65–71.
27. MICHAJLICK, A. and BRAGDON, J. H., Effects of carbohydrate on fat absorption. *Circulation*, 1959, **29**, 964.
28. POLONOVSKI, J., Biochimie du tissu adipeux. *Path. Biol.*, 1957, **5**, 1595–1606.
29. SCHRADE, W., BOHLE, E. and BIEGLER, R., Über den Polyensäuregehalt der verschiedenen Lipidfractionen des Blutes bei der Arteriosklerose und den Diabetes mellitus. *Klin. Wschr.*, 1959, **37**, 1101–9.
30. SCHRADE, W., BIEGLER, R. and BOHLE, E., Über den Polyensäurengehalt des Blutes bei verschiedenen Krankheiten. *Fette, Seifen, Anstrichmittel*, 1959, **61**, 10–15.
31. SWELL, L., FIELD, J. R. and TREADWELL, C. R., Correlation of arachidonic acid of serum cholesterol esters in different species with susceptibility to atherosclerosis. *Proc. Soc. Exp. Biol.*, 1960, **104**, 325–8.
32. THOMAS, W. A. and O'NEAL, R. M., Electron microscopy studies of butter and corn oil in jejunal mucosa. *Arch. Path.*, 1960, **69**, 121–9.
33. TIDWELL, H. C., Absorption of free and combined fatty acids. *Proc. Soc. Exp. Biol.*, 1958, **98**, 12–16.
34. TIDWELL, H. C., Lipid transport. *Amer. J. Clin. Nutrit.*, 1960, **8**, 310–14.
35. VAHOUNY, G V. and TREADWELL, C. R., Comparative effects of dietary fatty acids and triglycerides on lymph lipids in the rat. *Amer. J. Physiol.*, 1959, **196**, 881–3.

CHAPTER 5

Lipid Food Substances without Action in Relation to Atherosclerosis

SOME food substances containing mono-ethenoid fatty acids have no effect on the development of atherosclerosis.

Such substances are some natural oils, such as olive and arachis oil, or again substances of industrial origin, the action of which varies with the mode of preparation, such as margarine.

These heterogeneous elements will be grouped together in this chapter, although such grouping is undoubtedly a little artificial.

I. Olive Oil (Olea europea *L. Fam. Oleaceae*)

A. *Chemistry*

Its iodine index is about 85. The following is the fatty acid composition:

	Saturated				Unsaturated	
C_{14}	C_{16}	$C_{18} >$	C_{18}	$< C_{18}$	oleic	linoleic
1	7	1	0·5	0·5	80	10

B. *Biological Effect*

Malmros and Wigand[12] administered olive oil to healthy subjects and to 19 atherosclerotics. The oil was given in daily doses of 150 g, providing about 40 per cent of the calories in the diet. Its effect was favourable but slight.

Armstrong *et al.*[1] studied the effect of olive oil on 122 young males and 19 young females. They administered 57 g in addition to the subjects' food for a period of nine days. They observed a reduction of only 10·7 per cent in the blood cholesterol, although this reduction was statistically significant.

Schettler and Eggstein[14] administered olive oil, 80 g daily, to students who were on various diets for periods of 15–20 days. There was a reduction in the blood cholesterol of about 18 per cent. Other lipids were also reduced, only the phosphatides being unchanged. Similar, but irregular and smaller changes were seen in atheromatous subjects.

Keys *et al.*[11] thought that the oleic glycerides acted as an isocaloric quantity of glucides or, in other words, had practically no effect on blood cholesterol.

Holzner *et al.*[9] studied the comparative effects of olive oil and pork fat in rabbits which were also receiving cholesterol. Atherosclerotic lesions were less marked with olive oil.

Gounelle[5] experimenting with ten atheromatous subjects and using pure olive oil as the only source of fat found a decrease in the rate of lipids metabolized, in particular those of animal origin. He noticed a fall in blood lipids of about 26 per cent (14·2 per cent for cholesterol).

Johnson[10] replying to a question on the use of olive oil in a diet to counter hypercholesterolaemia could not obtain this last affect with other unsaturated fatty acids. He considered that a neutral fat should be used to improve the diet but one which does not increase the calories.

Grande[6] giving coconut fats and olive oil to the dog obtained the same result with or without these oils. He concluded that it is inactive but this does not take any account of the effect produced by the absorption of ethylenic acids.

II. Arachis Oil (Arachis hypogaea L. Fam. Leguminosae)

A. *Chemistry*

The iodine index is about 92. The fatty acid composition is as follows:

Saturated					Unsaturated	
C_{14}	C_{16}	C_{18}	C_{18}	C_{18}	oleic	linoleic
0·5	8	2·5	7	2	55	25

Its composition is thus close to that of olive oil, with slightly more linoleic and less oleic acid.

B. *Biological Results*

(1) Hammerl et al.[8] concluded that the oil increased cholesterol in 6 normal subjects given various doses.

(2) Finzi[4] would appear to have obtained more favourable results.

(3) Very large doses given to thirty-three rabbits produced macroscopic aortic lesions in 2 cases and microscopic lesions in ten cases after 12 months.[15]

Generally, the effect of arachis oil would appear to be only slightly atherosclerogenic, if the oil is not entirely without action.

III. Avocado Oil (Persea gratissima Goerth. Fam. Lauraceae)

A. *Chemistry*

The fatty acid composition of this oil is as follows:

Saturated acids			Unsaturated acids	
Palmitic acids	C_{16}	C_{18}	oleic	linoleic
	7·2	0·6	81	11·3

It is thus close to the preceding oils.

B. *Biological Investigations*

Grant[7] substituted avocado oil for the usual fats for periods of 2 to 12 weeks in sixteen subjects. Blood cholesterol was reduced by 12–21 per cent in half the cases and half exhibited no changes.

IV. Modified Milk Products

Milk concentrates with the natural fats removed are prepared in America. The fats are replaced by maize oil. As the emulsification is good, the illusion is complete. Ice cream and cheeses are prepared in the same way with milk artificially enriched in unsaturated fatty acids.

V. Frying Oils

Frying oils undergo profound chemical changes in the course of frying— oxidation, cyclization, polymerization. Unfortunately, the less saturated the oil, the more considerable are these changes. Unsaturated oil will, therefore, be used for atheromatous subjects and great care will be taken to avoid useless overheating and to renew the oil frequently. These precautions eliminate commercially fried products (chipped potatoes, fritters) from the ordinary diet of atherosclerotic patients, which should be replaced only by food fried with careful supervision.

Several points require further definition.

(1) Various factors must be considered in connexion with frying.

(a) The condition of the fat used. A common practice is to add fresh oil to the oil which has already been used for frying several times. This is a practice which is economic but dangerous as it retains and concentrates all the toxic products of cooking. The oil should, therefore, be renewed frequently and completely. The colour of the oil, which darkens gradually as it changes, can undoubtedly be used by the person responsible as a guide in this respect.

Custot's[3] measurements gave a minimum temperature of 150°C for the second frying. If a well-browned "fry" was desired the temperature had to be raised to 170°C, but there was no advantage in going much beyond these temperatures. This test operation was carried out with an initial 2 l. of oil and 500 g of raw potato.

(b) The body to be fried is plunged into the hot oil. The body introduces water which creates a protective vapour and, at the same time reduces the temperature, which falls to between 110° and 120°C. Finally, interactions are set up at this point between the body cooking and the oil, reactions which sometimes are protective to the oil but sometimes, on the other hand, hasten changes therein. In any case, this period is the least dangerous of all.

(c) The fried substance is drained. This is obviously a period in which the oil running off is very much exposed to oxidation by the air and undergoes considerable change. It is, therefore, recommended that the drops falling from the fry should not be received in the vessel containing the fat which will be used again for the next frying.

Certain quantities of the fats used—7–8 per cent in the case of frys, 16–18 per cent in fritters and 35–45 per cent in chips—always remained in the food substances.[3]

(d) Finally, the food is cooled. Its exposure to air and the spreading out of the food in too large and uncovered containers are factors which, even at this last period in the operation, favour oxidation harmful to the poly-ethenoid fatty acids of the fat employed.

(2) The effects of these oils on experimental atherosclerosis have been studied by Nishida et al.[13] Maize oil heated for 24 hours at 195°C still reduced blood cholesterol. It behaved in the same way as unheated oil in relation to atheromatous deposits.

VI. Modified Margarine

Initially, margarines are often composed of vegetable oils rich in un-saturated fatty acids but, in order to give them the consistency of butter, the manufacturers submit them to catalytic reductions which reduce the number of ethylenic bonds considerably and also change the positions of these bonds in the molecule. Hence, in relation to atheroma, they behave in the same way as butter, their consistency being similar.

In view of this disadvantage, margarine manufacturers in all countries have produced margarines which are modified by the addition of natural maize oil. An American margarine contained 34 per cent of linoleic acid and 52 per cent of total fatty acids of unsaturated type. A French margarine contained 44 per cent of unsaturated acids. Not only, therefore, are these products less atherogenic but, in the best forms, would even appear to have a favourable effect on blood cholesterol.

The experiments of Boyer et al.,[2] with a margarine containing 44·5 per cent of the total fats in the form of linoleic acid, demonstrated a reduction of 23 per cent in the blood cholesterol of man after eighteen weeks. Twelve weeks after the administration of this margarine was stopped the blood cholesterol had risen by 19 per cent.

To sum up, the oils used as the starting material for the manufacture of margarine are poly-ethylenic but during reduction to the consistency of butter some bonds become reduced. The biological effect is therefore the same as that of butter or even worse. In order to improve the margarine it is necessary to add some poly-ethylenic oil. As a result of this it becomes semi-liquid and has to be sold in boxes. It is only in this form that medical interest in it revives.

Vegetable butters of plant origin are usually solid and accordingly reduced; they have therefore become dangerous and the patient should not be deceived by their name.

Finally, foods which are rich in mono-ethenoid fatty acids appear to be inactive and neither diminish nor increase the blood cholesterol in man or animals or the arterial deposits in experimental animals.

References

1. ARMSTRONG, W. D., PILSUM, J. VAN, KEYS, A., GRANDE, F., ANDERSON, J. T. and TOBIAN, L., Alteration of serum cholesterol by dietary fats. *Proc. Soc. Exp. Biol.*, 1957, **96**, 302–6.
2. BOYER, P. A., LOWE, J. T., GARDIER, R. W. and RALSTON, J. D., Effect of practical dietary regimen on serum cholesterol levels. *J. Amer. Med. Ass.*, 1959, **170**, 257–61.
3. CUSTOT, F., Toxicité des graisses chauffés. Le problème des huiles de friture. *Ann. Nutrit.* (*Paris*), 1959, **13**, A, 416–48.
4. FINZI, M., Utilisation des mélanges de graisses végétales en diététique clinique. VIe Convoquo della Salute, Ferrare, 23–24 Mai 1959.
5. GOUNELLE, H., FONTAN, P. and DEMARE, M., Olive oil and blood cholesterol levels. *Amer. J. Clin. Nutrit.*, 1962, **10**, 119–23.
6. GRANDE, F., Effect of monoene fatty acid glycerides on šerum cholesterol concentration in the dog. *Fed. Proc.*, 1962, **21** (2), 100.
7. GRANT, W. C., Influence of avocados on serum cholesterol. *Fed. Proc.*, 1960, **19**, 18.
8. HAMMERL, H., PICHLER, O. and SIEDEK, H., Comparative studies on the serum lipid content after test doses of butter fat and different vegetable oils. *Wien. Klin. Wschr.*, 1959, **71**, 761–4.
9. HOLZNER, H., KRIEHUBER, E. and WENGER, R., Experimentelle Untersuchungen zur Arteriosklerosefrage. *Wien. Med. Wschr.*, 1960, **110**, 198–200.
10. JOHNSON, O. C., Olive oil. *J. Amer. Med. Ass.*, 1961, **176**, 642.
11. KEYS, A., ANDERSON, J. T. and GRANDE, F., Serum cholesterol in man: diet fat and intrinsic responsiveness. *Circulation*, 1959, **19**, 201–14.
12. MALMROS, H. and WIGAND, G., The effect on serum cholesterol of diets containing different fats. *Lancet*, 1957, **273**, 1–7.
13. NISHIDA, T., TAKENAKA, F. and KUMMEROW, F. A., Effect of dietary protein and heated fat on serum cholesterol and β-lipoprotein levels and on incidence of experimental atherosclerosis in chicks. *Circ. Res.*, 1958, **6**, 194–202.
14. SCHETTLER, G. and EGGSTEIN, M., Fette, Ernährung und Arteriosklerose. *Dtsch. Med. Wschr.*, 1958, **83**, 702–6, 709–10, 750–5.
15. STEINER, A. and DAYTON, J., Production of hyperglycemia and early atherosclerosis in rabbits by a high vegetable-fat diet. *Circ., Res.*, 1956, **4**, 62.

CHAPTER 6

Atherosclerogenic Food Substances

VARIOUS food substances have been found to give rise to atherosclerosis in man and animals and we shall consider four types.

I. Milk and Foods Derived from it: Butter, Cream and Cheese

Chemical similarity due to their common origin confers upon these foods the same effect on atherosclerosis but with varying intensity. These milk products have the same lipid make up as the fats of milk from which they are all derived.

The general composition of the lipid fraction of milk is weighted heavily on the side of the triglycerides (about 98 to 99 per cent). The phospholipids reach, at the most, 1 per cent and the sterols do not exceed 0·4 per cent. The free fatty acids, waxes and squalene are present in only trace amounts. Finally small quantities of vitamins A and E are detectable. The iodine number of the whole lipid fraction is about 38. It is therefore the triglycerides which supply nearly all the fatty acids present.

1. *The saturated fatty acids of the triglycerides of milk.* These are for the most part saturated fatty acids (60 to 75 per cent are saturated). The general composition can be expressed in the following ways, which are calculated from ten analyses published by different authors.

SATURATED FATTY ACIDS WITH EVEN NUMBER OF CARBON ATOMS
IN THE TRIGLYCERIDES OF MILK

Molecules per cent by weight			
$C_4 = 9·65$	$C_{10} = 3·7$	$C_{16} = 24·5$	$C_{22} = 0·07$
$C_6 = 3·0$	$C_{12} = 4·0$	$C_{18} = 10·5$	$C_{24} = 0·05$
$C_8 = 1·8$	$C_{14} = 11·3$	$C_{20} = 0·87$	$C_{26} = 0·06$

One can see the particular importance of the short-chain fatty acids and especially C_4, C_{14} and C_{16}.

Fatty acids less than C_{18} are synthesized from acetyl CoA in the mammal. Fatty acids of more than C_{18} are transported by the blood stream from fats absorbed from the diet of the animal.

Other fatty acids, although present in small quantities, should be noted since we must record how ignorant we are of their possible effect on atherosclerosis.

These are synthesized in the gut of the ruminant by the intestinal flora. They arise from propionic acid by the addition of acetyl groups and therefore contain an odd number of carbons. They represent about 1·7 per cent of the fatty acids from the triglycerides of milk. These are acids with C_{11} (trans) C_{13}, C_{16}, C_{17} (predominant), C_{21}, C_{23} (Shoreland *et al.*; Hansen *et al.*; Patton, Hallgren).

Others arise from the deamination and oxidative decarboxylation of certain amino acids (valinel, leucine, isoleucine). Branched chain acids of C_{13} to C_{18} amount to only 1 per cent.

2. *The unsaturated fatty acids of the triglycerides.* Among the main ones are the monoethylenic fatty acids. The following table gives the average of eight analyses.

Molecules per cent				
C_{10}	0·3	C_{14} 1·30	C_{18}	26·40
C_{12}	0·34	C_{16} 2·40	C_{20}	0·90

It can be seen that the type of acid which predominates more than any other is oleic.

The polyunsaturated fatty acids are non-conjugated of C_2, C_3, C_4, C_5 and C_6 with each one rarely exceeding 1 per cent. There is a slight predominance of the di-enoic acids, a small amount of which are generally conjugated. The di-enoic acids rarely exceed 1 per cent while the tri- and tetra-enoic acids are only of the order of 0·01 to 0·001 per cent.

It can be seen therefore that oleic acid and palmitic acid predominate, that there are also trans acids and conjugated diethylenic fatty acids.

The di-, tri- and tetra-enoic acids are present in only very small amounts, none of them greater than 3 per cent.

One can see two influences in their formation: the vegetable diet which imposes seasonal variations and the reducing action of the gut flora, which reduces the number of ethylenic bonds and even removes them at times.

3. *The fatty acids of the milk phospholipids.* About a third of the phospholipids are distributed into three practically equal groups as follows:

    1. Phosphatidylcholine.
    2. Phosphatidylethanolamine or phosphatidylserine.
    3. Sphingomyelin.

The importance that this last group plays in the atheromatous deposits in atherosclerosis is known.

In addition there are traces of cerebrosides, plasmalogens and phospho-inositols.

The fatty acids of these compounds are little known. We know that palmitic acid predominates, an analogue of arachidonic acid, oleic acid and an acid $C_{26}H_{52}O_2$.

On the whole, they are different to those of the triglycerides being less saturated. They appear to be synthesized in the liver and transported by the blood stream.

To sum up, the following facts should particularly be kept in mind: the fatty acids of milk are supplied by herbivorous animals and would be similar to those of plants if two organs did not intervene to modify them profoundly:

the udder which gives short carbon chains,

the gut which saturates these acids.

Furthermore, the considerable predominance of glycerides and the presence of sphingomyelin in trace amounts should be noted.

I. *Cow's Milk*

Cow's milk is, in effect, what concerns us. It has the following average composition per hundred millilitres:

Proteins 3·5; glucides, etc., 4·2; salts 0·70; water 88 and—what is the important point—lipids 3·60. A person who drinks 3 l. of milk daily, which is quite a large quantity, thus absorbs about 100 g lipids; as these lipids are, in fact, those found in butter, we can, therefore, reckon that the subject absorbs about 30–40 g of saturated fatty acids. Preformed cholesterol is minimal and of little account.

It must also be noted that milk contains 3·18 per cent casein among its proteins. The subject who absorbs 3 l. of milk thus has an absorption of 96 g casein. We shall see that casein, even when freed from all milk fats is atherosclerogenic[17, 47] and increases blood cholesterol.[2, 45, 52]

Even lactose has been suspected of causing hypercholesterolaemia by affecting lipid absorption (Wells *et al.* [64a]).

If these ideas are confirmed then milk would be really suspect, since only the water which it contains could be considered as not dangerous. It is necessary to await confirmation for casein and lactose before passing such a severe judgement.

The saturated fatty acid content, and possibly the considerable quantity of casein in milk, are probably responsible for many very important phenomena.

Various authors[62, 63] have observed that, among subjects with gastric ulcer submitted to various dietetic regimes, clinical accidents (infarct) were statistically much more frequent among those who had been on exclusively milk diets. In 1960 Briggs *et al.*[15] examined necropsy reports and showed that myocardial infarct was much more frequent (more than twice as frequent) in subjects who had been on milk diets than in ulcer subjects treated differently or in subjects free from ulcer. There was no significant difference between the last two types. This enquiry covered fifteen hospitals in the United States and Great Britain.

II. *Butter*

Butter is the food substance which has been most fully examined.

A. *Butter is rich in saturated fatty acids, a considerable fraction of these being short-chain acids.* Its iodine index is about 40.

Its (percentage) composition is:

Proteins 0·8; salts 0·07; water 6–20; but lipids are about 83 per cent and cholesterol 0·3 per cent.

The quantity of preformed cholesterol introduced by a diet rich in butter is still, therefore, minimal. The quantity of glycerides is considerable. Phosphatides represent only 0·03–0·1 per cent and are not of any importance.

The fatty acids of butter are distributed in the following manner:

(1) saturated fatty acids with short chains (from C_4 to C_{10}) 10 per cent
(2) myristic acid   10 per cent
(3) palmitic acid   20–30 per cent
(4) stearic acid   10 per cent

This gives a total of 50–60 per cent saturated fatty acids
(5) oleic acid   30–40 per cent

In addition there are very small quantities of acids with one unsaturated bond (C_{10}, C_{12}, C_{14}, C_{16}, C_{20}, C_{22}), with two unsaturated bonds (C_{18}, C_{20}), with three (C_{18}, C_{20}, C_{22}), and with four and five unsaturated bonds (C_{20}, C_{22}). There are also some fatty acids with odd numbers of carbon atoms. The points of essential importance are:

The large quantity of saturated fatty acids.
The presence among them of an appreciable quantity of short-chain fatty acids.

These two features are not balanced by the presence of poly-ethylenic acids in sufficient quantity. Oleic acid, which is neutral in relation to atherosclerosis, is the only acid present in considerable quantity.

B. *Butter increases cholesterolaemia in animals and man.* (1) Butter increases cholesterolaemia in the chicken (March and Biely, 1959;[46] Adamson, Leeper and Ross, 1961[1]).

(2) In 1960 Wigand[66] gave thirteen rabbits a semi-synthetic diet containing no cholesterol but 25 per cent of casein and 8 per cent of butter. The butter had the following composition: saturated fatty acids 58·6 per cent; acids with one unsaturated bond 38 per cent; with several unsaturated bonds 3·4 per cent; cholesterol 0·27 per cent. The diet was maintained for 18 weeks. The results are shown in the following table.

TABLE XXV. SERUM CONTENTS (mg/100 ml)

	Free cholesterol	Bound cholesterol	Total cholesterol	Triglycerides
Before	11·2	17·6	28·8	148·6
After	93·9	249·5	343·4	130·3
Difference	82·8	231·0	314·6	−18·3
p	<0·001	<0·001	<0·001	>0·05

	Phospholipids	Total lipids	Total cholesterol/ phospholipids	
Before	60·3	249·7	0·49	
After	180·2	823·5	1·94	
Difference	119·9	573·9	1·45	
p	<0·001	<0·001	<0·001	

Blood cholesterol and total lipids were thus considerably increased. Triglycerides were unchanged. Phospholipids were increased but to a much lesser extent than cholesterol. Esterized cholesterol was increased the most.

Funch[28] gave butter to nine rabbits and observed hypercholesterolaemia and hyperlipoproteiaemia in the seven rabbits which were alive at the end of the experiment. It is clear that the results are most often positive in the rabbit.

(3) Bragdon et al.[14] showed that butter, added to the regular diet, increased blood cholesterol in pigs.

(4) Two series of experiments concern monkeys. In 1956 Galapan et al.[29] studied the changes in blood cholesterol produced by large quantities of butter (56 per cent of the lipids in the diet) administered over a period of 2 months. Initially 0·14 per cent, the blood cholesterol reached 0·24 per cent at the end of the experiment. There was no increase from sesame oil, used as a control.

In 1959 Emerson et al.[26] studied the effect of a butter-rich diet in monkeys which also received 50 mg pyridoxine daily. The butter still increased the blood cholesterol.

(5) The results were similar in the case of man. In 1956 Beveridge et al.[12] administered quite large quantities of butter to forty-eight normal subjects over a period of 8 days. Blood cholesterol rose. The "most volatile" fractions

of butter, which were isolated by a process which is not described by the authors, were the most active. These were undoubtedly the short-chain acids.

In 1957 Keys et al.[43] administered 100 g butter daily (40 per cent of the total lipids in the diet) to twenty-six normal subjects. Their blood cholesterols were increased and were above those of controls given vegetable oils.

In 1957 Horlick and Graig[37] observed a reduction in the blood cholesterol of subjects deprived of butter, whether replaced by vegetable oils or not.

In 1957 Armstrong et al.[8] demonstrated on 122 subjects that butter produced a moderate, yet statistically significant, increase of blood cholesterol.

In 1958 Schettler et al.[58] showed that all lipids in the blood were increased in students who had consumed large quantities of butter, and that only the phosphatides were unchanged.

In 1959 Hammerl et al.[32] arrived at a similar conclusion in respect of total lipids in subjects who had consumed fairly large quantities. Various oils tested gave lower values.

In 1960 Hashim et al.[33] gave their subjects first butter and then synthetic saturated triglycerides. The latter, which are more saturated than butter, lowered the blood cholesterol. They concluded that butter had a specific action, increasing the blood cholesterol.

In 1961 Anderson, Grande and Keys[5] studied the effect on cholesterolaemia of butter compared with maize and olive oils, using a series of twenty-three schizophrenics. Butter gave a serum cholesterol of 233 mg per cent while olive oil and maize oil containing only the cis forms gave a value of 188 mg per cent.

It can be seen therefore that in the case of butter consistent observations are constantly found.

(6) In the rat thrombosis occurs after administration of a large quantity of butter in diets containing 40 per cent fat, 5 per cent cholesterol, 2 per cent cholic acid and 0·3 per cent thiouracil (Gresham et al., 1961 and 1962[31]; Naimi et al., 1962[50]).

C. *Butter produces the lesions of atherosclerosis in the pig and rabbit*, quite apart from any direct introduction of cholesterol.

(1) In 1959 Rowsell et al.[57] studied twelve pigs given a diet rich in butter and observed some development of atherosclerosis, although the blood cholesterol was only slightly increased.

More and his colleagues[49] studied pigs aged from $2\frac{1}{2}$ years. They gave them fodder rich in butter for 12 months and made a very large number of histological sections and compared them with a control series. The average number of aortic lesions was the same in the two groups, but the experimental series showed in addition fibrous lesions with smooth muscle cells in greatest quantity. Also it showed fatty cells and fat accumulation in smooth muscle.

(2) Post-mortem examination in the experiment of Wigand et al.,[66] referred to earlier, revealed one or more plaques (type + and + +, but no

type + + +) in twelve of the thirteen rabbits. There were no lipid deposits in the control rabbits (type 0).

In practice it will be remembered that, in the case of man, butter rations of 100 g daily will raise the blood cholesterol rapidly but that a similar effect can undoubtedly be produced by smaller doses if repeated daily over a number of years. Furthermore, in the animal butter itself can produce a type of atherosclerosis.

III. *Cream*

Cream has a fat content of from 30–50 per cent which is approximately half that of butter. Cholesterol is only 0·15 per cent. There have been no special investigations on cream but, from the practical standpoint, it probably behaves in the same way as butter, as cooks often use a weight of cream which is twice that of butter for preparations equivalent to those obtained with butter.

IV. *Cheeses*

Cheeses are rich in lipids, 30–35 per cent, and in casein, about 25–30 per cent. The lipids are those of butter.

They have not been studied as their importance in human nutrition is minimal. A reasonable portion of cheese, 50 g, is only the equivalent of 15 g of butter.

II. **Eggs, Normal or Modified**

Eggs have been extensively used for 50 years to induce atherosclerosis in rabbits. Their atherosclerogenic role would appear to be beyond doubt. In order that they may be used without danger, attempts had to be made to give fowls a diet rich in ethylenic fatty acids. We shall now describe these investigations.

I. *Normal Hens' Eggs*

Their composition affords part of the explanation of their activity.

A. *Composition of eggs.* Different analyses gave results which differ considerably, the eggs used being of widely varying origin.

(1) According to Terroine and Belin,[61] the general composition of an egg is as follows:

White 56·7 per cent; yolk 31·3 per cent and shell 11·4 per cent. As the weight of an egg is only very slightly above 50 g, it can be assumed that the yolk weighs about 17 g.

(2) According to Terroine and Belin,[61] the fatty acids are, for 100 g of

U.F.A.—5

yolk, 28·4 per cent of the fresh weight; an egg yolk contains, therefore, about 4·8 g of fatty acids.

(3) The distribution of the fatty acids (percentages of total fatty acids) is presented in Table XXVI.

TABLE XXVI

	Cruickshank[24]	James[42]
Saturated fatty acids	31·4%	43·12%
Unsaturated fatty acids	68·6%	56·88%
One egg therefore contains:		
Saturated fatty acids	1·5 g	2·07 g
Unsaturated fatty acids	3·28 g	2·73 g

According to James,[42] the saturated fatty acids are distributed as shown in Table XXVII.

TABLE XXVII

Acid	Percentage
Branched fatty acids	7·45
Myristic	0·33
n-Hexadecanoic	26·7
Stearic	8·64
Total	43·12

The unsaturated fatty acids are distributed as shown in Table XXVIII (percentage of total fatty acids):

TABLE XXVIII

Acid	Cruickshank[24] (percentage)	James[42] (percentage)
Palmitoleic		3·08
Oleic	46·7	46·9
Linoleic	19·0	
Linolenic	2·9	5·65
Arachidonic		1·28

Confining ourselves to the more recent analysis, we have the following values for an egg yolk (Table XXIX).

TABLE XXIX

Acid	Weight (g)	Acid	Weight (g)
Branched fatty acids	0·357	Palmitoleic	0·148
Myristic	0·016	Oleic	2·25
Hexadecanoic	1·28	Linoleic	0·27
Stearic	0·41	Linolenic	
Total saturated acids	2·063	Arachidonic	0·06
		Total unsaturated acids	2·73

An analysis by Fisher and Leveille[27] gave the results listed in Table XXX.

TABLE XXX

Acid		for one egg (g)
Linoleic	8·9	0·43
Linolenic	3·8	0·18
Total	12·7	Total 0·61

(4) The distribution between the constituent lipids was determined by Reiser[56] in 1951 (Table XXXI).

TABLE XXXI

Acids	Saturated	Oleic	Ethylenic				
			Di-	Tri-	Tetra-	Penta-	Hexa-
Glycerides	31	53	14·4	0·18	1·43	2·61	1·12
Phosphatides			20·1		9·1	9·2	3·79

The poly-ethylenic fatty acids would thus appear to be present in larger quantities in the phosphatides.

(5) Egg lipoproteins. In 1956 Schmidt et al.[59] centrifuged egg yolk at 20,000g.

There were two phases (see Table XXXII).

TABLE XXXII

Phase	Proteins (percentage of total)	Phospholipids (percentage of total)
Supernatant, clear yellow liquid	60	90
Granular	40	10

McIndoe[44] isolated from the upper phase a lipoprotein which represented almost the entire yolk lipids. A very close related lipoprotein is present in the serum of hens during the egg-laying period.

It yields two components on ultracentrifugation. It may possibly stand in some relationship to the spontaneous atherosclerosis which is frequent in the hen. It may also constitute an atherosclerogenic element in the subject who consumes eggs.

Experimental work with eggs showed that atherosclerosis was produced by regular use of increased quantities of cholesterol.

Chalatow[16] fed rabbits with enormous quantities of egg yolk. He found lipid deposits in the intima.

In 1913 Wesselkin[65] used a mixture of egg yolk and milk (one egg yolk daily for 6 months). He found crystalline lipid deposits in the intima.

Bailey[10] in 1916 and Anitschkow[7] in 1922 carried out experiments of a similar type. The latter gave a guinea-pig half an egg yolk daily for 6 months. These authors also observed lipid deposits.

In 1946 Altschul[3] produced cerebral atherosclerosis by giving egg yolk, milk or cholesterol. In 1950 the same author [4] produced atherosclerosis in the hamster by administering eggs and milk.

Nichols et al.[54] in 1956 had human subjects ingest seven eggs daily. They noted an increase of S_f 0–20 lipoproteins in these subjects who, previously, had been having little fatty foods.

In 1959 Wilgram[67] produced lipid deposits in the media and intima in the rat with a mixed diet containing 35 per cent of egg yolk and 25 per cent of lard.

In 1959 Rowsell et al.[57] noted hypercholesterolaemia and atherosclerotic deposits in twelve pigs fed with a diet in which 33 per cent of the calories was represented by egg yolks. Eggs appeared to be more active than butter.

Gordon et al.[30] administered ten eggs daily to a human subject. Blood cholesterol rose rapidly. This subject was thus receiving 3 g cholesterol daily in the eggs. The eggs were then omitted and were replaced by 3 g cholesterol daily. In 8 days the blood cholesterol had returned to its former level (it changed successively from 0·18 to 0·218 per cent and back to 0·18 per cent).

It would seem, therefore, that the effect produced by eggs is not due solely to the cholesterol that they introduce.

Horst et al., 1960[40] in experiments on the rat observed that the intravenous injection of egg yolk provoked lesions in the wall, which depended, moreover on primary lesions of the wall.

Wells and Bronte-Stewart[64] separated the lipids of egg yolk with acetone, the soluble fraction was itself fractionated into two parts both inactive, by saponification. Both the saponifiable fraction and the unsaponifiable fraction cause an increase of blood cholesterol in man if they are absorbed in less than 6 hours. It is thought, however, that this increase is due to association of cholesterol and a suitable fatty acid. A purely vegetarian diet which does not contain cholesterol could not, however, induce any symptoms.

These effects of egg yolk are denied by some authors who do not recognize that it has any special property: Anderson et al., 1962,[6] or even suggest a useful effect: Artemenko, 1960.[9]

It will be seen, therefore, that the doses of egg yolk administered were very large and that they were rarely consumed without the addition of foods which are also known to be atherosclerogenic (milk, lard). A definite conclusion is not easy. Two points do, however, emerge from these experiments generally:

(1) Eggs constitute a food which, in large doses, can produce increase of the blood cholesterol and lipid deposits in the arteries.

(2) Although the enormous numbers of eggs used by experimenters introduced considerable quantities of cholesterol it is improbable that this substance alone was responsible for the disturbances recorded. It is probable that the saturated fatty acids that accompanied them also constituted an important factor. Possibly also we should consider some special activity possessed by the forms of lipoprotein which we have discussed.

II. *Eggs Modified by Special Food Given to the Hens*

Attempts have naturally been made to modify the fatty acid composition of egg yolk by altering the diet of the hen, but it is not always easy to render the fatty acid selected or the corresponding oils acceptable to this bird. Fisher and Leveille[27] adsorbed these substances on calcium silicate, which the hens pecked readily. This, however, is not the only difficulty: the bird often reacts rather adversely to these attempts. Practically, therefore, the solution of the problem is quite difficult and the results would not appear to merit the effort required.

If one uses polyethylenic fatty acids in the diet of the chicken, these compounds increase in the egg but:

(1) The increase is extremely small compared with the large modification of the diet required (Horlick and O'Neil, 1958[38]).

(2) The increase of the polyethylenic acids is made at the expense of monoethylenic acids. The saturated acids are unaltered (Cruickshank, 1934;[24] Horlick and O'Neil, 1958[38]).

(3) There is little change in the total lipids, cholesterol and phosphatides (Reiser, 1951;[56] Fisher and Leveille, 1957[27]).

(4) Cholesterol detectable by the reaction of Zlatktis increases when the lipids are less saturated.

Moreover, a series of experiments shows the slight atherosclerogenic activity of these eggs.

(1) Horlick and O'Neil, 1960[39] studied two men receiving five modified eggs a day for 3 days. then ten eggs a day for 11 days. These diets were preceded by an intake of food poor in lipid except for soya-bean oil. The serum cholesterol fell continuously. It continued to fall in one of them but rose in the other.

In the subject who reacted favourably a return to normal a month later caused an increase of serum cholesterol: it settled down at 230 mg per 100 ml which was the value for the subject before all the experiments.

(2) In 1958 Gordon[30] and his colleagues used eggs from chickens fed on sunflower seeds. The subject of the experiment had first received ordinary eggs and the serum cholesterol increased. The substitution of the prepared eggs kept it at the same level.

When a second subject was treated in the same manner, the cholesterol continued to rise.

All these results can, therefore, be regarded as negative. It may be that some of these failures are due to the fact that sunflower seeds, the oil of which, as we shall see, has only a very limited effect on atherosclerosis, were often used to modify the hen eggs.

III. Lipids Associated with Meat

Butcher-meat comprises the striated muscles of the various domesticated mammalian animals. It introduces animal fats.

A. *Lipid Composition of Butcher-meat*

Even when the fat surrounding the muscle or present between the sheaths is removed, the meat still contains a considerable fraction of fats. They vary with the species of animal, its adiposity and age.

(1) Differences are, however, due largely to the anatomical position of the muscle used. Table XXXIII gives a classification in order of percentage of lipids in fresh tissue.[41]

TABLE XXXIII

Veal steak	9	Neck of pork	23
Veal sirloin	11	Loin of pork	23
Leg of veal	12	Beef sirloin	25
Beef steak	13	Shoulder of mutton	26
Chicken	13	Beef hamburger	28
Ox tongue	15	Beef ribs	31
Shoulder of beef	16	Fresh ham	31
Leg of mutton	17	Neck of pork (best end)	32
Mutton chops	17	Side of pork	32
Turkey	20	Smoked ham	35
Side of beef	23	Sausage meat	44

Storage in a refrigerator in which a certain amount of evaporation is possible increases the percentage of fats (by about 7 per cent). In grilled meats it is the intermuscular fats particularly which are lost, but in boiled meat there is no change in the relationship the fats bear to the raw weight. In practice these differences apply solely to the fats at the surface which one gets rid of mechanically or by grilling.

(2) The composition of these fats has been determined by a number of investigations.[11, 19, 25, 35]

(a) The iodine index of beef fat is about 40.

(b) The fatty acid compositions are given in Tables XXXIV and XXXV.

TABLE XXXIV. FATTY ACIDS

	Saturated			Mono-ethylenic	Poly-ethylenic	
	C_{14}	C_{16}	C_{18}	C_{18}	linoleic	arachidonic
Beef						
Banks et al.[11]	6·3	27·4	14·1	49·6	2·5	
Mutton						
Collin et al.[19]	4·0	25·0	31·0	36·0	4·0	
Pork						
Drogin et al.[25]	1·7	25·2	11·6	56·0	1·2	0·02
Hilditch						
Poor diet[35]	0·8	25·9	12·2	48·0	7·8	5·0
Rich diet	1·0	30·1	16·2	41·0	7·1	3·7

TABLE XXXV. FATTY ACIDS

	Beef (%)	Mutton (%)	Pork (%)
Saturated	48	60	38
Mono-ethylenic	49	36	40
Poly-ethylenic	2·5	4	2–10

These figures depend, of course, on the type of diet the animal receives.

A diet consisting mainly of soya given to a pig yielded a concentration of 36 per cent linoleic acid in the fat of this animal. The rearing of animals on these lines might possibly be considered.

B. *Biological Effects*

(1) In 1958 Copinski[22] studied the effect of a diet rich in animal fats on ten normal human subjects and observed definite increases of serum cholesterol and α-globulins and reduction of serum albumin.

(2) In the rabbit, Holzner *et al.*[36] noted that pig fat produced more frequent and more extensive deposits than olive oil, chosen for comparison, and which, as we shall see later, can be regarded as having little activity in either direction.

(3) Lard or chicken fat increased the blood cholesterol in chickens.[46]

(4) The effects of proteins on serum cholesterol in the rat using a casein diet show that the cholesterol is lowest when the proportion of protein is thirty to forty per thousand. The effects of pig fibrin are similar to those of casein. Zein exerts an hypercholesterolaemic effect which can be partly suppressed by casein. A protein from soya given in large quantity causes a reduction in serum cholesterol. On substituting wheat gluten for casein, the serum cholesterol level increases, while on the contrary the extraction of wheat gluten by alcohol reduces the level of cholesterol (Nath *et al.*, 1959[53]).

Forty per cent of proteins in the diet reduce serum cholesterol while the others behave in a variable manner. The reductions caused by wheat gluten are more regular. It is not difficult to feed rats since undernutrition can be induced by lysine, while the serum cholesterol is unchanged (Nath, 1958[52]).

Beveridge *et al.*[13] examined sixty-five students who had increasing quantities of meat; small quantities alone caused an increase in serum cholesterol. On the contrary with thirty-two students large quantities caused a reduction of cholesterol (Beveridge *et al.*[13]).

IV. Saturated Fats, Palm Oil

A certain number of experiments have been carried out with artificially reduced oils so that the effect of a saturated fat could be compared with that of an unsaturated oil, the latter varying in the different experiments. In other experiments the authors have chosen a naturally saturated oil, palm oil.

I. Chemical Study of these Fatty Substances

A. *Artificially reduced oils.* Reduction was generally produced by catalysis. These oils are not absolutely comparable with natural fats. Catalysis often leaves a certain number of ethylenic bonds. The iodine index was still 50 in a fat which was solid at ordinary temperatures, produced by the reduction of a maize oil. Furthermore, the reduction displaced the double bonds so that altogether one was dealing with an entirely new fatty substance.

B. *Palm oil* (*Elaeis guineensis* L. Fam. Palmaceae) is a naturally saturated oil. Its iodine index is about 50.

The distribution of its fatty acids is as follows:

Saturated C_8, C_{10}, C_{12}, C_{14}, C_{16}, C_{18}						Mono-ethylenic oleic	Poly-ethylenic linoleic
3	5	50	16	7	2	14	2

It will be seen that the main acids are lauric, myristic (one-third of the lauric acid) and oleic (slightly more than one-fourth of the lauric acid).

The general structure of the glycerides is as follows:

$$\text{glycerol} \begin{cases} \text{lauric (or myristic) acid} \\ \text{oleic (or myristic) acid} \\ \text{lauric (or myristic) acid} \end{cases}$$

The glyceride composition is therefore:

Completely saturated	63%
One unsaturated and two saturated	26%
Two unsaturated and one saturated	11%

C. *Coconut oil* (*Cocos nucifera* L. Fam. Palmaceae) has an iodine index of 8.

The average fatty acid composition can be shown in the following way:

Saturated C_8, C_{10}, C_{12}, C_{14}, C_{16}, C_{18}						Mono-ethylenic oleic	Poly-ethylenic linoleic
9	6	50	17	9	2	5	2

This is very similar to the preceding distribution.

The glycerides are essentially of the type:

$$
\text{glycerol} \left\{
\begin{array}{l}
\text{lauric acid} \\
\text{myristic or unsaturated acid} \\
\text{lauric acid}
\end{array}
\right.
$$

The glyceride composition is, then the following:

Completely saturated	84%
One unsaturated with two saturated	12%
Two unsaturated with one saturated	4%

II. *Animal Experiments*

Differing results must be reported.

(1) In 1959 Thomas[62] and O'Neil[55] noted renal and myocardial infarcts in a high percentage of rats even before the development of lesions in the arterial walls when the animals were given large doses of saturated fats and cholesterol.

(2) In 1960 Hegsted *et al.*[34] noted increase of blood cholesterol in chickens associated with a diet rich in saturated fats.

(3) Cottet *et al.*[23] observed a considerable increase of cholesterol and total lipids (Kunkel reaction) following administration of a diet rich in cholesterol and reduced maize oil.

(4) Wigand[66] gave reduced coconut oil without any addition of cholesterol to rabbits and noted considerable increase in the various forms of cholesterol, total lipids, lipid phosphorus, and β-lipoproteins in the serum, along with very extensive lipid deposits in the aorta.

Saturated fats are generally used for comparison when the anti-atherogenic effect of a food substance is being investigated experimentally.

Summary

The following food substances increase the blood cholesterol in animals and man and favour the development of, or actually create, deposits in the aorta in animals:

       milk, butter
       eggs
       animal fats
       vegetable fats artificially saturated
       palm and coconut oils

A final comment is called for from the work of Cohn *et al.* in 1961.[18] These workers placed chickens on two different types of feeding, one group was fed at regular intervals and the other allowed to nibble all day. The serum cholesterol declined more slowly after the finish of an atherosclerogenic diet and coronary lesions regressed less quickly in those chickens which had only two meals a day.

Increase in cholesterol is often accompanied by esterification, principally with oleic acid (Blomstrand and Christensen, 1963). Lastly, Hegsted et al.[34] consider myristic and palmitic acids the essential elements in hyper-cholesterolaemia.

References

1. ADAMSON, L. F., LEEPER, G. K. and ROSS, E., Influence of dietary fats and cholesterol on tissue lipids in chickens. J. Nutrit., 1961, 73, 247–58.
2. ALBANESE, A. A., HIGGONS, R. A., LORENZE, E. J. and ORTO, L. A., Effect of dietary proteins on blood cholesterol levels of adults. Geriatrics, 1959, 14, 237–43.
3. ALTSCHUL, R., Experimental arteriosclerosis in the nervous system. J. Neuropath., 1946, 5, 333–41.
4. ALTSCHUL, R., Experimental cholesterol arteriosclerosis II: Changes produced in golden hamster and in guinea pigs. Amer. Heart J., 1950, 40, 401–9.
5. ANDERSON, J. T., GRANDE, F. and KEYS, A., Effect on serum cholesterol in man of fatty acids produced by hydrogenation of corn oil. Fed. Proc., 1961, 20, 96.
6. ANDERSON, J. T., GRANDE, F., CHLOUVERAKIS, C., PROJA, M. and KEYS, A., Effect of dietary cholesterol on serum cholesterol level in man. Fed. Proc., 1962, 21, 100.
7. ANITSCHKOW, N., Über die experimentelle Atherosklerose der Aorta beim Meer-schweinichen. Beitr. Path. Anat., 1922, 70, 265–81.
8. ARMSTRONG, W. D., PILSUM, J. VAN, KEYS, A., GRANDE, F., ANDERSON, J. T. and TOBIAN, L., Alteration of serum cholesterol by dietary fats. Proc. Soc. Exp. Biol., 1957, 96, 302–6.
9. ARTEMENKO, E. M., Effect of dietary cholesterol (egg yolk) on blood cholesterol levels of atherosclerotic patients. Vop. Pit. Zdor. i Bol. Chel. Sbornik, 1960, 197–203.
10. BAILEY, C. H., Atheroma and other lesions in rabbits by cholesterol feeding. J. Exp. Med., 1916, 23, 69–84.
11. BANKS, A. and HILDITCH, T. P., The glyceride structure of beef tallows. Biochem. J., 1931, 25, 1168–82.
12. BEVERIDGE, J. M. R., CONNELL, W. F. and MAYER, G. A., The nature of plasma cholesterol elevating and depressant factors in butter and corn oil. Circulation, 1956, 14, 484.
13. BEVERIDGE, J. M. R., CONNELL, W. F., ROBINSON, C., Effect of the level of dietary protein with and without added cholesterol on plasma cholesterol levels in man. J. Nutrit., 1963, 79, 289–95.
14. BRAGDON, J. H., ZELLER, J. H. and STEVENSON, J. W., Swine and experimental atherosclerosis. Proc. Soc. Exp. Biol., 1957, 95, 282–4.
15. BRIGGS, R. D., RUDENBERG, M. L., O'NEAL, R. M., THOMAS, W. A. and HARTROFT, W. S., Myocardial infarction in patients treated with sippy and other high-milk diet. An autopsy study of fifteen hospitals in the U.S.A. and Great Britain. Circulation, 1960, 21, 538–42.
16. CHALATOW, J. J., Über das Verhalten der Leber gegenüber den verschiedenen Arten von Speisefett. Virchows Arch. Path. Anat., 1912, 207, 452–69.
17. CLARKSON, J. and NEWBURH, L. H., Relation between atherosclerosis and ingested cholesterol in the rabbit. J. Exp. Med., 1926, 43, 595–612.
18. COHN, C., PICK, R. and KATZ, L. N., Effect of meal eating compared to nibbling upon atherosclerosis in chickens. Circul. Res., 1961, 9, 139–45.

19. COLLIN, G., HILDITCH, T. P. and LEA, C. H., The component glycerides of a mutton tallow. *J. Soc. Chem. Ind. (Lond.)*, 1929, **48**, 46T–50T.

20. COOK, R. P., *Cholesterol*, Academic Press, New York, 1958.

22. COPINSKI, G., Effet d'un régime gras sur l'équilibre lipoprotéique de l'homme normal. *C.R. Soc. Biol.*, 1958, **152**, 1212–14.

23. COTTET, J., ENSELME, J. and GUICHARD, A., Action des acides gras non saturés sur l'athérosclérose expérimentale du lapin. *Arch. Mal. Cœur, Rev. Athéroscl.*, 1959, **1**, 256–63.

24. CRUICKSHANK, E. M., Studies in fat metabolism in the fowl. *Biochem. J.*, 1934, **28**, 965–77.

25. DROGIN, J. and ROSANOFF, M. A., On the detection and determination of halogens in organic compounds. *J. Amer. Chem. Soc.*, 1916, **38**, 711–16.

26. EMERSON, G. A., WALKER, J. B. and GANAPATHY, J. N., The effect of graded level of safflower oil and butter fat on the plasma cholesterol of monkeys receiving a minimal intake of pyridoxine. *Fed. Proc.*, 1959, **18**, 524 (No. 2064).

27. FISHER, H. and LEVEILLE, G. A., Observations on the cholesterol linoleic and linolenic acid content of eggs as influenced by dietary fats. *J. Nutrit.*, 1957, **63**, 119–29.

28. FUNCH, J. P. *et al.*, Effets du beurre, de quelques margarines et de l'huile d'arachide dans des diètes purifiées sur les lipides sériques et l'athérosclérose chez les lapins. *Brit. J. Nutrit.*, 1960, **14**, 355–60.

29. GALAPAN, C. and RAMANATHAN, R. S., Fats and diseases. *Lancet*, 1956, **271** (2), 1212–13.

30. GORDON, H., WILKENS, J. and BROCK, J. F., Serum cholesterol levels after consuming eggs with increased content of unsaturated lipids. *Lancet*, 1958, **275** (2), 244–5.

31. GRESHAM, G. A. and HOWARD, A. N., The effect of dietary fats and synthetic glycerides on the production of atherosclerosis and thrombosis in the rat. *Brit. J. Exper. Pathol.*, 1961, **42**, 166. *Circulation*, 1962, **25**, 421.

32. HAMMERL, H., PILCHER, O. and SIEDEK, H., Comparative studies on the serum lipids content after doses of butter fat and different vegetable oils. *Wien. Klin. Wschr.*, 1959, **71**, 761–4.

33. HASHIM, J. A. and VAN ITALIE, T. B., The effect of a medium chain triglyceride in man. *Fed. Proc.*, 1960, **19**, 19.

34. HEGSTED, D. M., GOBIS, A. and STARE, F. J., The influence of dietary fats on serum cholesterol levels in cholesterol-fed chicks. *J. Nutrit.*, 1960, **70**, 119–26.

35. HILDITCH, T. P., *The Chemical Constitution of Natural Fats*, Chapman, London, 1949.

36. HOLZNER, H., KRIEHUBER, E. and WENGER, R., Experimentelle Untersuchungen zur Arteriosklerosefrage. *Wien. Med. Wschr.*, 1960, **110**, 198–200.

37. HORLICK, L. and GRAIG, B. M., Effects of long-chain poly-unsaturated and saturated fatty acids on the serum lipids of man. *Lancet*, 1957, **274**, 566–9.

38. HORLICK, L. and O'NEIL, J. B., The modification of egg-yolk fats by sunflower-seed oil and the effect of such yolk fats on blood-cholesterol levels. *Lancet*, 1958, **275** (2), 243–4.

39. HORLICK, L. and O'NEIL, J. B., Effect of modified egg-yolk on blood-cholesterol levels. *Lancet*, 1960, **277** (1), 438.

40. HORST, A., ROZYNKOWA, D. and ZAGORSKA, I., Modifications de l'aorte du rat après injection d'allylamines et de jaune d'œuf. *Acta Med. Polona*, 1960, **1**, 1–9. *Excerpta Med.*, sect. 18, 1961, **5**, 417–18.

41. JACQUOT, R. and FERRANDO, R., Les caractéristiques alimentaires de la viande. *Ann. Nutr. (Paris)*, 1952, **6** C, 275–352.

42. JAMES, A. T. and WEBB, J. P. W., The behaviour of poly-unsaturated fatty acids on the gas-liquid chromatogram in *Essential Fatty Acids* (Ed. Sinclair), Butterworths, London, 1958.

43. KEYS, A., ANDERSON, J. T. and GRANDE, F., Essential fatty acids, degree of unsaturation and effect of corn (maize) oil on serum cholesterol level in man. *Lancet*, 1957, **272** (1), 66–8.

44. MCINDOE, W. M., Lipoprotein of high lipid content from egg-yolk. *Biochem. J.*, 1959, **73**, 45.

45. MAGEE, D. F. and FRAGOLA, L., Dietary protein and plasma cholesterol. *Fed. Proc.*, 1959, **18**, 96.
46. MARCH, B. E. and BIELY, J., Dietary modification of serum cholesterol in the chick. *J. Nutrit.*, 1959, **69**, 105–10.
47. MEEKER, D. R. and KESTEN, H. D., Effect of high protein diets on experimental atherosclerosis of rabbits. *Arch. Path.*, 1941, **31**, 147–62.
48. MILLER, W. L. and BAUMANN, C. A., Skin sterols. IV. Distribution of Δ 7-Cholesterol. *Proc. Soc. Exp. Biol.*, 1954, **85**, 561–4.
49. MORE, R. H., ROWSELL, H. C., LAINING, W. N., MUSTARD, F. J. and HAUST, M. D., The influence of butter feeding on the morphology of spontaneous focal lesions of pigs' aorta. *Fed. Proc.*, 1963, **22** (2), part I, 161.
50. NAIMI, S., GOLDSTEIN, R., NOTHMAN, M. M., WILGRAM, G. F. and PROGER, S., Cardiovascular lesions and changes in blood coagulation and fibrinolysis associated with diet-induced lipemia in the rat. *J. Clin. Invest.*, 1962, **41** (9), 1708–19.
51. NAKANISHI, K., BHATTACHARYYA, B. K. and FIESER, L. F., Cholesterol and companions. V. Microdetermination of Δ 7-sterols. *J. Amer. Chem. Soc.*, 1953, **75**, 4415–17.
52. NATH, N., HARPER, A. E. and ELVEHJEM, C. A., Dietary protein and serum cholesterol. *Arch. Biochem.*, 1958, **77**, 234–6.
53. NATH, N., HARPER, A. E. and ELVEHJEM, C. A., Effets des protéines alimentaires sur le cholestérol sérique du rat. *Canad. J. Biochem. Physiol.*, 1959, **37**, 1375–84.
54. NICHOLS, A. V., GOFMAN, J. W. and DOBBING, J., Fats and disease. *Lancet*, 1956, **271** (2), 1211–12.
55. O'NEAL, R. M., THOMAS, W. A. and HARTROFT, W. S., Dietary production of myocardial infarction in rats. Anatomic features of the disease. *Amer. J. Cardiol.*, 1959, **3**, 94–100.
56. REISER, R., The syntheses and intraconversions of poly-unsaturated fatty acids by the laying hen. *J. Nutrit.*, 1951, **44**, 159–75.
57. ROWSELL, H. C., DOWNIE, H. G. and MUSTARD, J. F., Comparison of effects of butter and egg-yolk on development of atherosclerosis in swine. *Circulation*, 1959, **29**, 970.
58. SCHETTLER, G. and EGGSTEIN, M., Fette, Ernährung und Arteriosklerose. *Dtsch. Med. Wschr.*, 1958, **83**, 702–6, 709–10, 750–5.
59. SCHMIDT, G., BESSMAN, M. J., HICKEY, M. D. and TANNHAUSER, J. J., The concentration of some constituents of egg-yolk in its soluble phase. *J. Biol. Chem.*, 1956, **223**, 1027–31.
60. STOKES, W. M., FISH, W. A. and HICKEY, F. C., Metabolism of cholesterol in chick embryo. *J. Biol. Chem.*, 1956, **220**, 415–30.
61. TERROINE, E. F. and BELIN, P., Influence de l'alimentation sur la composition quantitative de l'œuf de poule. *Bull. Soc. Chim. Biol.*, 1927, **9**, 1074–84.
62. THOMAS, W. A., O'NEAL, R. M., BRIGGS, R. D., RUDENBERG, M. L. and HARTROFT, W. S., High incidence of myocardial infarcts in ulcer treated with sippy and other high milk diets: a study of autopsied patients in fifteen hospitals. *Circulation*, 1959, **29**, 992.
63. THOMAS, W. A. and HARTROFT, W. S., Myocardial infarction in rats fed diets containing high fat, cholesterol, thiouracil and sodium cholate. *Circulation*, 1959, **19**, 65–72.
64. WELLS, Y. M. and BRONTE-STEWART, B., Egg yolk and serum cholesterol levels: importance of dietary cholesterol intake. *British Med. J.*, 1963.
64a. WELLS, W. W. and ANDERSON, S. C., The effect of dietary lactose on the serum cholesterol level of human subjects. *Fed. Proc.*, 1962, **21**, No. 2, 100.
65. WESSELKIN, N. W., Über die Ablagerung von fettartigen Stoffen in den Organen. *Virchows Arch. Path. Anat.*, 1913, **212**, 225–35.
66. WIGAND, G., Production of hypercholesterolemia and atherosclerosis in rabbits by feeding different fats without supplementary cholesterol. *Acta Med. Scand.*, 1960, **166**, suppl. 351, 1–92.
67. WILGRAM, G. F., Experimental atherosclerosis and cardiac infarcts in rats. *J. Exp. Med.*, 1959, **109**, 293–310.
68. WINDAUS, A. and STANGE, O., Über das Provitamin des Eisterins. *Z. Physiol. Chem.*, 1936, **244**, 218–20.

CHAPTER 7

Lipid Food Substances with Anti-atherosclerogenic Effects

A CERTAIN number of food substances appear to have the effect of reducing the serum concentrations of various lipids and attenuating the vascular manifestations of atherosclerogenic substances. This effect is generally attributed to the presence in their composition of unsaturated fatty acids, and particularly acids with several unsaturated bonds.

We are concerned here with various vegetable oils and fish oils.

I. Oils in which Linoleic Acid Predominates

1. *Oil from the Caryopsis of Maize* (*Zea mais* L. Gramineae)

This is the prototype of these oils.

A. *Chemistry*. The iodine index is about 120. The average fatty acid composition is as follows:

Saturated C_{14}, C_{16}, C_{18}			Mono-ethylenic oleic	Poly-ethylenic linoleic
0·2	10	3	48	40

B. *Maize oil and cholesterolaemia*. This is consumed as the oil or in Mexican tortillas. Authors generally stress the fact that maize oil lowers the blood cholesterol, but it should be noted that it facilitates the absorption of exogeneous cholesterol in the intestine. If then the latter is introduced in increased quantities, as it frequently is in animal experiments, the effect may be reversed.

(1) Effect on birds. In 1956 Jones et al.[36] noted that the blood cholesterol rose in chickens which had been given maize oil when the latter was replaced by cotton seed oil, the fatty acid composition of which is very much the same.

Alieva[5] observed a reduction of cholesterol by several vegetable oils. Marion et al.[54] had only negative results.

(2) Effect on rats. Maize oil appears to act in a peculiar way in the rat. Marshall et al.[55] and also Briot et al.[12] who gave very large doses of the oil, found that it increased blood cholesterol, whereas Lambiotte[47] and Lee et al.[49] found it to be without effect. This was with all introduction of cholesterol excluded. Nath in 1961 recalled the fact that rats subjected to diets

containing wheat gluten and 4 per cent maize or wheat oil sometimes lowered their serum cholesterol to a significant extent. He concluded that the hypo-cholesterolaemic effect is due to the polyethylenic fatty acids as well as the increased proteins in the diet which contribute methionine. In all cases it affects the blood lipoproteins (Nath et al., 1961).

(3) Effect on rabbits. Kritchevsky et al.[45] studied changes in blood cholesterol. It was increased in all the animals receiving cholesterol: the increase was, however, greater in the groups given maize oil also than in those receiving reduced maize oil in addition or cholesterol alone. The lipoproteins were increased in the same proportion.

In these experiments cholesterol was given in enormous doses, constituting 3 per cent of the diet. The duration of treatment was 2 months.

Cottet et al.[16] also used rabbits on a diet containing cholesterol (but only 1 per cent). Natural maize oil with pyridoxine added still permitted the blood cholesterol to increase but such increases were less than with the same oil reduced but still with pyridoxine added. Total lipids and the β/α_1 lipoprotein ratio were also lower. These differences would appear to be due to variable cholesterol absorption.

At the same time some groups of rabbits were also given intravenous injections of formaldehyde solution, this substance being intended to damage the serum protein and the proteins in the aortic wall.

Comparison of two groups, one consisting of rabbits given the athero-sclerogenic diet alone and the other given the same diet but formaldehyde injections in addition, shows that the latter had higher values for blood cholesterol, total blood lipids and for the β peaks of free electrophoresis.

When the rabbits receiving the atherosclerogenic diet and natural maize oil were compared with those having the same diet and the same maize oil but given injections of formaldehyde solution in addition, it was found that the latter group was again that in which the serum lipid abnormalities were greatest. Maize oil was thus inactive when the serum proteins were altered by formaldehyde.

On giving a semi-synthetic maize oil diet without cholesterol to rabbits, Wigand[82] observed a slight increase in the various forms of cholesterol and in phospholipids. This increase was very slight when compared with that produced by saturated fats.

MacMillan et al.,[57] however, failed to observe any differences in the increase of blood cholesterol produced by the introduction of exogeneous cholesterol whether the rabbits also received maize oil, butter or tristearin.

(4) Effects on the pig. Bragdon et al.[11] showed that maize oil, given as a supplement to the diet, did not produce hypercholesterolaemia.

(5) Effects on man. Ahrens et al.[1-3] examined a number of patients, six with obesity, four with hypercholesterolaemia, one with hyperlipaemia and three normal subjects. Maize oil reduced the blood cholesterol in all cases.

These authors considered that 4 g cholesterol had to be administered to a subject receiving maize oil in order to raise the blood cholesterol.

Beveridge et al.[9] found that the administration of maize oil reduced the blood cholesterol in forty-eight subjects.

Comparing it with other oils, Keys et al.[41] showed that maize oil was more active than all the other oils in reducing the blood cholesterol.

According to Horlick and Graig,[29] the blood cholesterol values in young persons given maize oil are the same as those obtained by elimination of fats from the diet.

Malmros stated in 1957[52] and again in 1959[53] that maize oil reduced blood cholesterol in the normal subject and in the subject with atherosclerosis.

Azerad et al.[8] administered 75 g maize oil daily for periods of from 29 to 73 days to atherosclerotic subjects. There was an average fall of 20 per cent in the blood cholesterol. There was also reduction of β-lipoproteins, as determined by the Burstein method. The improvement did not continue for more than a month after the end of treatment.

Shapiro et al.[73] studied six individuals of ages ranging from 24 to 27 years who were given 70 g maize oil daily. They noted reduction of serum cholesterol, particularly free cholesterol. Reduction of other lipids was somewhat slower.

Josey[37] tested a series of regularly administered doses on fifty-nine patients and concluded that maize oil reduced blood cholesterol.

In the same way Kuo and Carson[46] noted reduction in the blood cholesterol of normal man given a diet of fruit, rice and maize oil. The postcibal increase in triglycerides was also less marked. These improvements were unfortunately less evident in subjects with high blood cholesterols.

Pallone et al.[64] gave an emulsion of maize oil to twenty-four subjects with atherosclerosis and observed reduction of blood cholesterol and in the β/α_1 lipoprotein ration, symptomatic improvement and sometimes even restoration of a normal electrocardiogram.

Rhoads and Barker[71] observed that a diet poor in fats, given to nine atherosclerotic subjects, reduced blood cholesterol to a level which could be reduced still further if maize oil (90 g daily for 90 days) were added to the fat-free diet. The reduction was, however, only maintained for a few months.

Kinsell et al.[42] published favourable results from the use of maize oil in respect of the high blood cholesterol of diabetics but were unable to establish clinical improvement with certainty.

Pilkington et al.[67] reported similar results.

Hammerl et al.[26] showed that there was little increase in total lipids after administration of maize oil.

Carlson et al.[14] investigated three subjects from the same family, all with essential hypercholesterolaemia. Maize oil reduced their plasma cholesterol.

Björntrop et al.[10] showed that maize oil raised the level of poly-ethenoid fatty acids in the plasma of twelve subjects with hypercholesterolaemia in a remarkable manner.

Vignalou et al.[81] also published favourable results.

According to Alieva[5] maize oil effectively reduces the concentration of cholesterol whereas an olive oil diet has no effect.

Horlick[31] used 40 per cent olive oil on eight coronary patients with high serum cholesterol and caused a reduction of 24 per cent in the raised serum cholesterol.

There is one discordant opinion. Perkins et al.[66] were unable to produce any significant change in the blood cholesterol of twenty-two healthy students by the administration of 45 g maize oil with added pyridoxine in addition to their regular diet. The quantity of maize oil used in these experiments was much less than those employed by the preceding authors.

C. *Maize oil: deposits and arterial lesions.* Maize oil also has an action on the deposits. Kritchevsky et al.[45] noted less aortic atheroma in rabbits which were given cholesterol and maize oil, than in those which were given cholesterol alone.

Cottet et al.[16] noted that rabbits which were receiving cholesterol and natural maize oil exhibited much less extensive lipid deposits in the aorta than those receiving only cholesterol.

On the other hand, the deposits were of the same character and intensity, whether the animal was or was not ingesting maize oil, if at the time when it was receiving cholesterol it was given injections of formaldehyde which altered the wall. In this case the previous state of the wall appeared to be a factor of considerable importance.

Wigand[82] failed to observe any aortic deposits in rabbits on a semi-synthetic diet without cholesterol but with additional large doses of maize oil.

MacMillan et al.[57] found aortic deposits in rabbits on maize oil given cholesterol (1 g daily), but these deposits were less extensive than those observed in rabbits given the same dose of cholesterol but with butter or tristearin.

For the entire aorta, the areas invaded, expressed as a percentage of the area of the intima, were 51 for tristearin, 45 and 42 for butter, 30 for small doses of maize oil and 26 for large doses.

Clarkson et al.[15] comparing maize oil and coconut oil showed that maize oil diminished lesions in the pigeon in the absence of ingested cholesterol.

Gey et al.[23] did not see any modification of spontaneous lesions in old chickens who had received quite large quantities of maize oil.

Fisher et al.[20] found on the contrary that giving maize sterol delayed atherogenesis in small cockerels which had been given egg powder or oil.

The significance of the experiment is important since the oil of eggs strictly speaking causes not a true atherosclerosis but only damage by irritation of the intima. Perhaps the application of maize oil to the arterial wall after its ingestion protects it against the irritant action of oil from eggs.

Gerson et al.[22] gave maize oil to rats and observed an increase in tissue cholesterol and a large decrease of lipid and cholesterol in the serum.

This is not the same as Libert[50] who found no modification in the lesions of forty-four rabbits given peanut oil and even observed an increase of the atheroma with maize oil.

Moore[60] observed a decrease in hepatic deposits of cholesterol in hypo-cholesterolaemic rabbits given a diet rich in maize oil.

2. Soya Bean Oil (Soja hispida Moench. Leguminosae)

Soya bean oil is very similar to maize oil.

A. *Chemistry.* Its iodine index is about 150. The average fatty acid composition is as follows:

Saturated acids				Mono-ethenoid	Poly-ethenoid	
C_{14},	C_{16},	C_{18},	$> C_{18}$	oleic	linoleic	linolenic
0·2	10	1	1	25	50	5

It is a little richer in linoleic acid and poorer in oleic acid than maize oil.

Armstrong et al.[6] using rabbits and wheat oil found no effect on the hypercholesterolaemia or the atherosclerosis.

Andreenko et al.[7] using the dog showed an effect on lipid metabolism of maize oil.

Enselme et al.,[19a] comparing maize oil and palm oil, showed that maize oil brings about an elevation of serum cholesterol but less than that of palm oil. It is the same for all the lipids.

The detailed study of the lipid constitution showed paradoxically that maize oil introduced more cholesterol esters in the artery than palm oil but less triglycerides and phospholipids.

On the other hand, the aortic lesions are clear and numerous in the palm oil series but do not exist in the series with maize oil.

There is not therefore a parallel between the chemical structure of the artery taken as a whole and the deposits formed on its surface.

B. *Influence on lipidaemia.* There are two types of results to be considered. In man, reduction of the blood cholesterol and, more generally, of various forms of blood lipid has been noted.[30, 74, 78, 80, 67, 21, 25] In these various instances the oil replaced butter or margarine. The subjects were sometimes normal, sometimes atheromatous.

Nikkila et al.[63] who gave soya oil in excess, observed only reduction of phospholipids. It is the same in man according to Turpeinen.[79]

Swell et al.[76, 77] observed that, in rats, the blood cholesterol rose when the iodine index of their diet was increased by soya oil, more or less reduced. This experiment is difficult to interpret as we know little of the changes introduced into oils by reduction and as the changes observed in the blood cholesterol were slight. The diet did not introduce any cholesterol.

C. *Effect on arterial lesions.* There are two cases to be considered.

(1) The incidence of atherosclerosis was reduced by the ingestion of soya lecithin in rabbits on a cholesterol-rich diet.[40]

(2) Soya bean oil was added to the diet of two monkeys (*Coebus*) over a period of several months. Vascular lesions were much less considerable than in the experimental animals given saturated fats. No lesions, however, were noted in controls receiving only small quantities of fats.

Zemplenyl et al.[84] showed that soya oil has no influence on the development or regression of atheroma in the rabbit.

Klopotowski et al.[44] showed that soya oil increased the liver cholesterol in the rat.

Vles et al. in 1964[81a] established a good effect on the hypercholesterolaemic rabbit.

3. Sunflower Seed Oil (*Helianthus annuus* L. Compositae)

This oil belongs to the same series.

A. *Chemistry.* The iodine index is 125. The average fatty acid composition is as follows:

Saturated acids		Oleic acid	Linoleic acid
C_{16}	C_{18}		
5	3	30	60

B. The reports published on sunflower seed oil are not very favourable. It retarded the growth of rats[34] and increased total lipids much more than butter in man.[26]

Pleskov[68] studying sunflower oil obtained a reduction of serum cholesterol but especially during the first month of administration. After stopping the oil, the serum cholesterol rapidly rose to its original high level.

4. Oil of Carthamus or Bastard Saffron (*Carthamus tinctorius.* Compositae)

A. *Chemistry.* Its iodine index is 140. The fatty acid composition is of the following type:

Saturated acids		Oleic	Linoleic	Linolenic
C_{16}	C_{18}			
2	2	25	65	1

B. *Blood cholesterol* was reduced in man.[4, 48] In certain cases reduction was seen only in women.[63] According to Roen et al.[72] there was reduction in a third of the cases in man. Similar results were obtained with rabbits[58] and with rats.[19]

When the oil was added to the diet the vascular lesions produced in rabbits by coconut oil did not regress but they ceased to develop.[58]

According to Dayton et al.[17] saffron oil less readily allowed the transport of cholesterol from plasma to aortic wall than did palm oil.

5. Oat Plant Oil (Avena sutiva)

Let us only note that oat oil appears to have a marked hypocholesterolaemic effect on the rat (Potter et al.[69]). The same effect is observed in man (De Groot et al.[18]). These authors compared this with maize oil.

II. Oils in which Linolenic Acid Predominates

Linseed Oil (Linum usitatissimum L. Liliaceae)

A. *Chemistry*. Linseed oil has an iodine index of about 180. Its fatty acid composition is the following.

Saturated acids				Oleic	Linoleic	Linolenic
C_{14},	C_{16},	C_{18},	$> C_{18}$			
0·05	7	5	1	22	20	50

B. *Biological effects*. Linko[51] studied the effect of the oral administration of esterified linseed oil. He used twelve subjects suffering from cardiac atherosclerosis who had previously been subjected to a diet containing 50 g of butter and observed a reduction of cholesterol, lipoproteins and phospholipids in seven of them.

However, Hammerl et al.[26] found that its action on serum lipids in man was comparable with that of maize oil.[57]

In the experiment of MacMillan et al.[57] already mentioned, the deposits were less than those seen when butter was given to rabbits which were all also receiving cholesterol (1 g daily).

Hrstka et al.[33] showed that in sixteen atherosclerotic patients flaxseed extracts increased beta-lipoproteins, total cholesterol and esterified and unsaturated fats in serum but decreased phospholipid levels.

III. Oils with Long Unsaturated Carbon Chains

These may be of animal or vegetable origin.

1. Rapeseed Oil (Brassica [Sinapsis] campestris L. Cruciferae)

A. *Chemistry*. Its iodine index is in the neighbourhood of 100. The following is its fatty acid composition:

Saturated acids				Unsaturated acids			
C_{14},	C_{16},	C_{18},	$> C_{18}$	oleic	linoleic	linolenic	$> C_{18}$
0·1	2	2	4	16	14	8	55

B. *Biological investigations.* In the experiments of Wigand[82] already mentioned on rabbits given semi-synthetic diets, rapeseed oil behaved like maize oil. It produced very little change in the rabbit lipids. It produced no arterial lesion.

2. *Fish Oil and Seal Oil*

A. *Chemistry.* The compositions given in Table XXXVI have been arrived at by averaging values.

TABLE XXXVI

Oil	Saturated acids			Unsaturated acids					
	C_{14}	C_{16}	C_{18}	C_{14}	C_{16}	C_{18}	C_{20}	C_{22}	C_{24}
Fish:									
Menhaden									
(*Brevoortia tyrannus*)	5	14	1		15	30	20	15	
Cod liver									
(*Gadus morrhua*)	5	10			15	30	25	15	
Sardine									
(*Sardinops coerulea*)	5	15	3		12	18	18	14	15
Herring									
(*Clupea harengus*)	7	13			7	20	28	15	
Mammals:									
Seal									
(*Phoca vitulina*)	5	10	2	2	11	40	17	11	2

As these analyses are not sufficient, we give some additional information.

(1) Herring oil [Klenk, 1957] contains the following unsaturated acids:

with C_{18}: main constituent: tetra-ethenoid $\Delta^{9-12-15-18}$

  minor constituents: linoleic acid

  linolenic acid

with C_{22}: main constituent: hexaenoic acid $\Delta^{4-7-10-13-16-19}$

  minor constituent: pentaenoic acid $\Delta^{7-10-13-16-19}$

(2) According to Stoffel *et al.*[75] menhaden oil contains the following unsaturated acids:

with C_{16}: tetra-ethenoid $\Delta^{6-9-12-15}$ $\left. \begin{array}{l} 1 \cdot 9 \\ 0 \cdot 1 \end{array} \right\} 2$

    $\Delta^{4-7-10-13}$

  tri-ethenoid Δ^{6-9-12} $\left. \begin{array}{l} 1 \cdot 1 \\ 0 \cdot 2 \end{array} \right\} 1 \cdot 3$

    $\Delta^{7-10-13}$

  di-ethenoid Δ^{6-9} $\left. \begin{array}{l} 0 \cdot 4 \\ 1 \cdot 6 \end{array} \right\} 2$

    Δ^{9-12}

  mono-ethenoid Δ^{8} $\left. \begin{array}{l} 1 \cdot 4 \\ 8 \cdot 4 \end{array} \right\} 9 \cdot 8$

    Δ^{9}

with C_{18}: tetra-ethenoid	$\Delta^{6-9-12-15}$	3·2	3·2
tri-ethenoid	$\Delta^{9-12-15}$	1·0 ⎫	
	Δ^{6-9-12}	0·3 ⎭ 1·3	
di-ethenoid	Δ^{9-12}	2·2 ⎫	
	Δ^{6-9}	0·5 ⎭ 2·7	
mono-ethenoid	Δ^{9}		
with C_{20}: penta-ethenoid	$\Delta^{5-8-11-14-17}$	12·5	12·5
tetra-ethenoid	$\Delta^{5-8-11-14}$	0·2 ⎫	
	$\Delta^{8-11-14-17}$	0·4 ⎭ 0·6	
tri-ethenoid	Δ^{5-8-11}	1·0 ⎫	
	$\Delta^{8-11-14}$	0·6 ⎭ 1·6	
di-ethenoid	Δ^{11-14}	0·6	0·6
with C_{22}: hexa-ethenoid	$\Delta^{4-7-10-13-16-19}$		8·9
penta-ethenoid	$\Delta^{7-10-13-16-19}$		2

The total is less than given by the preceding authors.

The main acids are one of palmitoleic type, an acid with twenty carbon atoms and five ethylenic bonds and one with twenty-two carbon atoms and six ethylenic bonds.

B. *Biological investigations.* (1) Sardines (*Sardinops coerulea* Fam. Clupeidae). These contain oils which are themselves anti-atherosclerogenic and this action could be increased by the oil with which they are prepared and in which they remain for several months. Interpenetration could thus take place.

Bronte-Stewart *et al.*[13] have studied the effect of sardine oils on man. The subjects were three Bantus, whose blood cholesterol is naturally low. One aged 65 will be taken as an example here. When, after a cholesterol-free diet for 5 or 6 days, he was given sardine oil alone, his blood-cholesterol remained constant, but it fell when he was given sardine oil enriched with unsaturated acids of similar origin. This same oil reduced the subject's blood cholesterol even when he was having ten eggs daily, which normally would have increased it. There was parallel reduction of β-globulins. It may be that the presence of acids with long carbon chains is an important factor in the absorption of cholesterol.

Keys *et al.*[41] compared the effect of different oils on the blood cholesterol of man. Sardine oils had an action intermediate between those of sunflower seeds and maize.

Finally, in 1960, Mezzalma[56] gave sardine oil (2·5 g daily) to human subjects and confirmed earlier results.

Kelley *et al.*[39] studied the effect of sardines on fifty-nine men taking one tin a day for 26 weeks. Lipids were reduced as was cholesterol to a lesser degree.

Miller *et al.*[59] compared the effect of sardines and lard on the rat. They noted hypercholesterolaemia with the lard but observed no effect with the sardines. The sudanophile cardiovascular lesions are more marked in the group given lard than those given the sardines.

(2) The tunny, according to Howe et al.,[32] causes a reduction of serum lipids.

(3) Seal oil (*Phoca vitulina* Fam. Phocidae). The oil of the seal, a marine mammal, has, by reason of the nature of the animal's food, a composition similar to that of fish oil. It has the following fatty acid composition:

Saturated				Unsaturated					
C_{14}	C_{16}	C_{18}	C_{20}	C_{14}	C_{16}	C_{18}	C_{20}	C_{22}	C_{24}
5·1	10·7	1·3	0·6	1·8	10·5	39·6	17·6	10·6	2·1

These figures are from Burke and Jasperson.

The ethenoid bonds are very numerous (5 in the group with 24 carbon atoms).

(4) Herring oil (*Clupea harengus* Fam. Clupeidae) lowered the blood cholesterol of hens slightly (March et al., 1959). When cholesterol was given in sufficient quantity at the same time, the blood cholesterol was higher, probably as a result of the better absorption produced by the oil.

(5) Cod liver oil (*Gadus morrhua* Fam. Gadidae) reduced blood cholesterol[27]

It would perhaps be useful in practice to report secondary effects. Raulin et al.[70] have reported an infiltrating myocarditis following the consumption of deodorized herring oil.

Gran et al.[24] observed a transient lowering of cholesterol in the rat after the administration of cod liver oil.

(6) A lowering of lipids and in particular cholesterol is seen with a number of polyunsaturated fish oils. (Kinsell et al.,[43] Peifer et al.,[65] Nicolaysen,[62] Kahn,[38] Nesset et al.[61])

(7) Jagannathan[35] gave cotton seed oil to monkeys and prevented the increase in lipid caused by the reduced fats of peanuts.

Unfortunately the lesions remained the same for most of the time.

Conclusions

Certain points which will explain the different responses reported by some authors require clarification.

(1) Oils rich in poly-ethylenic acids favour the absorption of cholesterol and may thereby increase blood cholesterol but generally, when the dose of cholesterol introduced in the food is not high, these oils reduce the blood cholesterol.

(2) It is essential to distinguish between (*a*) the effect of substituting a poly-

ethylenic oil for a saturated fat, which generally reduces the blood cholesterol in man or animals and prevents or moderates vascular deposits in experimental animals, and (b) the effect of addition which leads to alimentary overloading in which the anti-atherogenic effects are less definite or are even suppressed. The former is comparable with the dietetic results obtained with small doses of oil used as replacement lipids for atherosclerogenic products; the latter can be likened to the effects it is sought to obtain by the therapeutic ingestion of large quantities given in addition to the diet.

(3) All oils do not appear to be equivalent. There is no definite relationship between the quantity of the various poly-ethylenic acids absorbed and the effects obtained.

References

1. AHRENS, E. H., BLACKENHORN, D. H. and TSALTAS, T. T., Effect on human serum lipids of substituting plant for animal fat in diet. *Proc. Soc. Exp. Biol.*, 1954, **85**, 872.
2. AHRENS, E. H., TSALTAS, T. T., HIRSCH, J. and INSULL, W. M., Effects of dietary fats on the serum lipids of human subjects. *J. Clin. Invest.*, 1955, **34**, 918.
3. AHRENS, E. H., INSULL, W., HIRSCH, J., STOFFEL, W., PETERSON, M. L., FARQUHAR, J. W., MILLER, TH. and THOMASSON, H. J., The effect on human serum-lipids of a dietary fat, highly unsaturated but poor in essential fatty acids. *Lancet*, 1959 (1), 115–19.
4. ALFIN-SLATER, R. B. and JORDAN, P., The effect of safflower oil on the nature of serum cholesterol esters. *Amer. J. Clin. Nutrit.*, 1960, **8**, 325–6.
5. ALIEVA, O. KH., Effect of some vegetable oils on blood lipids in atherosclerosis. *Vop. Pit. Zdr. i Bol. Chel. Sbornik*, 1960, 189–95.
5a. ANANTHA SAMY, T. S. and CAMA, H. R., Le rôle que jouent les graisses de régime dans la production d'hypercholestérolémie chez le rat. *J. Atheroscler. Res.*, 1964, **4**, 356.
6. ARMSTRONG, M. L., CONNOR, W. E. and MELVILLE, R. S., Failure of corn oil and triparanol to prevent hypercholesterolemia and atherosclerosis. *Proc. Soc. Exper. Biol. Med.*, 1963, **113**, 960–3.
7. ANDREENKO, G. V., BRAKSH, T. A., KURCIN, O. J. A., POPOVA, A. V. and KOMJAGINA, N. V., Sur le rôle de l'huile de maïs dans les troubles expérimentaux de la circulation. *Vopr. Pitan.*, 1963, **22**, 33–7.
8. AZERAD, E., LEWIN, J. and GHATA, J., Résultat d'un traitement de l'hypercholestérolémie athéroscléreuse par une huile riche en acides gras polyinsaturés. *Soc. Med. Hôp. Paris*, 1958, **74**, 707–9.
8a. BAVINA, M. V. and EVSTIGNEEVA, R. P., Influence des acides gras saturés et insaturés sur la composition lipidique du sang, du foie et de l'aorte, dans l'athérosclérose expérimentale. *Vopr. Pitan.*, 1964, **23**, no. 6, 56.
9. BEVERIDGE, J. M. R., CONNELL, W. F. and MAYER, G. A., The nature of the plasma cholesterol elevating and depressant factors in butter and corn oil. *Circulation*, 1956, **14**, 484.
10. BJÖRNTROP, P. and HOOD, B., Pattern of cholesterol ester fatty acids in serum in normal subjects and in patients with essential hypercholesterolemia. *Circ. Res.*, 1960, **8**, 319–23.
11. BRAGDON, J. H., ZELLER, J. H. and STEVENSON, J. W., Swine and experimental atherosclerosis. *Proc. Soc. Exp. Biol.*, 1957, **95**, 282–4.
12. BRIOT, C., CARLOTTI, J., LANDAT, PH., MONKHTAR, M. J., BAILLET, J. and DE GENNES, L., Etude de l'action comparée d'une huile de germe de maïs et du beurre dans la dyslipidose expérimentale du rat. *Presse Méd.*, 1959, **14**, 543–5.
13. BRONTE-STEWART, B., ANTONIS, A., EALES, L. and BROCK, J. F., Effects of feeding different fats on serum-cholesterol level. *Lancet*, 1956, **1**, 521–6.

14. CARLSON, L. A. and STERNER, G., Essential hypercholesterolaemia in two siblings. Effect of corn oil on serum-lipoïds. *Acta Paediat. (Uppsala)*, 1960, **49**, 168–74.
15. CLARKSON, T. B., PRICHARD, R. W., LOFLAND, H. B. and GOODMAN, H. O., Interactions among dietary fat, protein and cholesterol in atherosclerosis susceptible pigeons. *Circulation Res.*, 1962, **11**, 3 (part 1), 400–4.
16. COTTET, J., ENSELME, J. and GUICHARD, A., Action des acides gras non saturés sur l'athérosclérose expérimentale du lapin. *Arch. Mal. Cœur Vaisseaux*, 1959, **1**, 256–63.
17. DAYTON, S., HASHIMOTO, S. and JESSAMY, J., Les mouvements du cholestérol dans l'aorte du rat normal et l'influence de différentes sortes de graisses alimentaires. *J. Atheroscler. Res.*, 1961, **1**, 444–70.
18. DE GROOT, A. P., LUYKEN, R. and PIKAAR, N. A., Cholesterol-lowering effect of rolled oats. *Lancet*, 1963, **2** (7302), 303–4.
19. EMERSON, G. A. and WALKER, J. B., Protein fatty acid interrelationships. *Fed. Proc.*, 1960, **19**, 18.
19a. ENSELME, J., COTTET, J. and FRAY, G., Etude de diverses influences alimentaires sur l'athérosclérose provoquée par une alimentation privée de cholestérol. *Maladies du cœur (Revue de l'Athérosclérose)*, 1963, suppl. **3**, 52.
20. FISHER, H., WEISS, H. S., GRIMINGER, P., Corn sterols and avian atherosclerosis. *Proc. Exper. Biol. Med.*, 1963, **113**, 415–18.
21. GEILL, T., Soyabean oil and serum cholesterol. *Ugeskr. Laeg.*, 1960, *J. Amer. Med. Ass.*, 1960, **173**, 565.
22. GERSON, T. and SHORLAND, F. B., Effects of corn oil on the amounts of cholesterol and the excretion of sterol in the rat. *Biochem. J.*, 1961, **81**, 584–91.
23. GEY, K. F. and PLETSCHER, A., Inability of refined oil to influence spontaneous arteriosclerosis of old hens. *Nature*, 1961, **189**, 491–2.
24. GRAN, F. C. and NICOLAYSEN, R., Lowering of serum-cholesterol level in rats by intraperitoneal cod-liver oil. *Lancet*, 1961, **2**, 157.
25. GREENBERG, S. M., HERNDON, J. F., LIN, T. H. and VAN LOON, E. J., The antihypercholesterolemic effect of essential fatty acids in hypercholesterolemic dogs. *Amer. J. Clin. Nutrit.*, 1960, **8**, 68–71.
26. HAMMERL, H., PICHLER, U. and SIEDEK, H., Comparatives studies on the serum lipid content after test doses of butter fat and different vegetable oils. *Wien. Klin. Wschr.*, 1959, **71**, 761–4.
27. HAUGE, J. G. and NICOLAYSEN, R., The serum cholesterol depressive effect of linoleic, linolenic acids and cod liver oil in experimental hypercholesterolemic rats. *Acta Physiol. Scand.*, 1959, **45**, 26–30.
28. HOAREAU, E. and DELANOE, G., Les cardiopathies par athérosclérose et la cholestérolémie en milieu marocain musulman. *Arch. Mal. Cœur. Vaisseaux*, 1960, **2**, 333–45.
29. HORLICK, L. and GRAIG, B. M., Effect of long chain polyunsaturated and saturated fatty acids on the serum-lipids of man. *Lancet*, 1957, **273**, 566–9.
30. HORLICK, L., The effect of varying the dietary fats and fatty acids on the serum lipids in normal young men and women. *IIIème Congrès Mondial de Cardiologie, Bruxelles*, 1958, **2**, 291.
31. HORLICK, L., Dietary modification of serum cholesterol levels. *Canad. Med. Ass. J.*, 1961, **85**, 1127–31.
31a. HOWARD, A. N., GRESHAM, G. A., JONES, D. and JENNINGS, I. W., Traitement préventif de l'athérosclérose du lapin par l'emploi de farine de fèves de soja. *J. Atheroscler. Res.*, 1965, **5**, 330.
32. HOWE, E. E. and BOSSHARDT, D. K., A study of experimental hypercholesterolemia in the mouse. *J. Nutrit.*, 1962, **76**, 242–6.
33. HRSTKA, V. *et al.*, Modifying the lipid components of the blood. *Pharmadocyn.*, 1961, **132**, 197–204.
34. JACQUOT, R., ABRAHAM, J., BRUNAND, M., RAVEUX, R., SEGAL, V. and TREMOLIERES, J., Utilisation énergétique de diverses graisses d'un régime athérogène chez le rat. *Arch. Mal. Cœur Vaisseaux*, 1959, **1**, 275–84.
35. JAGANNATHAN, S. N., Effect of feeding fat blends of hydrogenated ground-nut (peanut) fat and cotton seed oil containing different levels of linoleic acid on serum cholesterol

levels in monkeys (macara radiata) and liver cholesterol concentration in cholesterol fed rats. *J. Nutrit.*, 1962, **77** (3), 317–22.

36. JONES, R. J., REISS, O. K. and HUFFMAN, J., Corn oil and hypercholesterolemic response in the cholesterol-fed chick, *Proc. Soc. Exp. Biol.*, 1956, **93**, 88–91.

37. JOSEY, A. I., Serum cholesterol in an office practice. *J. Amer. Med. Ass.*, 1959, **169**, 1238.

38. KAHN, S. G., Effect of the ethyl esters of the polyunsaturated fatty acids of fish oils on atherosclerosis and blood and tissue cholesterol of chickens. *Fed. Proc.*, 1962, **21** (2), 99.

38a. KAHN, S. G., VANDEPUTTE, J., WIND, S. and YACOWITZ, H., A study of the hypocholesterolemic activity of the ethyl esters of the polyunsaturated fatty acids of cod liver oil in the chicken. I. Effect on total serum cholesterol. *J. Nutrit.*, 1963, **80** (4), 403.

38b. KAHN, S. G., WIND, S., CLOCUM, A., PFEFFER, D. and YACOWITZ, H., A study of the hypocholesterolemic activity of the ethyl esters of the polyunsaturated fatty acids of cod liver oil in the chicken. II. Effect on serum and tissue cholesterol and aortic and coronary atherosclerosis. *J. Nutrit.*, 1963, **80** (4), 414.

39. KELLEY, T. F., BERNFELD, P., GOLDNER, M. G., GREENBERG, J. and HOMBURGER, F., Decrease of serum lipids in humans consuming canned Maine sardines. *Fed. Proc.*, 1962, **21**, 390e.

40. KESTEN, H. D. and SILBOWITZ, R., Experimental atherosclerosis and soya lecithin. *Proc. Soc. Exp. Biol.*, 1942, **49**, 71–3.

41. KEYS, A., ANDERSON, J. T. and GRANDE, F., Essential fatty acids, degree of unsaturation and effect of corn (maize) oil on the serum cholesterol in man. *Lancet*, 1957, **272**, 66–8.

42. KINSELL, L. W., WALKER, G., MICHAELS, G. D. and OLSON, F. E., Dietary fats and the diabetic patient. *New Engl. J. Med.*, 1959, **261**, 431–4.

43. KINSELL, L. W., MICHAELS, G. D., WALKER, G. and VISINTINE, R. E., The effect of a fish-oil fraction on plasma lipids. *Diabetes*, 1961, **10**, 316–19.

44. KLOPOTOWSKI, T. and SMIETANSKA, Z., Lipid synthesis in livers of rats maintained on soyabean oil diet. *Acta Biochim. Polon.*, 1960, **7**, 21–8.

45. KRITCHEVSKY, D., MOYER, A. W., TESAR, W. C., LOGAN, J. B., BROWN, R. A., DAVIES, M. C. and COX, H. R., Effect of cholesterol vehicle in experimental atherosclerosis. *Amer. J. Physiol.*, 1954, **178**, 30–2.

46. KUO, P. T. and CARSON, J. C., Dietary fats and the diurnal serum triglyceride levels in man. *J. Clin. Invest.*, 1959, **38**, 1384–93.

47. LAMBIOTTE, M., Relation entre la nature des lipides alimentaires et le métabolisme du cholestérol chez le rat adulte. *C.R. Acad. Sci. (Paris)*, 1960, **250**, 2282–4.

48. LECKERT, J. T., BROWNE, D. C., MacHARDY, G. and CRADIE, H. E., The result of the treatment of hypercholesterolemia associated with atherosclerosis with sitosterol and safflower oil derivatives. *J. Louisiana Sch. Med.*, 1958, **119**, 260.

49. LEE, C. C. and HERRMANN, R. G., Effect of vitamin D, sucrose, corn oil and endocrines on tissue cholesterol in rats. *Circ. Res.*, 1959, **7**, 354–9.

50. LIBERT, O. and ROGG EFFRONT, C., Experimental atherosclerosis and hyperlipidemia in rats and rabbits influence of some alimentary fats. *J. Atheroscler. Res.*, 1962, **2** (3), 186–98.

51. LINKO, E., Ethyl esters of linseed-oil fatty acids. Effects on serum lipids in atherosclerosis. *Ann. Med. Inter. Fenniae*, 1957, **46**, 129.

52. MALMROS, H. and WIGAND, G., The effect on serum cholesterol of diets containing different fats. *Lancet*, 1957, **273**, 1–7.

53. MALMROS, H., Cholesterol metabolism. *J. Amer. Med. Ass.*, 1959, **169**, 1788.

54. MARION, J. E., EDWARDS, Jr., H. M. and DRIGGERS, J. C., Influence of diet on serum cholesterol in the chick. *J. Nutrit.*, 1961, **74** (2), 171–5.

55. MARSHALL, M. V., HILDEBRAND, H. E., DUPONT, J. L. and WOMAK, M., Effect of fats on body composition and serum cholesterol of rats. *Fed. Proc.*, 1959, **18**, 535.

56. MEZZALMA, G., Sur un nouvel anticholestérolémiant obtenu par extraction de l'huile de poisson. *Minerva Med.*, 1960, **51**, 646.

57. MacMillan, G. C., Weigensberg, B. I. and Ritchie, A. C., Effects of dietary fats in rabbits fed cholesterol. *Arch. Path.*, 1960, **70**, 220–5.
58. Miller, J. P., Lambert, G. F. and Frost, D. V., Regression studies with safflower oil and sitosterol in rabbit atherosclerosis. *Circ. Res.*, 1959, **7**, 779–86.
59. Miller, S. A., Dymsza, H. A. and Goldblith, S. A., Cholesterolemia and cardiovascular sudanophilia in rats fed sardine mixtures. *J. Nutrit.*, 1962, **77** (4), 397–402.
60. Moore, J. H. and William, D. L., The influence of dietary fat on the liver lipids of the rabbit. *Canad. J. Biochem. Physiol.*, 1963, **41** (8), 1821–35.
61. Nesset, B. L. and Quackenbush, F. W., Influence of purified fatty esters and marine oils on hypocholesteremic effects of linoleate. *Fed. Proc.*, 1962, **21** (2), 100.
62. Nicolaysen, R., Lipids and diet. *Proc. Roy. Soc.*, Ser. B, 1962, **156** (964), 365–75.
63. Nikkila, E. A. and Jokipii, S. G., Effect on serum lipids of supplementation of diet with poly-unsaturated fat. A study with aged human subjects. *Acta. Med. Scand.*, 1960, **166**, 269–74.
64. Pallone, E., Cagianelli, G., Spremolla, G. and Gustinicci, Recherches cliniques sur l'effet thérapeutique des acides gras essentiels dans la maladie athéromateuse. *G. Clin. Med.*, 1959, **40**, 1143–58.
65. Peifer, J. J., Janssen, F., Muesing, R. and Lundberg, W. O., The lipid depressant activities of whole fish and their component oils. *J. Amer. Oil Chem. Soc.*, 1962, **39**, 292–6.
66. Perkins, R., Wright, I. S. and Gatje, B. W., Safflower oil pyridoxine and corn oil pyridoxine emulsion. Their effect on serum cholesterol levels in young adult males when used as supplements to a normal diet. *J. Amer. Med. Ass.*, 1959, **169**, 1731–4.
67. Pilkington, T. R. E., Stafford, J., Hankin, V. S., Simmonds, F. M. and Koerselman, H. B., Practical diets for lowering serum lipids. A long term study on outpatients with ischemic heart disease. *Brit. Med. J.*, 1960, 23–5.
68. Pleskov, A., L'influence de certaines huiles végétales sur le taux de cholestérine et de lécithine chez les artérioscléreux. *Klin. Med.*, 1962, **3**, 126–30, in *Sem. Hôp.*, 1962, **38** (38–9), 2257.
69. Potter, G. C., Hensley, G. W. and Bruins, H. W., The effect of oat oil on serum cholesterol in rats fed a hypercholesteremic diet. *Fed. Proc.*, 1963, **22** (2), part I, 268.
70. Raulin, J., Richier, C., Escribano, L. and Jacquot, R., Répercussions nutritionnelles et pathologiques de l'usage alimentaire de l'huile de poisson désodorisée par chauffage. Description d'une myocardite infiltrante. *C.R. Acad. Sci.* (*Paris*), 1959, **248**, 1229–32.
71. Rhoads, E. V. and Barker, N. W., Effect of reduction of dietary fat and additional ingestion of corn oil on hypercholesterolemia. *Proc. Mayo Clin.*, 1959, **34**, 225–9.
72. Roen, P., Perry, J. and McDonald, J. B., The effect of safflower oil on serum lipids. *Amer. J. Gastroent*, 1960, **33**, 587–91.
73. Shapiro, W., Estes, E. H. and Hilderman, H. L., The effect of corn oil on serum lipids in normal active subjects. *Amer. J. Med.*, 1957, **23**, 898–909.
74. Soukupova, K., Les régimes lipidiques. *Diet. et Nutrit.*, 1958, **9**, 51–7.
75. Stoffel, W. and Ahrens, E. H., The unsaturated fatty acids in menhaden body oil: the C_{18}, C_{20}, C_{22} series. *J. Lipid Res.*, 1960, **1**, 139–46.
76. Swell, L., Flick, F., Field, H. and Treadwell, C. R., Role of fat and fatty acid absorption of dietary cholesterol. *Amer. J. Physiol.*, 1955, **180**, 124–8.
77. Swell, L., Boiter, A., Field, H. and Treadwell, C. R., Absorption of dietary cholesterol esters. *Amer. J. Physiol.*, 1955, **180**, 129–32.
78. Turpeinen, O., Roine, P., Pekkarinen, M., Karvonen, M. J., Rautenene, Y., Runeberg, J. and Alivirta, P., Effect on serum cholesterol level of replacement of dietary fat by soyabean oil. *Lancet*, 1960, **1**, 169–98.
79. Turpeinen, O. *et al.*, Effects of serum cholesterol level of changes in dietary fat composition. *J. Atheroscler. Res.*, 1961, **1**, 307–16.
80. Verdonk, G., Investigation of the influence of diet on atheromatosis. *Verh. Kon. Acad. Geneesk. Belg.*, 1958, **20**, 147–203.
81. Vignalou, J., Berthaux, P. and Lalanne, F., Effet d'un supplement d'acide linoléique

sur la cholestérolémie des sujets soumis à un régime hypolipidique. *Presse Méd.*, 1960, **68**, 933.

81a. VLES, R. O., BULLER, J., GOTTENBOS, J. J. and THOMASSON, H. J., L'influence de différentes graisses diététiques sur l'athérosclérose du lapin provoquée par le cholestérol. *J. Atheroscler. Res.*, 1964, **4**, 170.

82. WIGAND, G., Production of hypercholesterolemia and atherosclerosis in rabbits by feeding different fats without supplementary cholesterol. *Acta Med. Scand.*, 1960, **166** (suppl. 351), 1–91.

83. WISSLER, R. W., FRAZIER, L. E., HUGHES, R. H. and RASMUSSEN, R. A., The development of atheromatous disease in cebus monkeys using saturated and non-saturated fats. *Proc. Soc.*, 1960, **19**, 17.

84. ZEMPLENYL, T., LOJDA, Z., GRAFNETTER, D., FODOR, J. and FELT, V., The effect of soya oil on experimental atheromatosis of the aorta and some enzymes of the arterial wall in rabbits. *Excerpta Med.*, sect. 18, 1961, **5**, 495.

CHAPTER 8

The Phospholipids

SEVERAL lipids contain phosphoric acid, and are derived from the phosphatidic acids or from an alcohol called sphingosine. The latter are of most interest to us, particularly sphingomyelin. We have already given some tables which contain data on the phospholipids from the point of view of normal subjects and those suffering from atherosclerosis, and it will be necessary to refer the reader back to these tables.

In 1963 Böttcher[1] gave a list of the principal phospholipids found in the aorta of normal and atherosclerotic subjects.

> Many types of phospholipids were found, including phosphatidic acids, lecithins, several types of cephalins, plasmalogens, lysocompounds and sphingolipids.
>
> In healthy tissue each type of phospholipid has its own characteristic fatty acid composition, which changes in the direction of increasing saturation with atherosclerosis.

In 1940 Weinhouse and Hirsch[3] showed that the proportion of ether-soluble phospholipids became lower as the illness progressed, whereas that of ether-insoluble ones became higher.

Smith in 1960[2] showed that the sum total of the phospholipids did not vary much.

Böttcher (see table, pp. 9–10) separated the phospholipids which he called lecithins and sphingomyelins and emphasized the very important rise in the sphingomyelins and the corresponding fall in the lecithins. The phospholipid group as a whole tended to fall, the clearest variation occurring in the intima.

In 1963 he came to this conclusion:

"The sphingolipids (sphingomyelins, galactoceramides, and sulphatides) are the dominating phospholipid fraction. Even in young intima, they represent more than 40 per cent of the total phospholipids, and this percentage can rise in all types of lesions to almost 70 per cent. In particular, the galactoceramides are interesting."

In conclusion, the evolution of the sphingomyelins in the course of atherosclerosis appears to be quite different from that of the other phospholipids.

Evolution was not always in evidence in the early stages; it appeared late enough to make one regard it as a result rather than a cause of the disease.

No attempt has been made to produce experimental atherosclerosis with sphingomyelins.

References

1. BöTTCHER, C. J. F., *Evolution of the Atherosclerotic Plaque*, Chicago, 1963 (R. J. JONES, Ed.), 360 pp.
2. SMITH, E. B., Intimal and medial lipids in human aorta. *Lancet*, 1960, 799–803.
3. WEINHOUSE, J. and HIRSCH, E. F., Atherosclerosis. II. The lipids of the serum and tissues in experimental atheroscleroses of rabbits. *Arch. Path.*, 1940, **30**, 856–67.

CHAPTER 9

The Lipoproteins

THE lipoproteins constitute a most interesting group of compounds from the point of view of atherosclerosis. They are made up of a spherical envelope which is probably perforated, since the amount of protein present is insufficient to contain all of the lipid in a sphere. Beneath this envelope are linked the phospholipids (usually phosphatidyl choline) and deeper within the sphere are found the fatty acids, the glycerides and especially cholesterol.

The bond between the protein and phospholipid parts is made by ionic attraction between the positively and negatively charged groups present in each part. The bond between the phosphatidyls and cholesterol or tri-glycerides is brought about by Van der Waals forces which are considerably weaker than the protein-phospholipid link. A source of strain is immediately apparent in the lipoprotein sphere where the phosphatidyl–cholesterol bond occurs. This can affect the stability of the whole structure and one can well imagine the conformational stresses between the parts of the lipoprotein as possibly being concerned in the mechanism of transport or deposition of cholesterol. The quality of these proteins can be judged by the Nbt value, as also can the quality of the lipids.

The lipoproteins of the aorta will be considered in both the normal and pathological state.

Some extracts of normal serum were made by Kayahan in 1960[2] from an homogenate of dried aorta. The author found on paper electrophoresis a distinct difference between the healthy aorta which showed three globulins each containing lipid, and the atherosclerotic aortas which contained only one globulin very rich in lipid. In addition we described with Frey in 1960[1] some experiments carried out on atherosclerosis and normal aortas. The extracts represented the infiltrations of serum as well as soluble collagen. We have not confirmed the results of Kayahan by free electrophoresis. Certain serum proteins extracted from the wall of the aorta were characterized by the number of free amino groups and the soluble collagen by estimation of hydroxyproline. Finally, Kayden et al. in 1960[3] extracted some lipoproteins from the aortic intima which gave immunochemical reactions similar to those of the serum lipoproteins. This was probably due to infiltration.

Finally, the role of lipoproteins seems to be under suspicion from an experiment by Stewart in 1960.[5] An apparatus was specially constructed so that a fragment of rabbit aorta could be perfused with lipoproteins from the serum of rabbits subjects to an atherosclerogenic diet. He obtained histological changes which suggested the early stages of atherosclerosis. Perfusion with triglycerides did not give the same effect. Tracy, Merchant and Kao showed in 1961,[6] by the use of immunoelectrophoresis, that lipoproteins of *very* low density (α_2) migrated more rapidly to the anode and diffused more slowly in agar than those lipoproteins of low density (β for example). However, these two fractions cannot be distinguished from each other by antigenic properties. In extracts of the aortic intima one does find lipoproteins with physical characteristics of the β-lipoproteins, the only ones found in raised concentration in the perfused aortas. The intima seems to concentrate the β-lipoproteins of the serum which are present before one can see a fatty band or plaque. It is more concentrated in recent atheromatous plaques than in the aortas without any. One cannot show it in old plaques. Maggi *et al.*, in 1964[4] showed that in the normal aorta of the dog, in the area surrounding the plaques and in the wall of the human atherosclerotic femoral artery, the quantity of free lipids is low. A phospholipid containing double bonds is tightly bound to the wall.

Such are the ideas that we have today on the role of these lipoproteins. Certainly we cannot arrive at any certain and precise conclusions from these but we consider that an abnormal colloidal state allows them to fasten readily on the arterial wall and we draw the practical conclusion that a diet consisting of lipoproteins should be avoided. We can also ask ourselves if an abnormal weakness of the serum lipoproteins, which seem to be the same as those of the aortic wall, does not allow some unexpected separation of the cholesterol they contain. Therefore the determination of these lipoproteins loses its significance since their abnormality is not quantitative but qualitative.

This is thus one field of research for all those who are interested in the problem of the pathogenesis of atherosclerosis.

References

1. FREY, J., Recherches relatives à l'extraction des protéines aortiques sur des fragments normaux et athéroscléreux. Thèse, Lyon, 1960, 55 pages.
2. KAYAHAN, S., Cholesterol-binding capacity of serum globulins in normal and atherosclerotic subjects. *Lancet*, 1960, **1**, 255–6.
3. KAYDEN, H. J., SEEGAL, B. C. and HSU, K. C., Immunochemical reactions of low density lipoproteins of human serum and aortic wall. *Circulation*, 1959, **20**, 978.
4. MAGGI, V., CHAYEN, J., GAHAN, P. and BRANDER, W., A histochemical study of the bound lipids of arteries: their possible role in arteriosclerosis. *Exper. Molec. Pathol.*, 1964, **3**, no. 5, 413–20.
5. STEWART, G. T., The production of animal deposits of lipid in isolated rabbit's aorta. *Brit. J. Exp. Path.*, 1960, **41**, 389–95.
6. TRACY, R. E., MERCHANT, E. B. and KAO, V. C., On the antigenic identity of human serum beta and alpha-2 lipoproteins and their identification in the aortic intima. *Circul. Res., U.S.A.*, 1961, **9** (2), 472–8.

CHAPTER 10

Mucopolysaccharides

THE study of mucopolysaccharides started in 1922 when Levene[21] of the Rockefeller Institute published the results of his investigations of the hexosamines, mucins and mucoids. The application of these findings to the aorta is due to Meyer.[25, 26]

The problems which such studies present arise from many different sources. These compounds are difficult to isolate and some changes may occur as a consequence of necessary manipulation. Isolation can, in spite of all precautions, still leave impurities attached to the product. One usually works with groups having similar analytical reactions in common, but in this case the role of the constituents cannot be decided upon. In addition the simple anatomical separation of the three layers which make up the artery itself constitutes a great difficulty.

A. *Determination of Total Hexosamines*

Determining the total hexosamines involves measuring a complex composed of glucosamines and galactosamines which are not distinguishable from each other. Furthermore, the ionized hexosamines, the hyaluronic acids and the chondroitin sulphates are not separated, nor the unionized hexosamines. The results obtained therefore only represent a net amount of little significance. What can we learn from this? In general, the presence in the intima of a lot of hexosamines which is just about all one can expect from a measurement so complex and variable. An exception, however, is the marked increase of hexosamines in the histological forms called fibro-hyalines. The details are as follows.

The aorta only has been investigated. The Elson Morgan method is generally used for the estimation of hexosamines. The contents in the aorta and various normal arteries are given in Table XXXVII.

In man Kirk *et al.*[12, 13] found that the hexosamine content of fragments of aorta fell slightly as the atherosclerotic lesions increased. The successive figures for hexosamine were 0·34, 0·30 and 0·28 per cent of dry tissue on transition from normal tissue to increasingly advanced plaques. This investigation was on the intima and media together. Noble *et al.*[30] gave the same sequence but with extremely small variations.

According to de Maurizi *et al.*,[24] healthy fragments from the aorta of atheromatous subjects have a normal content, the zones of lipid deposits a normal or slightly raised content, and only in the zones in which fibro-hyaline degenerations predominate is the hexosamine content definitely increased. These investigations were on isolated intima.

Men: 0·034   0·031   0·035
Women: 0·046   0·048   0·046
(Total hexosa./grammes protein)

TABLE XXXVII. HEXOSAMINES *

Species	Artery	Intima	Media	Externa	Total	References
Rabbit	Aorta	1·5		0·5	1·07	Kuzin et al.[18a]
Pig	Aorta	0·7		0·47	0·83	Kuzin et al.[18a]
Dog	Aorta Arch Thoracic Abdominal				1·0 0·85 0·74	Shetlar[32a]
Man	Aorta	1·34	1·23	0·66	Intima and Media	Kuzin et al.[18a]
	Peripheral artery		0·4			Kuzin et al.[18a]
	Aorta Coronary Cerebral Pulmonary				1·2 1·0 0·72 1·08	Kirk et al.[12, 13] Kirk et al.[12, 13] Kirk et al.[12, 13]

* % dry weight. The author's figures have been reduced to dry weight by assuming a water content of 75 per cent.

B. Determination of Uronic Acids

In all cases except one, this concerns glucuronic acid. In chondroitin sulphate B one finds in its place iduronic acid. Here are the results obtained:

Mucopolysaccharides: uronic acids. Uronic acids are estimated by two techniques which are not very specific, namely colour reactions with orcinol and with carbazol. The proteins are removed with 0·5 N sodium carbonate. The mucopolysaccharides are precipitated with protamine. The following are the results.

(1) Normal uronic acid values for the aorta (percentage of dried tissue) are given in Table XXXVIII.

(2) Regarding the effects of experimentally produced atherosclerosis, Bollet et al.[5] failed to observe any increase of uronic acids in either the arteries or plasma of rabbits during 6 months of atherosclerogenic treatment (1 g

cholesterol daily), despite the development of the abnormalities usually seen in induced atherosclerosis. Thereafter, however, there was a marked increase, the percentage reaching 0·51 with carbazol and 0·4 with orcinol. A similar observation was made by Antonini et al.[1] The carbazol/orcinol value ratio was itself increased. The authors concluded that the changes in the muco-polysaccharides were secondary to lipid changes and that the rise in the carbazol/orcinol ratio indicated qualitative change.

The total amount of acid mucopolysaccharide is raised in atherosclerosis (Böttcher et al., 1963,[6] Schmidt et al., 1964[31]).

TABLE XXXVIII

	Colour reaction with carbazol	Colour reaction with orcinol	References
Rabbit	0·34	0·29	Bollet et al.[5]
Man	0·2		Kirk[16]

C. Mucopolysaccharides Containing Sulphur

The presence or absence of sulphur can give us some information on the distribution of the groups of glycoproteins. One can in effect distinguish:

the glycoproteins not containing ionized sulphur such as chondroitin acid and hyaluronic acid;

the glycoproteins containing ionized sulphur such as chondroitin sulphates (A, C and B or β heparin), the keratin sulphates, α heparin, heparin sulphate or heparin monosulphate as well as sulphohyaluronic acid.

Mucopolysaccharides containing SO_4 groups. Estimation of the hydro-lysable SO_4 groups affords information on variations occurring in the sulphur-containing mucopolysaccharides. Kirk's technique[12, 13, 15, 16] is as follows. He heats the substance to 118°C with HCl in sealed ampoules for 15 hours, after which he precipitates the sulphates with benzidine and ends with spectrophotometric measurements.

(1) Table XXXIX shows the normal values for various species. Percentages given for wet tissue have been multiplied by four (75 per cent water) to render them comparable.

(2) Practically no changes with age have been noted.[16]

(3) Changes have been observed with the development of atheromatous lesions.

(a) Buck[7] studied the aorta in rabbits given cholesterol and observed the following changes in the SO_4 values:

normal	0·132–0·189	average: 0·165%
atheromatous	0·181–0·226	average: 0·203%

(b) Kirk and Dyrbye[12-14] studied the hydrolysable sulphates in fresh human tissues and obtained the following figures:

normal artery: 0·085; moderate atheroma: 0·07; severe atheroma: 0·077 per cent.

There was, in fact, little or no change.

(c) When cholesterol and radioactive sulphur, ^{35}S, were administered simultaneously to rabbits, autoradiography revealed an excess of this sulphur in the atheromatous plaques. This sulphur was still increased after dialysis.[7] By contrast, there was extremely little in the media subjacent to the plaques.[7]

In atherosclerosis Böttcher et al. in 1963[6] showed a rise of acid mucopolysaccharides during the period of formation. Similarly Curran et al.[8] found during this period a rise of mucopolysaccharides containing SO_4H_2 in the intima and the media in man. The rate of fixation of sulphate ^{35}S of the mucopolysaccharides of the aorta and the increase of serum protein-bound hexoses, hexosamines and serum acids in animals fed on cholesterol (Gero et al., 1962[10-11]).

Mucopolysaccharides not containing SO_4 *groups.* Kirk et al.[14] made the calculation:

Mucopolysaccharides without SO_4 = total hexosamines − (hydrolysable

$$\text{sulphate} \times 1·86)$$

TABLE XXXIX

Animal	Aorta		Arteries				References
	Thoracic	Abdominal	Iliac	Coronary	Cerebral	Pulmonary	
Cat	0·423	0·132	0·168				Jorpes et al.[11a]
Dog	0·279						Jorpes et al.[11a]
Horse	0·279	0·087	0·192				Jorpes et al.[11a]
Pig	0·180	0·165	0·336				Jorpes et al.[11a]
Rabbit	0·23						Buck et al.[7]
Man	0·3			0·216	0·168	0·28	Kirk et al.[14]

TABLE XXXIXa

	Aorta	Coronary arteries	Cerebral arteries	Pulmonary arteries
Percentage of dry tissue	0·16	0·15	0·102	0·135
Percentage of total hexosamines	54·0	60·0	57·0	50·0

D. *Hyaluronic Acid*

More information may possibly be obtained by the study of various glyco⁻ proteins carefully isolated from each other. Hyaluronic acid has been isolated from the ox aorta by Meyer *et al.*[26] and by Berenson *et al.*[3] The fact that a protein fraction was sensitive to bacterial hyaluronidase enabled Kirk[14-15] to confirm the presence of hyaluronic acid in the human aorta.

The glucosamines which represent the hexosamines of heparin, heparitin and hyaluronic acid constitute 21 per cent of the total hexosamines of the mucopolysaccharides in the human aorta.[16]

The greater part of the mucopolysaccharides in an atherosclerotic plaque from an elephant was destroyed by hyaluronidase, the importance of hyaluronic acid in this lesion in a frugivorous animal being thus demon- strated.[22a]

In the aortas affected by atherosclerosis Berenson *et al.* (1963)[4] found a marked decrease of hyaluronic acid. Enselme *et al.* (1959)[9] found on the contrary an increase in this acid.

E. *Chondroitin Sulphuric Acid*

The complex chondroitin sulphuric acid ($-C$ protein) is separated from normal or atherosclerotic aortas by chromatography. The yield from a normal aorta is about 0·13 per cent and from a diseased aorta about twice as much.

It has long been known that chondroitin sulphuric acids could be extracted from the vessels with sodium carbonate solutions. They have thus been extracted by Morner[27] from the intima and from the internal part of the media of the cat and from the aorta of man, by Krawkow[18] from the aorta of the horse, by Levene and Lopez-Suarez[22] and Levene[21] from the aorta of the cat, by Stallman[33] from the aorta of the horse and by Bassiouni[2] from the human aorta.

Some recent works merit sustained attention.

(1) Meyer *et al.*[25] isolated acid chondroitin sulphates B and C from the cat aorta. Acid chondroitin sulphate B has also been isolated from the pig aorta.[26] And in 1956 Meyer *et al.*[26] isolated acid chondroitin sulphate A

from the aorta of the ox. Acid mucopolysaccharides constituted about 1 per cent of the dry weight of the tissue. Acid chondroitin sulphate A accounted for about one-third of this extract.

(2) By chromatographic separation Berenson[3] isolated acid chondroitin sulphates A and B from ox mucopolysaccharides. Chondroitin sulphate A represented about 75 per cent of the sulphomucopolysaccharides.

(3) Kirk et al.[14, 15] extracted mucopolysaccharides from human aortas. They contained 24·8 per cent of hexosamines. Galactosamines constituted 79 per cent of the hexosamines. As they correspond to chondroitin sulphates, it would appear that the latter predominated. To this should be added a comparative study of the effect of testicular hyaluronidases, which hydrolyse chondroitin sulphates A and B as well as hyaluronic acid and the effect of staphylococcal hyaluronidase which acts only on hyaluronic acid.

This examination demonstrated the presence of chondroitin sulphates A or C, or else A and C. Paper electrophoresis at pH 8·6 separated a rapid group which contained an enzyme for galactosamines and a slow group which contained hexosamines of which 56 per cent were galactosamines. The components in the rapid band of this electrophoresis which were among the chondroitin sulphates were partly eliminated by the action of testicular hyaluronidase. The author concluded that chondroitin sulphate B (fraction remaining) and chondroitin sulphates A and/or C (fraction eliminated) were present.

(4) Manley et al. in 1965[23a] showed that the ratio of hyaluronic acid to chondroitin sulphate is lower in the wall of the abdominal aorta than in the wall of the thoracic aorta. Moreover, this ratio is likewise diminished in the left coronary artery if one compares it with those peripheral vessels of the same size. Finally the intra-cranial arteries and the middle cerebral ones show a significant deficiency in hyaluronic acid.

These vascular troubles are localized in the parts of the vessels which are the constant site of atheroma at a more advanced age, which precedes the visible lesions.

(5) According to Berenson in 1963[4] there is in the atherosclerotic aorta a relative rise in condroitin sulphate B whereas the A and C forms are decreased.

F. Glycoproteins with Covalent Bonds

Covalent bonds. These substances are generally neutral, in which case they are composed of hexosamines and various sugars (galactose, mannose, glucose, pentose). Sometimes they are acid, the acidity being generally due to sialic acid. On glucide content, they are divided into:

(a) Mucoids: containing more than 4 per cent glucides;

(b) Glucoproteins: containing less than 4 per cent of glucides.

One can approach the study of these substances in two ways, namely by estimating one of their constituents, either hexosamine or the esterified sulphates, or by isolating them.

We shall examine the state and the role of each of these in the artery. Mucopolysaccharides are generally isolated by delipidation of the tissue followed by treatment with pancreatinases to eliminate other proteins. They are then precipitated with alcohol. The techniques employed by different authors vary considerably. Separation of the different mucopolysaccharides is effected by zonal electrophoresis and by chromatography.

Noble *et al.*[30] detected hexosamines which were soluble in saline solutions; they were dealing with free polysaccharides and insoluble hexosamines which were bound to fibrous proteins. With the development of atherosclerosis the values of the soluble hexosamines fell, whereas those of the insoluble hexosamines increased. The hexosamine-sclero-protein linkage would thus appear to increase as the disease develops.

The chromatographic separation of galactosamines and glucosamines enabled Kirk and Dyrbye[14] to estimate these two types of hexosamines. In the aorta the glucosamines constituted an average of 21 per cent of the hexosamines and appeared to diminish with age. The galactosamines were 79 per cent of the hexosamines and were increased in old age.

The α_2 glycoproteins are raised in diabetes and atherosclerosis which appears to correlate with a degenerative tendency of the artery (William *et al.*, 1964[34]).

There is also an increase of α_2 glycoproteins in the atherosclerotic aorta in parallel with the serum level (Schonebeck *et al.*, 1962[32]).

The role of the mucopolysaccharides can be summarized thus:

1. hyaluronic acid separates the tissue elements;
2. heparin plays an anticoagulant role, particularly the sulphate compounds;
3. heparin clarifies the serum;
4. they have a protective action against colloidal properties.

G. *Oxygen Consumption in the Atherosclerotic Aorta*

The need for oxygen is very great in the atherosclerotic artery (Lazzarini-Robertson, 1962;[20] Munro[28]).

Ksabyan showed an accumulation of ascorbic acid in the media of the aorta but this diminishes in lipidosis of the aorta and is absent in atheroma.

References

1. ANTONINI, F. M. and MINNINI, G., Studio sui mucopolisaccaridi plasmatici e dell'aorta nell aterosclerosi sperimentale da colestero. *Arch. Ist. Biochem. Ital.*, 1955, **17**, 119–36.

2. BASSIOUNI, M., The estimation of heparin and similar substances in human blood and tissue using a combined biological and colorimetric method with paper electrophoretic studies. *J. Clin. Path.*, 1954, **7**, 330.

3. BERENSON, G. S., A study of acid mucopolysaccharides of bovine aorta with the aid of a chromatographic procedure for separating sulfated mucopolysaccarides. *Biochim. Biophys. Acta*, 1958, **28**, 176.

4. BERENSON, G. S., DALFERES, E. R., ROBIN, R. and STRONG, *Evolution of the Atherosclerotic Plaque*. The University of Chicago Press, Chicago and London, 1963, **1**, 139.

5. BOLLET, A. J., CHUNI WANG and ADLERSBERG, D., Acid mucopolysaccharide content of the aorta in cholesterol-fed rabbits. *Circulation*, 1958, **18**, 481.

6. BÖTTCHER, C. J. F. and KLYNSTRA, F. B., Acid mucopolysaccharides in human aortic tissue. Their distribution at different stages of atherosclerosis. *Lancet*, 1963, **2**, 439.

7. BUCK, R. C. and HEAGY, F. C., Uptake of radioactive sulfur by various tissues of normal and cholesterol-fed rabbits. *Canad. J. Biochem. Biophys.*, 1958, **36**, 63.

8. CURRAN, R. C. and CRANE, W. A. J., Mucopolysaccharides in the atheromatous aorta. *J. Pathol. Bacteriol.*, 1962, **84**, 405.

9. ENSELME, J., COTTET, J. and Mme CLERC, Le séromucoïde perchlorosoluble du sérum au cours des phases évolutives de l'athérosclérose. *Revue de l'Athérosclérose*, 1959, **1**, 40.

9a. FORMAN, D. T., MacCANN, S., MOSHER, R. E. and BOYLE, A. J., The influence of experimentally induced atherosclerosis on the sulfate content of the aortic wall. *Circ. Res.*, 1960, **8**, 267–70.

10. GERO, S., GERGELY, J., FARKAS, K., DEVENYI, T., KOCSAR, L., JAKAB, L., SZEKELY, J. and VIRAG, S., Rôle des substances mucoïdes de l'intima dans la pathogénie de l'athérosclérose. *J. Atheroscler. Res.*, 1962, **2**, 276.

11. GERO, S., GERGELY, J., DEVENYI, T., VIRAG, S., SVEKELY, J. and JAKAB, L., Inhibitory effect of some mucopolysaccharides on the lipolytic activity of the aorta of animals. *Nature*, 1962, **194**, 1181.

11a. JORPES, F., HOLMGREN, H. and WILANDER, O., Über das Vorkommen von Heparin in den Gefässwänden und die Augen. *Z. mikr. Anat. Forsch.*, 1937, **42**, 279.

11b. JORPES, F., *Heparin in Treatment of Thrombosis*. Oxford University Press, London, 1946.

12. KIRK, J. E. and DYRBYE, M., Studies on the mucopolysaccharides of human tissue. *Circulation*, 1956, **14**, 480.

13. KIRK, J. E. and DYRBYE, M., Hexosamine and acid hydrolysable sulfate concentrations of the aorta and pulmonary artery in individuals of various ages. *J. Geront.*, 1956, **11**, 273.

14. KIRK, J. E. and DYRBYE, M., Mucopolysaccharides of arterial tissue. II. Analysis of total isolated mucopolysaccharides material. *J. Geront.*, 1957, **12**, 23.

15. KIRK, J. E., WANG, J. and DYRBYE, M., Mucopolysaccharides of human arterial tissue. IV. Analysis of electrophoretically separated fractions. *J. Geront.*, 1958, **13**, 362–5.

16. KIRK, J. E., Mucopolysaccharides of arterial tissue, in Lansing. *The Arterial Wall*, 1 vol., 259 pp., Baillière, Tindall, London, 1959, pp. 161–91.

17. KLEMER, A. and HOMBERG, K., Recherches chimiques sur les complexes chondroïtine sulfurique-protéine pour l'étude de l'artériosclérose et des processus de vieillissement. *Angew. Chem. Dtsch.*, 1964, **76**, no. 13, 591.

18. KRAWKOW, N. P., Beiträge zur Chemie der Amyloidentartung. *Arch. Exp. Path. Pharmak.*, 1898, **40**, 195.

18a. KUZIN, A. M. and GLADYSHEV, B. N., Distribution of easily hydrolyzable compounds containing hexosamine in different tissues of animals and man. *Biokhimija*, 1950, **15**, 316.

20. LAZZARINI-ROBERTSON, A., Respiration of human arterial intima and atherogenesis. *Feder. Proc.*, *U.S.A.*, 1962, **21** (2), 101 (March–April).

21. LEVENE, P. A., *Hexosamine, their Derivatives and Mucins and Mucoids*, Rockefeller Institute, New York, 1922, monogr. no. 18.

22. LEVENE, P. A. and LOPEZ-SUAREZ, J., Mucin and mucoids. *J. Biol. Chem.*, 1918, **36**, 105–26.

22a. LINDSAY, S., SKAHEN, R. and CHAI KO, H. J. L., Arteriosclerosis in the elephant. *Arch. publ.*, 1956, **61**, 207–18.

23. LINKER, A., HOFFMAN, P. and MEYER, K., Heparitin sulfate. *Fed. Proc.*, 1958, **17**, 264.

23a. MANLEY, C. and HAWKSWORTH, J., Distribution des mucopolysaccharides dans l'arbre vasculaire humain. *Nature*, 1965, **206**, 1152.

24. MAURIZI, DE M., DINA, M. A. and GALETTI, R., Contributo allo studio dei mucopolisaccharidi e dei lipidi nelle placche arteriosclerotiche. *G. Geront.*, 1959, **2**, 107–13.

25. MEYER, K. and RAPPORT, M. M., The mucopolysaccharides of the ground substance of connective tissue. *Science*, 1951, **113**, 596–9.

26. MEYER, K., DAVIDSON, E., LINKER, A. and HOFFMAN, P., The acid mucopolysaccharides of connective tissue. *Biochim. Biophys. Acta*, 1956, **21**, 506–18.

27. MORNER, C. T., Einige beobachtungen über die Verbreitung der Chrondoitin-Schwefelsäure. *Z. Phys. Chem.*, 1895, **20**, 357.

27a. MUIR, H., Chondroitin sulfate in human aorta. *IVth Confer. Chronic Biologique*, section 2, p. 18.

28. MUNROE, J. and SHIPP, J. C., Effect of sulfonylurea compound on hyperlipemia and hypercholesterolemia in the diabetic. *Clin. Res.*, 1962, **10**, 88.

29. MURATA, K. and KIRK, J. E., La teneur en acide sialique chez l'homme du tissu d'artère et de veine. *J. Atheroscler. Res.*, 1962, **2**, 452.

30. NOBLE, N. L., BOUCEK, R. J. and KAO, K. Y. T., Biochemical observations of human atheromatosis. Analysis of aortic intima. *Circulation*, 1957, **15**, 366–72.

31. SCHMIDT, M. and DMOCHOWSKI, A., The acid mucopolysaccharides of normal and atherosclerotic human aorta. *Acta Biochim. Polon.*, 1964, **11**, no. 2–3, 371–7.

32. SCHONEBECK, L., WERBER, U. and VOIGT, K. D., Les composants du sérum et de la paroi artérielle contenant des hydrates de carbone liés aux protéines dans l'athérosclérose. *J. Atheroscler. Res.*, 1962, **2**, 332.

32a. SHETLAR, M. R., Mucopolysaccharides in atherosclerosis. Presentation at Meeting of Veterans, Administration's Advisory Committee on Problems of Aging, 5 Nov., 1956, Saint Louis.

33. STALLMAN, B., Beiträge zur Physiologie des Alterns. XI. Untersuchungen verschiedenalter Pferdeaorten auf ihren Gehalt an chondroitin-Schwefelsäuren. *Z. Ges. Exp. Med.*, 1937, **101**, 175.

34. WILLIAM, S. FRANKL, Glycoproteins in diabetes mellitus and atherosclerosis. *Amer. J. Med. Sciences*, 1964, 118/588.

35. WILANDER, O., Studien Über Heparin. *Skand. Arch. Physiol.*, 1939, suppl. 15.

CHAPTER 11

The Glycoprotein Origin of Lipid Deposits

Since 1956 John Yudkin,[5, 6] Professor of Nutrition and Dietetics in the University of London at Queen Elizabeth College, has attributed to sucrose an important role in the pathogenesis of atherosclerosis.

The author distinguishes between hunger and appetite in these terms: "For the present purpose we may say that hunger is a sensation which makes one want to eat, appetite is a sensation which makes one want to eat a particular food. The quality of a food which evokes appetite is what I have earlier called palatability." The arguments presented by the author are the following:

(1) The wealthier countries are those most affected by atherosclerosis. This incidence corresponds to an excess of calories which is provided by lipids or carbohydrates. To quote the author: "The failure to reduce caloric intake comes from an increased consumption of highly palatable food. My own view is that we should also look to the specific effect of sugar as well as to the general effect of carbohydrates." One can object to these assertions that in grams of simple food and taking account of the digestability of the foods in the organism, the carbohydrates supply 3·88 calories and the lipids 8·65. Can the attraction of sugar for man make up the difference? Also one sees that sucrose is no different to the other carbohydrates, since after digestion sucrose, like many polysaccharides which are broken down to monosaccharides, gives glucose as the end product.

(2) "National levels of fat and sugar consumption are very similar." The graphs do show some aberrant points.

"Statistics relating fat intake to ischaemic heart disease in different populations may therefore express only an indirect relationship and the causal relationship may be with sugar." It is necessary perhaps to choose.

(3) If one prepares a comparative table of the utilization of sugar and frequency of infarcts one obtains the following results for men aged 45–65 (Table XL).

(4) We can readily give our own interpretation of these facts: the carbohydrates, like the lipids, are degraded to acetyl CoA, a precursor of cholesterol but all the carbohydrates and not only sucrose which is emphasized so much. Moreover, for eighteen carbon atoms the carbohydrates give nine molecules of CoA, whereas the saturated fatty acids give six. Those from the

94

carbohydrates which avoid this fate are burnt to CO_2 and H_2O and therefore cannot contribute to cholesterol.

The conclusions of Yudkin are certainly very interesting but they require to be confirmed in some way. We give here some additional information.

Wells and Anderson[4] had published some similar results concerning lactose but they attributed the increase in atherosclerosis in the rabbit and rat to an increase of cholesterol absorption by the action of this sugar. They studied it in man and summarized their results as follows: "Four male students (ages 21–23) were fed a controlled natural diet for 8 weeks. For the first 5 weeks, important daily components of the diet were: total calories

TABLE XL. SUGAR INTAKE OF SUBJECTS WITH MYOCARDIAL INFARCTION (MI), OR PERIPHERAL ARTERIAL DISEASE (PA) AND OF CONTROL SUBJECTS (C) MEN AGED 45-65

| Group | Number | Age (mean years) | (Sugar intake (g per d)) | |
			Mean	Median
MI	20	56 −4	132	113
PA	25	56 −5	141	128
C	25	56 −0	77	56

Significance of difference in sugar intake: MI and control
P   0·0005
PA 0·0005
P   0·00003

2685, protein 85 g; lipid 28 per cent of calories; cholesterol 1·01 g; lactose 160 g. During the following three weeks, the lactose was replaced by an equivalent amount of sucrose. The free and total serum cholesterol of the subjects were determined before, during and after the controlled diet periods. The average total serum cholesterol increased from the 'normal' level of 185 mg per cent to 231 mg per cent during the lactose feeding period and decreased to 162 mg per cent when sucrose was substituted for lactose."

We have ourselves given rabbits two types of feed, one composed of a standard diet and the other composed of potatoes to which were added a little grass or cabbage leaves to render it more acceptable to the animal. The results appeared so surprising to us that we have not published them (Enselme and Cottet[1]). The following table shows the values obtained. All these animals received 1 gram per day of cholesterol. Each group consisted of twelve rabbits.

	Serum				Aorta			
	Cholesterol		Total lipids		Number of lesions		Percentage of animals with lesions	
	Before	After	Before	After	Diet+cholesterol Normal	Potato	Diet+cholesterol Normal	Potato
Exp. I Controls	0·45	2·4						
Treated	0·67	6·0			0·66	1·83	50%	91%
Exp. II Controls	0·58	5·88						
Treated	0·75	7·0			0·87	1·1	50%	90%
Exp. III Controls	0·41	6·1						
Treated	0·42	8·39	1·85	17·26	1·4	1·4	83%	83%

Larsen and Bortz[3] made a study of the health of some employees on a sugar plantation in Hawaii over a period of 17 years.

Half of the workers were Japanese, and half were Filipinos. The striking increased age of the workers—a mean of nine years based on the data for eight plantations—could account for some of this rise. Improved diagnosis may also have been a factor. Improved economic conditions, with the associated dietary changes, likewise played a part.

DEGREE OF AORTIC SCLEROSIS COMPARED WITH DEGREE OF CORONARY SCLEROSIS IN THE POST-MORTEM SERIES, BY RACE AND SEX

Race and sex	Per cent of patients and various grades of sclerosis				
	Grade 0	Grade 1	Grade 2	Grade 3	Grade 4
Caucasian males	3 (4)*	9 (10)	21 (20)	22 (23)	42 (41)
Caucasian females	7 (9)	11 (14)	22 (21)	21 (16)	37 (37)
Japanese males	6 (10)	19 (23)	31 (32)	23 (18)	18 (14)
Japanese females	8 (23)	27 (22)	27 (20)	20 (3)	16 (19)

* The percentages of patients showing coronary sclerosis are in parentheses.

One can see the expected effect of carbohydrates and not only sugars but these experiments are carried out on only one type of diet, very different from human food which is in equilibrium with lipids which should be studied. The exaggeration of these special diets should warn us when drawing our conclusions and persuade us to give a more balanced diet.

References

1. ENSELME, J., COTTET, J. and FRAY, G., Action d'un pool d'acides aminés sur l'athérosclérose expérimentale du lapin. *Arch. Mal. Cœur (Rev. Athérosclérose), Fr.*, 1962, **4** (2), 15–20.
2. HODGES, R. E. and OHLSON, M. A., Total serum lipids, cholesterol and triglycerides following ingestion of diets with 2 sources of carbohydrate. *Fed. Proc.*, 1963, **22** (2), part 1, 209.
3. LARSEN, N. P. and BORTZ, W. M., Atherosclerosis: a comparative study of Caucasian and Japanese citizens in the Hawaiian islands. *J. Amer. Geriatr. Soc.*, 1960, **8** (11), 867–72.
4. WELLS, W. W. and ANDERSON, S. C., The effect of dietary lactose on the serum cholesterol level of human subjects. *Fed. Proc., U.S.A.*, 1962, **21** (2), 100.
5. YUDKIN, J., Diet and coronary thrombosis. Hypothesis and fact. *Lancet*, 1957, **273** (2), 155–62.
6. YUDKIN, J., Dietary fat and dietary sugar in relation to ischaemic heart-disease and diabetes. *Lancet*, 4 July 1964.

CHAPTER 12

Proteins

THE various types of protein found in the aorta will now be considered in turn.

I. The Elastic Tissue

Elastic tissue, which is widely distributed in the body, is present in very large quantity in the aorta. It is not certain that we are dealing with a single chemical entity. It may possibly represent a mixture of proteins. Its isolation and analysis are rendered very difficult by reason of its insolubility, which is not changed by boiling or by prolonged autoclaving. Furthermore, it is in direct relationship with another tissue, collagen, and histological examination shows that these tissues are often so intermingled that elastic tissue must often still contain fragments of collagen even after the most careful purification. The traces of hydroxyproline which are found among its amino acids after hydrolysis and the faint glucide reactions which it sometimes gives are probably due to collagen and mucopolysaccharides present as impurities. Its resistance to pepsin is not absolute, the fact that it is rendered soluble by elastase is not absolutely specific, and if impure trypsin attacks it, it is because the trypsin contains cellulase. Its behaviour when examined by X-ray diffraction and in the electron microscope is in no way characteristic. Its identification must, therefore, be essentially analytical. Elastin is the protein which is insoluble in 0·1 N sodium carbonate and is not converted into gelatin.[38, 50]

Variations of this definition will be observed. Some authors[50] estimate the hydroxyproline and employ conversion factors. This procedure is incorrect if it is accepted that this amino acid belongs to the collagen impurities. In general, it is sufficient to purify and weigh the insoluble residue but, as we have said, there is nothing to prove that we are dealing with a single protein.

This definition is valid only for mammals. Certain teleosteans (*Lophius pescatorius*) have an elastic tissue which, although exhibiting the other characteristics of elastin, is soluble within 15 minutes in 0·1 N sodium carbonate.

A. *The Quantities of Elastin Contained in the Arteries*

Table XLI shows the values found by various authors.

The variations seen from one author to another arise from various causes such as differences in the extraction (sodium carbonate or urea), differences in the tissue preparations, whether media alone or media plus intima.

The average of 42 per cent for the media of man found by Lansing[34-36] should perhaps be retained.

TABLE XLI

Aorta of	Age (years)	Elastin, % of dry tissue	Notes and references
Rat		24·0	Lowry et al.[38]
		47·7	Extraction with urea, 20%
			Estimation by hydroxyproline
		47·0	Neuman et al.[50]
Ox		39·8	Neuman et al.[50]
		37·8	
Pig		51·7	Neuman et al.[50]
		53·4	
Man		30·0	Lowry et al.[38]
	0–10	48·5	
	11–20	48·2	(Media)
	21–30	43·3	Lansing[35, 36]
	31–40	41·4	(Average: 42)
	41–50	44·1	
	51–60	41·4	
	61–70	43·8	
	71–80	43·8	
	81–90	41·1	

B. *Evolution of Elastin in the Course of Ageing*

The various changes seen have been well assessed by Lansing.[34-36]

(1) When the media alone is considered, quantitative changes appear to be minimal and elastin does not seem to be reduced in the aged.

(2) Chemical analysis by Lansing [34-36] shows that the composition of elastin changes slightly with age. Among its amino acids there was an increase in the amino diacids (aspartic and glutamic) and a reduction in the apolar acids (glycine, valine, proline).

(3) Histologically, there was fragmentation of the elastic layers with fenestration. These changes were observed in the external elastic membrane of the renal arteries.

(4) Estimations of the calcium in the elastic tissue revealed an increasing content (from 1 to 6 per cent). This was probably in the form of hydroxyapatite (Weissmann et al., 1960).

In 1960 Shin Yeh Yu and Blumenthal[66] also showed that the calcium in the elastic tissue of the media of the aorta increased with age. The calcium which could be extracted by chelation diminished with age. Only a small fraction of this calcium could be replaced. There would thus appear to be two types of calcium in elastic tissue, the one bound to the tissue and the other unlinked. Furthermore, these phenomena could not be reproduced in the case of very old subjects. Their elastin behaved differently.

These changes can be interpreted either as change in one protein, elastin, or as evidence of the disappearance of one of the proteins which perhaps constitute the entity that is elastic tissue.

C. Changes Due to Atherosclerosis

(1) The investigation of quantitative changes is difficult. The percentage of elastic tissue is greatly reduced at the level of a plaque, and the latter introduces an excess of lipid elements.

(2) The changes in this tissue described by histologists are generally considerable in the media subjacent to the plaques. Fredman (1963) thinks that initially there is a rapid disintegration of the elastic layer by the accumulation of lipids both in and around it, during experimental atherosclerosis of the rabbit.

(3) These changes are associated with a considerable increase of fixed calcium. The investigations of Blumenthal et al.[6, 7] have demonstrated calcification preceding the atheromatous plaques. When the intimal lesion was established, calcification increased at that level. These investigations were effected by histological techniques involving micro-incineration.

As Lansing[35, 36] suggests, the evolution of the plaques is probably as follows: normal tissue, fibrous plaque, fatty plaque, necrotic plaque. Increase of calcium in the intima was observed with change from the normal to the fibrous type. In the media the main increase occurred during the change from the fibrous to the lipid type, that is after a certain degree of evolution had taken place. These analyses were made on lipid-free tissue.

(4) The effect of the ingestion of elastase on the development of experimental atherosclerosis has been the subject of a considerable number of investigations.

There was, after 6 weeks, a considerable increase of blood cholesterol and, according to Lansing,[34] of atherosclerosis in a rabbit receiving small doses of cholesterol (0·3 g daily). The atherosclerosis was less conspicuous if the rabbit ingested elastase at the same time. Two facts here seem remarkable, namely the development of atherosclerosis from so small a dose of cholesterol administered over a period which is also short, and the action of an enzyme introduced by the digestive route. Tennent[69] repeated these experiments on cockerels treated for 8 weeks with a larger dose of cholesterol (2 per cent of the diet). He failed to observe changes resulting from the ingestion or injection of elastase.

Finally, in 1953 Balo and Banga[3] reported that the pancreas of subjects who had died from vascular affections contained very little elastase, whereas there were considerable quantities in the pancreatic glands of individuals who had died as a result of violence or from diseases other than vascular affections.

Elastin and collagen are present in larger quantities in the aorta of the cock than in that of the hen. It may be that this is one of the reasons for their different susceptibilities to atherosclerosis.[12]

Hall has attempted to treat atherosclerosis using an impure preparation containing elastase, an acid polysaccharide and an enzyme E, which is probably the clearing factor. The results obtained were very irregular.

Tracy *et al.* (1961)[70a] showed that there are early on some lipoproteins in the plaques which later decrease.

Reay *et al.* in 1963[61] showed that initially a large soluble fraction of elastin was formed in pigs deprived of food containing copper. The copper deficiency in the layers was studied using pancreatic diastase for 12 hours at 37°C.

II. Collagen

Collagen exhibits the following analytical characteristics:

(1) The X-ray (large angle) diffraction patterns present a picture in the meridian line in which a periodicity of 2·86 Å is discernible. This characteristic would appear to be a constant and adequate sign of the presence of this protein.

(2) Observation of collagen with the electron microscope reveals fibrils with alternating bands of high and low density. The dark bands are 640 Å distant from one another. This alternation is also found in the X-ray (small angle) diffraction patterns. This characteristic may be lacking particularly in the collagen of invertebrates.

(3) Insoluble collagen subjected to a temperature of 60°C for a sufficient length of time yields a closely related and soluble protein, gelatin. On free electrophoresis the latter yields a band which can be identified from the value of its mobility and, in consequence, the presence of collagen can be affirmed.

(4) Collagen is probably the only protein which contains hydroxyproline (14 per cent). Very pure elastin undoubtedly contains none.

(5) Natural collagen is not hydrolysed by trypsin or cathepsin. It is hydrolysed by pepsin and denatured by collagenase. These properties may be utilized for certain microscopic observations.

(6) Collagen is generally insoluble. Three types of soluble collagen are, however, accepted and are often called procollagens, namely acid (*p*H 3·62) soluble collagen,[55] alkali (*p*H 9·0) soluble collagen [Neuberger and Harkness] and collagen soluble in 0·45 M NaCl in neutral medium [Gross]. Orekhovitch *et al.*[55] have shown that the three collagens have the same composition. The differences in solubility are explained by their state in the morphological structures and by the different degrees of aggregation.

The particles concerned would appear to be asymmetrical and have a molecular weight of about 500,000, a length of 3000 Å and a thickness of 15 Å. There would also appear to be two other components, a β component with a molecular weight of 125,000 and an α component with a molecular weight of 290,000.

The authors have formulated an analytical method based on these definitions. Collagen is the protein which is insoluble in 0·1 N NaOH and which is convertible into gelatin. The quantity of gelatin gives the quantity of collagen. This is arrived at by estimating the content of hydroxyproline and multiplying this by the coefficient 7·46.

A. Collagen Content of the Aorta

In Table XLII some values are given in percentages of dry weight of artery.

TABLE XLII. COLLAGEN CONTENT OF THE AORTA

Animal	Collagen (% wt. of dry artery)	Author
Rat	25·6	Neuman et al.[50]
	31·0	Lowry et al.[38]
Pig	16·0	Neuman et al.[50]
Ox	23·1	Neuman et al.[50]
Man	28·0	Lowry et al.[38]

B. Collagen in Atherosclerosis

In the course of atherosclerosis, collagen (as judged by hydroxyproline) increases as the lesion advances.

Enselme et al.[15a, 15b] showed in 1961 that the insoluble collagen is increased most in the atheromatous fragments.

Levene[37a, 37b] in a general review attributed an important role to collagen. In fact there is an appreciable problem in determining exactly what is the origin of this proliferation of collagen in atherosclerosis. And one wonders if it is not possible to modify it and thus to prevent the arterial obstruction.

Shimamoto in 1963[65] pointed out that one of the characteristics of the micro-structure of the large arteries and surrounding cells is seen in the muscular layers below the endothelial cells which show a clear cut contrast with the veins. He observed that the administration of compounds such as cholesterol which are capable of inducing experimentally an atheromatous change, provoke an oedematous reaction as well as swelling of the extracellular space. These oedematous changes are considered by this author to be an important mechanism of atherogenesis and thrombogenesis.

Enselme and his colleagues[14, 15] showed in addition that when the NH_2

groups of the cell wall proteins are blocked with formaldehyde, acetaldehyde or propionaldehyde there is an increase of atherosclerogenesis which then develops more rapidly.

In addition Frey and his colleagues[19] at the Biochemistry Laboratory at Lyon compared two series of rabbits, one submitted to a normal diet and the other to an atherosclerogenic diet. They demonstrated that although both groups took practically the same amount of proline, the latter group showed a reduction in the formation of hydroxyproline in insoluble collagen. This fall of activity is statistically significant for the skin but it is particularly definite in the case of the aorta.

III. Other Proteins

A fairly large number of other proteins are found in the vessel walls. Their recognition is essentially histochemical and is still generally incomplete. The following should be mentioned.

A. *Proteins of the Vessel Endothelium*

The vessel endothelium is composed of cells whose chemistry is complex. The proteins of these cells, which are rich in glycogen and phosphatases, are virtually unknown.

The endothelium represents about 2 per cent of the total weight of the artery[17] but the fraction ascribable to proteins cannot be exactly determined. This leaves 3 per cent of non-endothelial tissue in the intima. The presence of an intercellular cement would appear to be discounted by electron microscope examinations. There is, however, a basal membrane. The outstanding sign of ageing is diminution in the capacity for return to a normal type once a disturbing agent has appeared.[72]

Buck[9, 10] using the electron microscope, observed that endothelial cells from rabbits having provoked lesions of atherosclerosis, were different to the cells from the normal animal, even after a return to a non-atherosclerogenic diet.

B. *The Proteins of Smooth Muscle*

Smooth muscle represents 20 per cent of the walls of elastic arteries and 40 per cent in muscular arteries. The arteries which we are studying belong particularly to the former type. This value corresponds to between 14 and 15 g of proteins.

The latter are of various types, the most important being the following:
myosin: (without actin) soluble in solutions of pH 7, $p/2 = 0\cdot2-0\cdot3$ actin: water-soluble;

natural actomyosin: soluble in solvents of pH 7, p/2 = 0·3–0·5; tropomyosin: extractable under high ionic pressures after delipidation of myoglobin.

C. *Enzyme Proteins*

Enzymes are found in the muscular wall. They are the enzymes of the great metabolic systems. We shall return to this subject. They constitute the main fraction of myogen.

D. *The Proteins of the Nucleoproteins*

Nucleoproteins are present in the cytoplasm and more particularly in the nuclei of the cells of various types in the arterial wall.

Various facts point to the activity of proteins.

(1) There is change in and reduction of elastin and a more or less definite increase of collagen in atherosclerotic aortas.

(2) There have been a large number of experiments on the importance of proteins in the spontaneous or experimentally produced atherosclerotic process.

(a) For the most part authors have found that the blood cholesterol was reduced by a supply of proteins and increased when these were replaced by glucides. This is stated for fowls by Kokatnur *et al.*,[29, 31] Johnson *et al.*, [24, 25] Stamler *et al.*,[67] Nishida *et al.*,[52] Picketrol (1958, 1959), None *et al.* (1959), March *et al.*[43] and Mann *et al.*;[42] for the dog by Allison *et al.*:[1] for the rat by Nath *et al.*;[48] and for man by Mellinkoff *et al.*[46] and Barnes *et al.*[4]

(b) Lipid deposits in the arteries have been reduced in the same way in fowls[27, 52, 57, 67] and in rabbits.[21, 59]

(c) Casein, on the other hand, appears to increase the blood cholesterol in the rabbit.[13, 40, 41, 45] In the rat Magee[40] failed to observe any change but Nath[48] stresses the large quantities of casein required to raise the blood cholesterol, Finally, Fragola and Magee[18] showed that casein reduced cholesterol excreted in the faeces.

Increase of the blood cholesterol in man was observed by Albanese *et al.*[1a] Reduction of blood cholesterol was seen by Nath *et al.*,[48] but the diet had to contain 30–40 per cent of casein.

(d) The favourable effect of proteins of animal origin is questioned by a certain number of authors in respect of rats,[71] rabbits[20, 23, 51, 53, 68] and man.[54]

All these authors found, in fact, increase of blood cholesterol after the ingestion of proteins. All, however, stress the fact that these proteins had not been defatted.

(e) Finally, certain authors found that the addition of animal proteins made no difference.[2, 39, 51, 70]

(f) These contradictory opinions can be explained in various ways.

The protein/energy ratio of the diet is undoubtedly important.[11, 30, 33]

The supply in the food of some amino acids, such as methionine and the essential amino acids generally, would appear to be a factor of primary importance.[8, 21, 25, 32, 33, 46, 52, 64]

(g) Almost all authors have found that vegetable proteins have a favourable effect. This is true of soya.[16, 37, 44, 45, 47, 48, 62] According to Nath et al.,[48] zein increases the blood cholesterol.

(h) The capacity of proteins to fix lipids varies in atherosclerosis with hyper-cholesterolaemia. It is increased in the serum and in the aortic intima.[28]

(i) It is fitting that experiments in which the formation of lipid deposits was produced by damaging the arterial intima, that is by altering its proteins, should be appended to these examinations of the importance of proteins.

Such were the results obtained by cauterization,[63] by the introduction of a nylon thread,[26] by papain injections[56] and by thromboendarterec-tomy.[22] Likewise Bjorksten[5] readily obtained fixation of cholesterol, in fine dispersions and coloured with carbon, by exposing fragments of aorta for forty-eight hours in formol or solutions of chromium sulphate-lead acetate or lead nitrate, which have an irritant effect on the wall.

In the dog subjected to atherosclerogenic treatment homografts were more prone to become the seat of changes than the receptor tissues.[26] The same was found in man in the case of operations for coarctation of the aorta.

Enselme and Gauthier[15] gave very small doses of cholesterol (0·3 g daily) to rabbits. This cholesterol was administered as an oxalate or acetate complex. They obtained quite considerable lesions. The caustic effect of the complexed acid created a special receptivity in the wall.

In 1958 Netsky et al.[49] injected a suspension of cholesterol into the media of the brachiocephalic artery of fowls. They obtained a response collagen reaction which provided histological pictures close to those of spontaneous atherosclerosis.

Good, wholesome proteins would appear, then, to favour a normal state of the wall but proteins which have been changed would seem to cause fixation of lipid deposits.

Polcak et al.[58] showed with rabbits submitted to a standard diet and one enriched with cholesterol, the amount of cholesterol, phospholipids, total lipids and serum cholesterol were significantly lower when the diet was enriched with meat.

Renaud in 1964[60] demonstrated the protective effect of a protein, casein on the thrombotic syndrome in the rat.

References

1. ALLISON, J. B., WANNEMACHER, R. W., SPOERLEIN, M. T. and MIDDLETON, E. J., Protein reserves and plasma lipids. *Fed. Proc.*, 1959, **18**, 516.
1a. ALBANESE, A. A., HIGGONS, R. A., LORENZE, E. J. and ORTO, L. A., Effect of dietary proteins on blood cholesterol levels of adults. *Geriatrics*, 1959, **14**, 237–43.

2. ASCHKENAZY, A., BLANPIN, O. and COQUELET, M. L., Etude des protéines et lipides stromatiques et de l'hémoglobine chez des rats carencés en protéines. *Sang*, 1959, **30**, 566–73.

3. BALO, J. and BANGA, J., Changes in elastase content of the human pancreas in relation to arteriosclerosis. *Acta Physiol.*, 1953, **4**, 187–94.

4. BARNES, B. O., RATZENHOFER, M. and TSCHERNE, G., Arteriosclerosis in 10,000 autopsies and the possible role of dietary protein. *Fed. Proc.*, 1960, **19**, 19.

5. BJORKSTEN, J., A mechanism of cholesterol deposition on arterial walls. *Proc. Soc. Exp. Biol.*, 1952, **81**, 350–3.

6. BLUMENTHAL, H. T., LANSING, A. J. and WHEELER, P. A., Calcification of the media of the human aorta and its relation to intimal arteriosclerosis, ageing and disease. *Amer. J. Path.*, 1944, **20**, 665–79.

7. BLUMENTHAL, H. T., LANSING, A. J. and GRAY, S. H., The interrelation of elastic tissue and calcium in the genesis of arteriosclerosis. *Amer. J. Path.*, 1950, **26**, 989–1010.

8. BOSSHARDT, D. K., KRYVOKULSKY, M. and HOWE, E. E., Interrelation of cholesterol, palmitic acid and unsaturated fatty acids in the growing mouse and rat. *J. Nutrit.*, 1959, **69**, 185–90.

9. BUCK, R. C., Uptake of radioactive sulfur by vascular tissue. *Circulation*, 1954, **10**, 595.

10. BUCK, R. C. and HEAGY, F. C., Uptake of radioactive sulfur by various tissues of normal and cholesterol-fed rabbits. *Canad. J. Biochem. Biophys.*, 1958, **36**, 63.

11. CAMPBELL, A. M. and SWENDSELD, M. E., Effect of varying dietary nitrogen intakes on serum cholesterol. *Fed. Proc.*, 1959, **18**, 520.

12. CEMBRANO, J., LILLO, M., VAL, J. and MARDONES, J., Influence of sex difference and hormones on elastin and collagen in the aorta of chickens. *Circ. Res.*, 1960, **8**, 527–9.

13. CLARKSON, S. and NEWBURGH, L. H., The relation between atherosclerosis and ingested cholesterol in the rabbit. *J. Exp. Med.*, 1926, **43**, 595–612.

14. ENSELME, J., Protéines et athérosclérose. *Path. Biol.*, 1959, **7**, no. 19–20, 2119–22.

15. ENSELME, J. and GAUTHIER, M., Action athérosclérogène des complexes oxalique et acétique du cholestérol. *Presse Méd.*, 1960, **68**, 1337.

15a. ENSELME, J., FREY, J. and HENRY, J. C., Comparaison de la constitution du tissu aortique normal et athéromateuse. *Bull. Soc. Chim. Biol.*, 1967, **43**, 1085–95.

15b. ENSELME, J., HENRY, J. C. and FREY, J., Recherches sur l'état des protéines sériques dans l'athérosclérose. *Arch. Mal. Cœur*, 1961, **3**, 44–50.

16. FISHER, H., The biochemical evaluation of atherogenesis in roosters fed purified diets with varied levels of protein, corn oil and cholesterol. *Fed. Proc.*, 1959, **18**, 525.

17. HOLMAN, R. L., MACGILL, H. C., STRONG, J. P., GEER, J. C. and GUIDRY, M. A., The arterial wall as an organ, in PINCUS, G., *Hormones and Atherosclerosis*, Academic Press, New York, 1959, pp. 123–9.

18. FRAGOLA, L. and MAGEE, D. F., Role of the pancreas in reduction of fecal fat and cholesterol by dietary protein. *Amer. J. Physiol.*, 1960, **198**, 354–6.

19. FREY, J., Recherches relatives à l'extraction des protéines aortiques sur des fragments normaux et athéroscléreux. Thèse, Lyon, 1960, p. 55.

20. FREYBERG, R. H., Relation of experimental atherosclerosis to diets rich in vegetable protein. *Arch. Intern. Med.*, 1937, **59**, 660–6.

21. GROOT, DE, A. P., Protéine alimentaire et taux de cholestérol dans le sérum du rat. *Nature (Paris)*, 1959, **184**, 903–4.

22. GRYSKA, P. F., The development of atheroma in arteries subjected to experimental thromboendarterectomy. *Surgery*, 1959, **45**, 655–60.

23. IGNATOWSKI, A., Über die Wirkung des tierischen Eiweisses auf die Aorta und die parenchymatösen Organe der Kaninchen. *Virchows Arch. Path. Anat.*, 1909, **198**, 248–70.

24. JOHNSON, D. and FISHER, H., Dietary factors other than fat which influence plasma cholesterol level in the chicken. *Fed. Proc.*, 1958, **17**, 480.

25. JOHNSON, D. and LEVEILLE, G. A. and FISHER, H., Influence of amino acid deficiencies and protein level on the plasma cholesterol of the chick. *J. Nutrit.*, 1958, **66**, 367–76.

26. JORDAN, G. L., BAKEY, M. E. DE, HALPERT, B., Lipid changes produced by chronic hypercholesterolemia in nylon and orlon replacements of canine thoracic aorta. *Proc. Soc. Exp. Biol.*, 1958, **99**, 484–7.

27. KATZ, L. N., Experimental atherosclerosis. *IIIe Congrès Mondial de Cardiologie, Bruxelles*, 1958, **4**, 403–9.
28. KAYAHAN, S., Cholesterol-binding capacity of serum globulins in normal and atherosclerotic subjects. *Lancet*, 1960, **1**, 255–6.
29. KOKATNUR, M. G., RAND, N. T., KUMMEROW, F. A. and SCOTT, H. M., Dietary protein: a factor which may reduce cholesterol levels. *Circulation*, 1956, **14**, 962.
30. KOKATNUR, M. G., RAND, N. T., KUMMEROW, F. A. and SCOTT, H. M., Effect of dietary protein and fat on changes of serum cholesterol in mature birds. *J. Nutrit.*, 1958, **64**, 177–84.
31. KOKATNUR, M. G., RAND, N. T. and KUMMEROW, F. A., Effect of the energy to protein ratio on serum and carcass cholesterol levels in chicks. *Circ. Res.*, 1958, **6**, 424–31.
32. KOKATNUR, M. G. and KUMMEROW, F. A., The relationship of corn oil and animal fats to serum cholesterol: values at various dietary protein levels. *J. Amer. Oil Chemists Soc.*, 1959, **36**, 248–50.
33. KOKATNUR, M. G., KLAIN, G., SNETSINGER, D., KUMMEROW, F. A. and SCOTT, H. M., Effect of various amino acids on serum cholesterol levels in chicks. *Fed. Proc.*,1959, **18**, 532.
34. LANSING, A. I., Ageing of elastic tissue and the systemic effects of elastase. *Ciba Foundation Colloquia on Ageing*. Eds. G. E. W. WOLSTENHOLME and M. P. CAMERON, Little & Brown, Boston, 1945, pp. 88–102.
35. LANSING, A. I., Elastic tissue. *The Arterial Wall*, Baillière, Tindall & Cox, London, 1959, pp. 136–60.
36. LANSING, A. I., Elastic tissue, in PAGE, J. H., *Atherosclerosis, Connective Tissue and Thrombosis*, Academic Press, New York and London, 1959, pp. 167–80.
37. LEVEILLE, G. A. and FISHER, H., Plasma cholesterol in growing chicken as influenced by dietary protein and fat. *Proc. Soc. Exp. Biol.*, 1958, **98**, 630–2.
37a. LEVENE, C. I. The electron-microscopy of atheroma. *Lancet*, 1955, 1216–17.
37b. LEVENE, C. I. Collagen as a tensile component in the developing chick aorta. *Brit. J. Exp. Path.*, 1961, **42**, 89–94.
38. LOWRY, O. H., ROURKE-GILLIGAN, E. and KATERSKY, E. M., The determination of collagen and elastic tissues with results obtained in various normal tissues from different species. *J. Biol. Chem.*, 1941, **139**, 795–804.
39. LUTZ, R. N., BARNES, R. H., KWONG, E. and WILLIAMS, H. H., Effect of dietary protein on blood serum cholesterol in men consuming mixed diets. *Fed. Proc.*, 1959, **18**, 534.
40. MAGEE, D. F. and FRAGOLA, L., Dietary protein and plasma cholesterol. *Fed. Proc.*, 1959, **18**, 96.
41. MALMROS, H. and WIGAND, G., Atherosclerosis and deficiency of essential fatty acids. *Lancet*, 1959, 749–51.
42. MANN, G. V., Decompensation of sterol metabolism in monkeys. *Fed. Proc.*, 1960, **19**, 15.
43. MARCH, B. E. and BIELY, J., Dietary modification of serum cholesterol in the chick. *J. Nutrit.*, 1959, **69**, 105–10.
44. MEEKER, D. R. and KESTEN, H. D., Experimental atherosclerosis and high protein dets.i *Proc. Soc. Exp. Biol.*, 1940, **45**, 543–5.
45. MEEKER, D. R. and KESTEN, H. D., Effect of high protein diets on experimental atherosclerosis of rabbits. *Arch. Path.*, 1941, **31**, 147.
46. MELLINKOFF, S. M., MACHELLA, T. E. and REINHOLD, J. G., The effect of a fat free diet in causing low serum cholesterol. *Amer. J. Med. Sci.*, 1950, **220**, 203–7.
47. NATH, N., HARPER, A. E. and ELVEHJEM, C. A., Dietary protein and serum cholesterol. *Arch. Biochem. Biophys.*, 1958, **77**, 234–6.
48. NATH, N., HARPER, A. E. and ELVEHJEM, C. A., Alimentary protein effects on the serum cholesterol of rat. *Canad. J. Biochem. Physiol.*, 1959, **37**, 1375–84.
49. NETSKY, M. G. and CLARKSON, T. B.,Response of arterial wall to intramural cholesterol. *Proc. Soc. Exp. Biol.*, 1958, **98**, 773–4.
50. NEUMAN, R. and LOGAN, M. A., The determination of collagen and elastin in tissues. *J. Biol. Chem.*, 1950, **186**, 549–56.

51. NEWBURGH, L. H. and CLARKSON, S., The production of atherosclerosis in rabbits by feeding diets rich in meat. *Arch. Intern. Med.*, 1923, **31**, 653–76.

52. NISHIDA, T., TAKENAKA, F. and KUMMEROW, F. A., Effect of dietary protein and heated fat on serum cholesterol and β-liproprotein levels, and on incidence of experimental atherosclerosis in chicks. *Circ. Res.*, 1958, **6**, 194–202.

53. NUZUM, F. R., SEEGAL, B., GARLAND, R. and OSBORNE, M., Arteriosclerosis and increased blood pressure. *Arch. Intern. Med.*, 1926, **37**, 733.

54. OLSON, R. E., VESTER, J. W., GURSEY, D. and LONGMAN, D., Effect of low protein diets upon serum cholesterol in man. *J. Clin. Invest.*, 1957, **36**, 917–18.

55. OREKHOVITCH, V. N., CHPIKITER, V. O., MAZOUROV, V. I. and KOUNINA, O. V., Procollagènes. Classification, métabolisme, action des protéinases. *Bull. Soc. Chim. Biol.*, 1960, **42**, 505–18.

56. PARONETTO, F. and ADLESBERG, D., Papain atherosclerosis. *Circulation*, 1959, **20**, 975.

57. PICK, R., STAMLER, J. and KATZ, L. N., Effects of high protein intakes on cholesterolemia and atherogenesis in growing and mature chickens fed high-fat, high-cholesterol diets. *Circ. Res.*, 1959, **7**, 866–9, and *J. Amer. Med. Ass.*, 1960, **172**, 984.

58. POLCAK, J., MELICHAR, F., SEVELOVA, D., DVORAK, I. and SKALOVA, M., L'effet d'un régime enrichi de viande sur le développement de l'athérosclérose expérimentale du lapin. *J. Atheroscler. Res.*, 1965, **5**, 174–80.

59. RAAB, W., Möglichkeiten der Arterioskleroseverhütung. *Münchner Med. Wschr.*, 1939, **86**, 689.

60. RENAUD, S. and ALLARD, C., Effect of dietary protein level on cholesterolemia, thrombosis, atherosclerosis and hypertension in the rat. *J. Nutrit.*, 1964, **83**, 149.

61. REAY, D. T., WEISSMAN, N. and CARNES, W. H., Effects of elastase digestion and formic acid extraction on aortas from copper deficient pigs. *Fed. Proc.*, 1963, **22** (2), part I, 161.

62. SALTYKOW, S., Arterienveränderungen (Atherosklerose und verwandte Krankheiten des Menschen). *Zbl. allg. Path. Anat.*, 1908, **19**, 321.

63. SCHLICHTER, J. B., KATZ, L. N. and MEYER, J., The occurrence of atheromatous lesions after cauterization of the aorta followed by cholesterol administration. *Amer. J. Med. Sci.*, 1949, **218**, 603–9.

64. SEIDEL, J. C., NATH, N., HARPER, A. E. and ELVEHJEM, C. A., Effect of dietary protein and sulfur-containing amino acids on serum cholesterol in the rat. *Fed. Proc.*, 1960, **19**, 18.

65. SHIMAMOTO, T., La relation d'une réaction oedémateuse dans les artères avec l'athérosclérose et la thrombose. *J. Atheroscler. Res.*, 1963, **3**, 87.

66. SHIN YEH YU and BLUMENTHAL, H. T., Nature of calcium-elastin binding. *Fed. Proc.*, 1960, **19**, 19.

67. STAMLER, J., PICK, R. and KATZ, L. M., Effects of dietary protein and carbohydrate level on cholesterolemia and atherogenesis in cockerels on a high-fat, high-cholesterol mash. *Circ. Res.*, 1958, **6**, 447–51.

68. STEINBISS, W., Über experimentelle alimentare Atherosklerose. *Virchows Arch. Path. Anat.*, 1913, **212**, 152.

69. TENNENT, D. M., ZANETTI, M. E., OTT, W. H., KURON, G. W. and SIEGEL, H., Influence of crystalline elastase on experimental atherosclerosis in the chicken. *Science*, 1956, **124**, 588.

70. TOLSTOI, E., The effect of an exclusive meat diet on the chemical constituents of the blood. *J. Biol. Chem.*, 1929, **83**, 753–8.

70a. TRACY, R. E., MERCHANT, E. B. and KAO, V. C., On the antigenic identity of human serum β and α_{21} lipoproteins and their identification in the aortic intima. *Circulation Res.*, 1961, **9**, 472–8.

71. TREMOLIERES, J., BRUNAUD, M., MELIK, T. and SEGAL, V., Hypertension et artériosclérose chez le rat par un régime hyperlipidique et hyperprotéique. *Sem. Hôp.*, 1958, **34**, 1266.

72. ZWEIFACH, B., Structure and behaviour of vascular endothelium, in LANSING, A. I., *The Arterial Wall*, Baillière, Tindall & Cox, London, 1959, pp. 15–45.

CHAPTER 13

Calcium Deposited in Plaques

ALL arteries have some calcium salts in a diffuse form, in fact the normal type contains about 2 per cent of calcium per dry weight of tissue. Concentration of calcium in the arteries occurs at high and low levels of diffuse calcification. With low calcification at a level of 0·5 μg/mg, one finds 0·5 μg/mg in the plaques. With higher calcification, for example 3·2 μg/mg, the plaques contain 5 μg/mg. Therefore the calcification of atheromatous plaques depends on the effect of previous diffuse calcification of the aorta and in elderly subjects there is an interaction between the degeneration due to age and previous absorption of the aorta (Blankenhorn[1]).

Calcification of the abdominal aorta is more frequent in atherosclerotic subjects than in normal subjects (Eggen et al.[2]).

It is interesting to recall that Ruffer in 1910[3] discovered similar calcification to that of atherosclerosis in some mummies of the "21st dynasty and a more general type in subjects mummified between 1580 B.C. and A.D. 525." Moreover, Shattock[4] reported that the mummy of Pharoah Menephtah II of Thebes also contained some calcified senile plaques of calcium phosphate.

These phenomena seem therefore secondary to a peculiar inclination of certain aortic tissue to form calcium on the one hand and to some change due to the great age of the subject on the other.

References

1. BLANKENHORN, D. H., Calcium deposits in the plaque. *Evolution of the Atherosclerotic Plaque*. Ed. R. J. Jones, 1963, 360 pp.
2. EGGEN, D. A., STRONG, J. P. and McGILL, H. C., Calcification in the abdominal aorta. *Archives of Pathology*, 1964, **78**, 575.
3. RUFFER, M. A., On arterial lesions found in Egyptian mummies. *J. Path. and Bact.*, 1911, **15**, 453–62.
4. SHATTOCK, S. G., Microscopic sections of the aorta of King Menephtah. *Lancet*, 1909, **1**, 318–19.

CHAPTER 14

The Effects of Diet on Atherosclerosis as Seen in Epidemiological Investigations

THE incidence of vascular accidents and the serum levels of the different lipids in groups with their own regular diet may help to clarify some aspects of the problem with which we are concerned.

Two types of group can be considered, limited groups, such as religious monastic groups, and others extending even to all the inhabitants of a country or certain categories in the population.

It must always be remembered that the problem is complicated by the large number of factors which intervene—climate, social mode of life, race and so on. The results which we are about to describe must, therefore, be carefully interpreted. Their explanation must often be to a large extent hypothetical.

I. Monastic Societies

Published investigations generally compare two religious orders living in the same region (excessive climatic differences being thus avoided) who enjoy similar mental states free from shocks, as a result of their detachment from worldly events, and who perhaps experience the same metaphysical anxieties. Benedictines, whose diet is practically that of the country in which they live, are generally compared with Trappists, whose diet is much stricter and almost exclusively vegetarian.

There is also a more recent study of the Buddhist monks of Korea, where the discipline is extremely strict but the climate and psychological environment is different to those previously mentioned.

The following are the results of various investigations.

(1) Groen[36] studied 181 Trappists and 167 Benedictines. The blood cholesterol of the Benedictines was comparable to that of the general population in the same region. Trappists of middle or more advanced age had lower values.

Clinical examinations which included electrocardiography and radiography revealed less cardiovascular sclerosis in Trappists than in Benedictines of the same age.

Coronary occlusion was equally uncommon in both groups.

(2) Quinlau et al.[83] observed lower lipid levels in Trappists than in Benedictines. There were, however, considerable individual variations.

(3) Barrow in 1960 and 1962[9, 10] published some important results which serve as the basis of our table.

(4) Lee and his colleagues in 1962[62] contributed some valuable information on the manner of life and various chemical values of the serum of the Buddhist monks. This data will be considered with that of Barrow but let us first look at the work of Groen, who studied some Flemish orders. The studies concerning the Trappists are rendered complicated because of the division in the text into two periods: the one from 15 September to Easter which is very strict, and the other during which the diet is more liberal. The findings are shown in the following table:

	Benedictines	Trappists	
		Summer	Winter
I Number of subjects	181	168	168
II Diet:			
Average daily calories	2523	3450 2625	1800
Calories percentages from:			
Protein	13	14	14
Animal protein	6	5	1
Fat	35	26	7·5
"Animal" fat	20	10	3
Carbohydrate	52	60	78

There are certainly some differences between the groups but they seem of little importance.

The values of the serum cholesterol are readily expressed by the two curves shown on page 112 and the relevant clinical data are in the table also on page 112.

In fact we readily accept the conclusions of the author.

The average blood cholesterol level was significantly higher among the Benedictine monks than among the Trappist monks. However, there was no difference in prevalence of myocardial infarcts, angina pectoris, hypertension and electrocardiographic signs of diffuse atherosclerotic (ischaemic) heart disease between the two groups. It appeared as if myocardial infarction, the result of an occlusion of one of the major coronary arteries, was rarer among both orders than among other groups of the Netherlands and Belgian population; whereas the frequency of electrocardiographic signs of diffuse myocardial damage (possibly due to coronary sclerosis) and angina pectoris

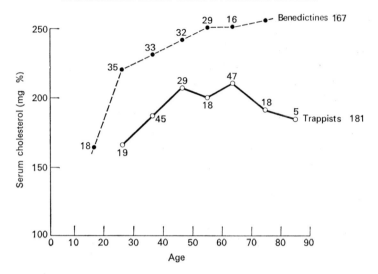

among both groups were not found to be markedly different from that of the general population.

The studies of Barrow carried out on American orders and those of Lee are collected together in the table on page 113.

The following conclusions can be drawn from this data:

(1) The serum values show a lowering of the cholesterol, total lipids and β-lipoproteins in proportion to the reduction in the daily calories of lipid origin. This was greater with vegetable lipids.

(2) We know little about the morbidity and mortality of these monastic groups from atherosclerosis. The authors state that in general they are

EFFECTS OF DIET AND STRESS IN TRAPPIST AND BENEDICTINE MONKS

	Trappist Monks			Benedictine Monks		
	Fathers	Brethren	Both	Fathers	Brethren	Both
Obesity (no. of cases)	40	23	63	23	7	30
Average blood pressure:						
Systolic (mm Hg)	147	147	147	136	136	136
Diastolic	83	80	82	85	83	84
Number with diastolic hypertension (100)	9	4	13	7	3	10
Number with myocardial infarct	1					
Number with angina pectoris	2	1	3	3	1	4

Serum levels in mg per cent	Bene-dictines	Trappists	Buddhists (male) 17–29	35–50	50–79	Buddhists (female) 17–29	30–49	50–79
I. *No. of subjects examined*	1253	684	90			39		
II. *Diet*								
Average daily calories	3200	2896	2600 on average					
from proteins (%)	13	10	11					
from carbohydrates (%)	42	64	82					
from lipids (%)	45	26	7					
Lipids of animal origin (%)	75	43	0					
Lipids of vegetable origin (%)	25	57	100					
III. *Serum values*								
Total cholesterol	236	205	120	120	150	151	159	159
Maximum cholesterol at 60	258	220						
Free cholesterol	57	40	34	34	40	40	43	43
Esterified cholesterol	179	165	86	86	110	111	116	116
Phospholipids	265	247						
P. content of lipids			6	6·3	6·7	5·7	6·6	6·6
Triglycerides (m equ/l)			3·5	5·6	4·1	3·2	4·6	3·9
Total lipids	700	650						
lipoprotein ultra centr.	50	45						
lipoprotein	180	160						
Total esterified fatty acids (m equ/l)			8·8	10·7	10·9	9	11·4	12·2

extremely low but these statements are not based on statistics. Also we are obliged to consider certain climatic differences between the two orders of Benedictine and Trappist on the one hand and the Buddhists on the other. Finally, the Buddhist monks are generally accepted into the order at a very early age and consequently are affected early on by the diet and for a considerable time.

All told, we find there an argument in favour of the activity of polyethylenic lipids on the various lipids which appears indisputable. It is based on quite solid evidence but assumes a relationship between serum cholesterol and the manifestation of clinical signs.

II. Comparisons of Various African Types—Bantus, Blacks of Various Origin, Whites, Immigrant Asiatics

Climatic influences were very much the same for this group. The investigations dealing with ethnic groups in Africa comprised studies made at different centres.

A. *Centres and races.* Geographically, the following have to be distinguished.

(1) The Transvaal, a plain with equatorial forests between two mountain massifs. There are several towns—Pretoria, Johannesburg. In the population here there are:

    (a) Bantus: 9 million,

    (b) Eurafricans: 1 million,

    (c) An immigrant white population: 3 million,

    (d) Immigrant Asiatics: 500,000.

(2) Uganda, in which live:

    (a) African negroes,

    (b) Immigrant Asiatics (Hindus and Muslims),

    (c) An immigrant white population.

(3) The Congo and Nigeria, also inhabited by blacks and whites.

The Bantu population is more or less scattered throughout the whole of South Africa.

B. *Diet.* The Bantu and black populations live a more frugal life than the others, while the negroes have a diet closer to that of the whites, who live much as in Europe.

The Asiatics have introduced their own particular types. The following details can be given.

(1) The Bantus and blacks generally make two meals a day with vegetables, potatoes, bananas, maize and cereals, and a certain amount of grilled meats and fish (twice a week in Uganda).

The lipids of the diet are estimated at 16–20 g per day.[57]

Different types of diet have been adopted by the Bantus, depending on whether they are in the country or in the town; their diet can, however, be summarized generally in the following way.

The diet is rich in:

    (a) cereals (50–90 per cent of the calories): maize, millet (*Sorghum vulgare*);

    (b) vegetables: pumpkins, sweet potatoes (*Ipomea batatas*), green vegetables.

The diet is poor in fats which constitute 15–20 per cent of the calories: it is poor in milk, eggs, fish, meat. According to Keys *et al.*[53] this value is only about 10 per cent.

The diet is rich in phosphorus, iron, vitamin A and thiamine, and poor in calcium, riboflavin and vitamin D.

(2) The Hindus are lacto-vegetarians, consuming some eggs but not very many, polished rice and no alcohol.

(3) The Muslims live on eggs and fish with polished rice as the staple article of diet.

These peoples use cotton seed oil* and little butter. Lipids represent 30–40 per cent of the total calories.

C. *Racial peculiarities.* It is difficult to say what racial peculiarities there may be which interfere with the effects of the diet. There is, at any rate, one important point to be recorded in connection with the Bantus.

The Bantu male has an abnormally high excretion of oestradiol, oestrone and oestriol in comparison with the excretion of the whites.[13, 14] On the other hand his excretion of 17-ketosteroids is slightly less.[14, 57]

Finally, gynaecomastia with a slight degree of testicular atrophy is common.

There is thus a definite general tendency to femininity. And they also suffer frequently from siderosis and portal fibrosis.[42]

D. *The physical activity* of the Bantus and negroes is much greater than that of the European populations who live in contact with them.

E. *Pathological states.* One can make the following clinical statements:
(1) Hypertension is common among the Bantus.[11, 15]
(2) Atherosclerosis.

(a) Bantus. The lesions of aortic atherosclerosis seen at post-mortem were the same for whites and Bantus up to the age of 40, after which they advanced more rapidly in the whites.[104]

In 1946 Becker[11] found lesions of atherosclerosis in 27·6 per cent of 3000 post-mortem examinations on subjects between 1 and 60 years of age. In 1959 Anderson[4] noted an incidence of only 10 per cent.

The incidences given for coronary artery involvement have varied with the type of case. Laurie *et al.*[61] have recently shown that it is much more frequent than has been stated, although still less than in Europeans. It was present in 1·4 per cent of autopsies.

The frequency of infarct is less than in other negroes or in whites.[15, 90]

In 1960 Schrire[93] published the following figures (Table XLIII) for patients of the Groote Schuur Hospital, Cape Town.

TABLE XLIII

	Percentages		
	Whites	Coloured	Bantus
Coronary disease	26·0	13·0	1·1
Possible coronary diseases	5·5	3·5	0·5
Hypertension	46·0	51·0	35·0

These would appear to support the generally accepted ratios.

* Cotton seed oil. Iodine index 110: saturated acids 26, linoleic acid 47.

TABLE XLIV

	Negroes				Immigrant Europeans	Immigrant Asiatics	
	Bantus	Transvaal	Nigeria	Senegal	Transvaal	Vegetarians	Non-vegetarians
Iodine index	179·0 (c)				160·0 (c)		
Total cholesterol (mg/100 ml)	166·0 (a) 168·0 (b) 145·0 (f)	204·0 (a)	129·0 (e)	<166 (g)	234·0 (a) 242·0 (b)	236 (f)	274 (f)
Free cholesterol Esterified cholesterol Cholesterol of β-lipoproteins	91·0 (c) 72·0 (a)	76·8 (a)			141·0 (c) 82·6 (a)		
Cholesterol/phospholipids	0·8 (d)				0·84 (d)		
Sf 12–20 Sf 20–100			25·4 (e) 40·1 (e)				
Total lipids	393·0 (a)	544·0 (a)			850·0 (a)		

(a) Bronte-Stewart et al.[17]
(b) Keys and Anderson, according to Brock.[15]
(c) Lewis.[63]
(d) Walker.[114]

(e) Mann et al.[67]
(f) Shaper et al.[97]
(g) Fernex.[28]

Cerebral lesions were also higher than in the other groups of the population.[15, 115]

(b) In Rhodesia coronary artery involvement is very rare among the negroes, and severe and moderate atheromas are less frequent.[40]

(c) In Uganda an infarct rate of 3 per cent has been noted among negroes. On the other hand, coronary artery involvement is an important cause of death (43 per cent for males, and 9 per cent for females) after thirty years among the Asiatic population.[69]

(d) In the Congo Vandeputte[112] found cases of atherosclerosis as frequent among the Congolese as among the whites (119 autopsies).

(e) Coronary insufficiency was rare among the Senegalese of Dakar.[78]

To sum up, the populations can be arranged in two groups:

(1) A group with a low vascular morbidity: Bantus, the negroes of Rhodesia and the negroes of Uganda.

(2) A group with a high vascular morbidity: Europeans, Asiatics and Congolese negroes.

Since 1960 these various investigations have been pursued with ideas which varied from one author to the next. In 1961 Schrire[93] of Cape Town Hospital gave some important results on 9000 hospital cases at the Groote Schuur Hospital, all with electrocardiograms. The author only exceptionally found symptoms of coronary trouble in the Bantu, whereas white subjects showed them far more frequently.

Wainwright[113] has given a number of extremely expressive graphs which show that coronary atherosis is less frequent in the Bantu of Johannesburg than in the European or American population. These results were based on post-mortem examinations. The nature of the lesions examined and the area of development are expressed by the graphs.

Reef et al.[84] also insist that atheroma in the Bantu is less severe than that described in the U.S.A. Finally the most serious types of lesion are hardly ever seen beyond the aorta and some iliac vessels.

Fernex,[29] having studied the histological aspect of the question, observed that with the Africans rarely struck by coronaries, the number of tissue basophils (or mast cells which will form heparin and histamine) is two to three times greater than in the European control group. He was also able to show some raised or lowered values, in favour of hyperplasia or hypoplasia of the system. The number of mast cells is low when there is an atheromatous coronary manifested and especially in the case of coronary stenosis. Skin biopsies enable the number of mast cells of the subject to be determined.

Scott et al.[96] compared 117 subjects of East Africa with 137 from New York. They saw some cases of atherosclerosis in both groups but whereas they found seventeen myocardial infarctions in the Americans they found none among the Africans.

It is necessary when considering results which are the opposite of the above

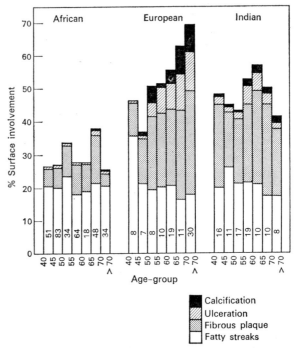

FIG. 1. Aorta: average percentage area of intima involved by atheroma in Africans, Europeans, and Indians.

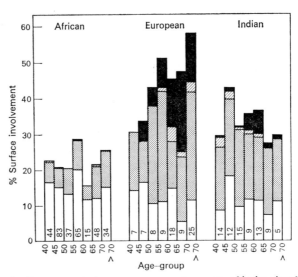

FIG. 2. Coronary arteries: average percentage area of intima involved by atheroma in Africans, Europeans, and Indians.

that Charters[23] reported a number of inconsistencies in the work of Malhotra and Pathania,[65] in the Punjab. Peage, Lewis and Gilbert are also considered in the same way: a diet rich in fats was not necessarily associated with a high incidence of infarction. The results are criticized by Queez.

Table XLV, taken from Anderson et al.,[4] gives a picture of the chemical changes seen in the aorta. There is greater acceleration in the increase of lipids, including cholesterol, in the whites than in Bantus.

TABLE XLV

	Aorta of			
	Bantu		Whites of Transvaal	
	Under 45 years	Over 45 years	Under 45 years	Over 45 years
Total lipids	13·9	15·5	14·5	19·3
Total cholesterol	1·42	2·84	1·83	3·16
Phospholipids	2·5	3·04	2·68	3·11
Collagen	24·6	21·7	24·3	21·5
Elastin	27·5	31·8	29·2	28·4
Hexosamines	0·88	0·95	0·7	0·89
Ash	3·6	5·6	2·95	5·8
Calcium	1·0	1·6	0·9	2·29

Figures are in g/100 g dry weight.

In conclusion, the following points should be noted:

(1) The privileged position of the Bantus is due to their diet, but it may also be due to a tendency to femininity.

(2) The black type (except perhaps in the Congo) is very different from the white type. There are characteristic features in the serum and in the arterial wall of the latter which bring him very close to coronary types, whereas the blacks are much further removed therefrom. It is difficult to separate racial and dietetic influences. The Asiatics exhibit the two effects operating simultaneously.

The clinical frequency of atherosclerotic accidents is in keeping with these chemical observations.

The large quantities of poly-ethenoid fatty acids (particularly linoleic and arachidonic acids) in the serum of Bantus, who are little affected, the slightly smaller quantities in the blacks, who are relatively safe, in comparison with the figures recorded for the whites, who stand in greatest danger, seem to justify the importance which is generally attached to these substances.

F. *Chemical state of the serum.*

(1) The lipids generally:

(a) From birth up to the age of 40 years, the blood cholesterol differed little in the Bantus and the immigrant whites, but differentiation developed thereafter.[12, 114] The same would appear to apply to lipoproteins.[47]

(b) For the period after the age of 40, see Table XLIV.

(2) The fatty acids of the esters are distributed in the manner shown in Table XLVI.

TABLE XLVI

Percentages	Bantus (a)	Congo Blacks (b)	Whites Transvaal (a)	Coronary patients (a)
Saturated and mono-ethylenic acids	18·0		28·3	41·5
Poly-ethylenic acids				
Di-ethylenic acids				
Linoleic	55·4		53·2	40·6
Linolenic	8·6	Increased	5·1	5·4
Tetra-ethylenic				
Arachidonic	13·6	Increased	9·5	7·6
Penta-ethylenic	1·2		1·4	2·1
Hexa-ethylenic	3·2		2·5	2·8

(a) Lewis,[63] 1958.   (b) Roels *et al.*,[85] 1959.

Antonis[5] also noted the high content of di-ethenoid and tetra-ethenoid acids in the serum of Bantus. The triglycerides themselves are fairly low in Bantus.[6] The S_f 12–100 lipoproteins are very low.[89] It should also be noted that differences have been observed in coagulation factors. In Bantus the plasma prothrombin is reduced, factor VII is also reduced,[68] and fibrinogen is abnormally increased.[30, 61, 68]

In 1962 Antonis *et al.*[7] studied the behaviour of the blood lipids of some Bantu and white prisoners, submitted to the same diet, which contained about 15 per cent of the calories in the form of fat. They observed a similarity between the two groups in the figures obtained. On increasing the amount of fat to 40 per cent of the calories, the same changes were produced after rather a long period. The ratio of cholesterol/phospholipids is influenced by the diet. Oils are less active on the level of cholesterol but cause a sharp rise in the amount of phospholipids. It is mainly the triglycerides which effect the influence of the diet.

Shaper *et al.*[98] studied the effect of a poor diet caused through the milk and exceptionally through the meat. They observed that in the adult and aged

African one finds the same values for the cholesterol, phospholipids, fatty acids and triglycerides as in Africans from Uganda living on a diet poor in fats.

Roels[86] studied three groups of black Africans from the Congo, the first took 6·8 per cent and the second 37·8 per cent of their calories in the form of vegetable oil. The third group consumed 48·3 per cent of the calories in the form of animal fat. This third group had the highest cholesterolaemia but there was little difference in the serum cholesterol of the other two groups. The total fatty acids are the same in all three groups.

III. Types of Population in America: Citizens of the U.S.A., American Indians, Neapolitan Immigrants

This collection consists of widely varying ethnic groups and social classes living, however, under relatively similar climatic conditions.

A. *Typical American subjects, representing an earlier adaptation to the ways of life of the country.*

(1) Notable characteristics of the diet are the large consumption of preserved foods and milk products, and the high percentage of lipids which, according to Keys et al.[53] constitute 41 per cent of the diet.

Gore et al.[32] summarized the diet of the U.S.A. in the following manner:

Calories: 3220 (proteins 12 per cent, lipids 41 per cent, glucides 47 per cent).

(2) The quite exceptional importance of deaths from vascular affections in that country is well known (see Table XLVII).

TABLE XLVII. DEATHS FROM CORONARY DISEASE IN THE U.S.A. (1955)

	Whites		Coloured subjects	
	Males	Females	Males	Females
Cardiac involvement of coronary origin	242,246	139,385	13,606	10,025

Differences in mode of life and particularly in diet are undoubtedly more important here than the racial differences (Keys et al.[55]).

Among 4914 subjects between the ages of 40 and 59 in good health initially, eighty-two certain cases of complications of atherosclerosis (or about 1·7 per cent) were identified within 3 years. These were subjects who showed no signs of predisposition (hypertension, diabetes, etc.) and had had no previous signs of vascular disturbances: they were subjects indulging in moderate physical activity and belonging to the middle social class.[31]

In 1959 White[117] reported that 843,410 of 1,565,000 deaths were due to diseases of the heart and vessels and 428,800 were the result of cardiopathies from coronary arteriosclerosis.

However, Moses in 1963[71] tried to show that this increase is more apparent than real. He attributed it to the fact that the expectation of life has increased, and it is this which raises the frequency of the symptoms that one sees in the elderly.

(3) The various authors have all found a high blood cholesterol.[31, 49, 50, 77, 92] We have been able to compile Table XLVIII.

TABLE XLVIII. BLOOD CHOLESTEROL IN U.S.A.

Geographic origin	Sex	Age (years)	Average (mg/100 ml)	Reference
New York	M	40–60	317	92
	F	40–60	246	
	M & F	40–60	240–252	31
California	M	40–60	240–263	31
Pittsburgh	M	33–36	200	49
Minnesota	M	40	222	50
		45	242	
		50	249	
		65	233	
New Haven	M	20–40	214	77
		50	250	
		>50	230	

Comparing young Guatamalians with North Americans, Guidry[38] noted that after separation on silicic acid only the sterols have a higher value in the Americans; the other lipids are no different.

(4) The S_f values in Table XLIX give the averages for normal subjects aged 40–59 years.[31]

TABLE XLIX

	S_f 12–20	S_f 20–100
Cleveland	33·3	81·1
California	50·1	98·6
Boston	40·0	84·0
Pittsburgh	43·2	102·3

Rosenman and his colleagues, however, in 1961[88] did not observe any clear correlation between serum cholesterol and the diet in Californian subjects.

Stamler thought that "For the middle-aged, mortality from this disease has increased since the early decades of the century particularly for white males". He defined the ideal diet to reduce the hypercholesterolaemia as "A reduction in food and also a diet low in total fats and cholesterol or a diet low in saturated fats and cholesterol and containing vegetable and fish oils".

He leaves then a place for other influences, such as obesity, hypertension, excessive smoking and physical inactivity.

B. *American Indians.*

(1) These are subjects living in reserves.

(2) The blood cholesterol of these subjects varies with age,[1] as shown in Table L.

TABLE L

Age (years)	Average	Age (years)	Average
20–29	193·5 mg %	40–49	217·8 mg %
30–35	227·4 mg %	50–59	216·4 mg %

Reference to the preceding tables will show that the blood cholesterol is the same as that of the Americans up to the age of 40 years but that divergence begins after that age.

Table LI gives the values found in various reserves.

TABLE LI

	M	F
Crow	223·8 mg %	200·0 mg %
Yank Town	209·9 mg %	209·1 mg %
Acoma	223·0 mg %	191·7 mg %
San Carlos	193·5 mg %	189·4 mg %
Lac Courtes Oreilles	212·6 mg %	199·9 mg %

The usual sex difference is apparent here.

Certain groups of American Indians from the south (Arizona, New Mexico) only rarely show any symptoms of atherosclerosis. Their serum cholesterol stays low although their diet is similar to the American one. The authors Kositchek et al.[59] suspected ethnic influences.

Stuart and his colleagues in 1962[105] gave some important information about a West Indian reserve (St. Kitts, W.I.). The diet of these Indians is made up of rice, bread, jam, plantain, bananas, peas, beans, salt pork, fish and young chickens, although these last three are reserved for the week-ends.

Also there are citrus fruits. The fats are for the most part from cotton seed oil. There are only very small quantities of butter. They use a small amount of lard.

The serum cholesterol is as follows:

	Age	Average
Men	20 to 29	161 mg/100 ml
	30 to 39	182 mg/100 ml
	40 to 49	190 mg/100 ml
Women	20 to 29	182 mg/100 ml
	30 to 39	192 mg/100 ml
	40 to 49	196 mg/100 ml

The average values are low and high figures are rare, hardly ever exceeding 289 mg/100 ml. Also the women have slightly higher figures than those found in the men.

C. *Neapolitan Immigrants in Boston.*[69] These were a group of 189 subjects who left Naples many years previously. Their ages were from 20 to 50 years. Their diet had become that of the Americans. Fats represented 43 per cent of the total calories (only 20 per cent in Naples). The hospitalization rate for all cardiovascular affections was 18 per cent (3 per cent only in Naples). Total blood cholesterol was 239·2 mg/100 ml (in Naples: 184·7 mg/100 ml).

Broell *et al.* in 1962[16] stress the fact that the mortality in subjects between 55 and 64 is only rarely due to atherosclerosis, when the parents come directly to America from Italy or Ireland. Therefore it seems that one is able to conclude that these subjects had assumed the American type; it would seem, therefore, that racial influences were of little moment here and that diet was an important factor.

IV. Eskimos

The Eskimos appear to comprise special types of population. There is, however, a certain degree of homogeneity. The following types should be distinguished.

A. *The Eskimos of the Arctic and Canada* (*Eastern Arctic Canada*). This is a population living according to ancestral custom. Its diet consists of fish and seal (see the analysis pp. 73–74). The lipids ingested thus introduce fatty acids with chains which are often long and very unsaturated.

According to Corcoran *et al.*,[24] the lipid constants (mg/100 ml serum) are those given in Table LII.

TABLE LII

Total blood cholesterol	144	Total fatty acids	351
Free cholesterol	46	Phospholipids	164
Esterified cholesterol	98		

After 3 days of fasting, Eskimos excreted no acetone in the urine, a fact which would appear to indicate a considerable ability to oxidize lipids.[41]

B. *The Eskimos of Alaska.* These have introduced the use of preserved foods into their diet. Blood cholesterol values, as measured by various authors,[3, 25] are given in Table LIII.

TABLE LIII

Age (years)	Total blood cholesterol (mg %)			Free
	Males (a)	Females (a)	Mixed (b, c)	
15–19	184	191		
20–29	187	205		
30–49	207	210	214 173	47
50 and over	226	225		

(a) Pett *et al.*[81]
(b) Scott *et al.*[95]
(c) Sinclair *et al.*[101]

Statistics for morbidity and mortality. Unfortunately, it is impossible at present to give any exact statistics for morbidity or mortality from vascular disease among Eskimos. Death certificates are signed by witnesses who are not always doctors and cannot, therefore, provide statistical data.

V. Italians

Special investigations have been carried out in two towns, Naples and Bologna, and also in a penitentiary centre at Perugia.

A. *Bologna.* The remote origin of the inhabitants was a fusion of Villanovian, Etruscan and Roman elements. This is the North Italian type.

The diet is abundant and rich in milk products in the very fertile region of Emilia. According to Keys *et al.*,[54] lipids represent 29 per cent of the total calories.

B. *Naples.* The inhabitants are of Greek and Roman stock with a slight Etruscan influence.

The diet is mainly one of oils and fish. Lipids, according to Keys *et al.*,[54] constitute 20 per cent of the total calories.[72]

C. *Perugia.* The prisoners examined at Perugia were of the Bolognan type. Because of certain restrictions, their ration averaged 2355 calories and the food lipids represented only 19·5 per cent of the calories in the ration.

Table LIV summarizes the results of these investigations.

TABLE LIV

Town	Blood cholesterol (mg/100 ml)		Authors
	Males	Females	
Bologna			
Firemen	220		Keys et al.[51·54]
Various	226	244	Azzolini et al.[8]
Perugia			
Prisoners			
5 years	228		
10 years	220		Picchio et al.[82]
Naples			
Firemen	164		Keys et al.[53]
Hard labour prisoners	160		

Several observations have been made. In Naples the blood cholesterol increased up to the age of 40 years, after which it became relatively stable. In Bologna high blood cholesterols were more frequent in women (65 per cent) than in men (53 per cent). In Perugia the high blood cholesterol, despite the low proportion of the dietary fats, should be noted.

Jankelson and his colleagues, 1962,[46] studied 146 subjects living in the locality of Boston, but whose parents were born in Naples. They did not find any correlation between electrocardiogram anomalies and serum cholesterol.

VI. The South Baltic Group

Some communities whose ethnic origin is of the Viking type can be found in this group which consists essentially of the inhabitants of Sweden and Denmark. The climatic influences are fairly uniform. According to Brock,[15] who examined death certificates signed between 1952 and 1954, the frequency of acute forms of infarct was about 0·15–0·20 per cent of total deaths at Malmo (Sweden).

According to Keys et al.[54] lipids represent 38 per cent of the dietary calories in Sweden. The blood cholesterols as given by Kornerup[58] and Malmros et al.[66] are shown in Table LV.

TABLE LV. BLOOD CHOLESTEROLS (mg %)

Sønderberg (Denmark)			Malmo (Sweden)
Children and adolescents	Males	201	
	Females	218	
First ten years of life	Males	203	
	Females	224	Both sexes 223
Second ten years of life	Males	237	
	Females	235	Both sexes 232

In Sweden, Svanborg et al. in 1961[106] published a table of the average composition of the serum lipids from a population in good health.

DATA OBTAINED PER 100 ML

	Men	Women
Total lipids	609·7±15·3 mg	648·1±21·1 mg
Total cholesterol	191·5± 7·3 mg	185·4± 7·1 mg
Free cholesterol	64·0± 2·4 mg	57·5± 3·5 mg
Phospholipids	207·8± 4·4 mg	232·4± 8·2 mg
Triglycerides	83·5± 6·2 mg	88 mg
Free fatty acids	0·750±0·034 m moles/l	0·781±0·045 m moles/l

VII. North Africans

A. *Moslem classes*. A paper by Hoareau et al.[44] deals essentially with the poor Moslem classes in Morocco. Among hospital cases he noted:
 Coronary sclerosis—8·13 per cent, as compared with Paris—4·4 per cent.
Hypertension—3·38 per cent, as compared with Paris—31·9 per cent.
Angina and infarct—3·66 per cent, as compared with Paris—24·0 per cent.
(The values given for Paris in the paper of Hoareau et al. are from Goumenakis and Lenegre.[35])
The blood cholesterol values were (mg/100 ml):

normal subjects of average age 62 years	154
coronary subjects	180
infarct and angina	179

Values noted at Casablanca were:

normal subjects	136
subjects with infarct	169

(This vinestigation covered 1000 hospital patients.)

It will be seen that the accidents, which were rare, occurred in subjects with low blood cholesterol.

B. *Algerians* (*Paris*). Rollen *et al.*[87] studied Algerians in Paris. Their diet, which was not considered by the authors, was undoubtedly modified. Blood cholesterol was still, however, below that of Parisians. Some correlation between blood cholesterol and weight was noted, particularly in the women.

VIII. The Various Populations of Honolulu

Honolulu has a large population belonging to a great variety of ethnic groups. Diet seems to be fairly homogeneous. Forty per cent of the energy is supplied by fats. Twelve per cent of this comes from fats of vegetable origin and 28 per cent from those of animal origin. The general type is similar to the American diet, with meat and eggs forming an important element.

Blood cholesterols as given by Adamson[2] are shown in Table LVI.

TABLE LVI

Ethnic origin	20–39 years (mg %)	40–49 years (mg %)	50–59 years (mg %)	All ages (mg %)
Caucasians	226	266	269	256
Chinese	247	278	282	272
Philippinos	196	251	263	250
Hawaiians	240	252	289	251
Japanese	230	269	276	257

The Philippine group with the lowest average belongs to the first generation of immigrants. The Chinese group with the highest blood cholesterol is third generation.

Serum lipid phosphorus values are as shown in Table LVII.

TABLE LVII

Ethnic origin	20–39 years (mg %)	40–49 years (mg %)	50–59 years (mg %)	All ages (mg %)
Caucasians	9·95	10·7	10·44	10·43
Chinese	10·22	11·04	11·01	10·83
Philippinos	9·35	10·45	10·93	10·50
Hawaiians	10·4	10·79	11·81	10·54
Japanese	10·02	10·63	11·28	10·66

It would appear that diet is much more important than race.

IX. Comparisons of the Diets of Several Races
in Various Countries

In 1960 Gore et al.[32] published a combined anatomical and pathological study of four peoples with the types of diet (grams and percentage of the calories) shown in Table LVIII.

TABLE LVIII

Country	Calories	Proteins (g)	Lipids (g)	Glucides (g)
U.S.A.	3220	97 (12%)	148 (41%)	384 (47%)
Japan	2025	70 (13·8%)	22·8 (10·1%)	385 (75%)
India	1724	47 (10·9%)	19 (9·9%)	349 (79·2%)
Jamaica	2276	65 (12%)	44 (17%)	405 (71%)

Aortic and coronary changes were more frequent in the U.S.A. group than in the others. In Japan and Jamaica aortic changes were more prominent than coronary changes.

X. Investigations in Australia and New Guinea

There are several investigations to be reported, mainly those of Southwood[102] in 1959, Schwartz et al.,[94] Casley-Smith[22] and De Wolfe et al.,[120] all in 1958.

The natives of this country have a diet which is poor in lipids (5 per cent) in comparison with that of the whites in the same regions (40 per cent). The incidence of coronary accidents is low. Blood cholesterol is low. Blood pressure is rarely increased.

XI. The Special Problem Presented by Israel

All the material refers to Israelites. The question is then one of subjects with the same ethnic origin but separated for varying periods of time, sometimes several centuries.

The following have to be considered.

A. *The Yemenite group.* This group is composed of tribes which have lived for two thousand years in the centre of Arabia. They were in the habit of consuming very little dietary lipids. On their arrival they used only 30 g daily but now use 50 g.

The values of the serum constants are shown in Table LIX.

TABLE LIX (mg %)

	Age		Date of arrival			
	Young	Adult	Recent		Much earlier	
			Males	Females	Males	Females
Total cholesterol	161·0	159	146–158	172–190	198–206	194–228
Cholesterol of α-proteins	40·0	41				
Cholesterol of β-proteins	121·0	121				
Total lipids			556			
α-Lipoproteins	28·1	31				
Phospholipids	218·0	213	207–212	219–237	217–233	228–252

It will be seen that the values rise with the duration of residence. Cerebral accidents were most frequent in this group. There was a considerable number among new arrivals but, after twenty years of residence, mortality would appear to be four times higher.

There was an equal incidence in men and women.

In some more recent publications, Brunner[20, 21] showed that the Yemenites benefit from a low cholesterol. Also only a small amount is present as α-cholesterol (about 14 per cent); which hardly varies in the extremely rare cases of coronaries.

Toor et al.[108] compared these groups of European Israelites and Yemenites over the age of 70 who had lived in the same place for 5 to 9 years but the Yemenites had kept a diet less rich in animal fats than the Europeans. They observed that electrocardiogram anomalies are rarer and severity of atherosclerosis less in the Yemenites than in the Europeans who show about three times more abnormalities.

B. *Immigrants from Europe.* These represent a prosperous social class which undoubtedly has a more plentiful diet which is richer in fats.

Their serum values were as shown in Table LX.

TABLE LX

	Subjects (mg %)	
	Young	Old
Total cholesterol	198·0	217·0
Cholesterol of α-lipoproteins	54·0	44·5
Cholesterol of β-lipoproteins	135·0	171·0
α-Lipoproteins	28·8	21·0
Phospholipids	240·0	286·0

Briefly, the values for the serum lipids in adults are in the upper zone of the general average.

Vascular accidents involve mainly the coronary arteries and were more frequent in men. They were generally more frequent than among the Yemenites. They increased little with the duration of the stay.

These excellent studies of Brunner *et al.*,[18,19] Kallner[48] and Toor[107] lack, however, exact analysis of the nature of the lipids employed.

XII. Argentinians

Coronary accidents would appear to be half as frequent as in England.

The population consumes 82 g of animal fats and 24 g of vegetable fats daily, or 7 per cent more than the population of the United States. Blood cholesterol in a group of clinically healthy individuals of ages between 40 and 51 years (average 44·6 years) was 210·6 mg/100 ml.[70]

XIII. Dakar

Payet[80] has given us a great deal of information about Dakar. The diet is very rich in linoleic acid from peanut oil. He records that among the Senegalese, as in the various populations of under-developed countries, a resistance to coronary disease is seen due to the following factors:

    contribution from lipids derived from vegetable fats and rich in essential fatty acids;
    slight metabolic deviations dominated by a low serum cholesterol;
    coronary and cerebral thrombosis exceptional.
These things are the exact opposite in the European and North American:
    contribution from lipids lacking in essential fatty acids;
    important metabolic deviations;
    frequent coronary and cerebral thrombosis.

The humoral profile in Western Europe corresponds then particularly to a biochemical syndrome of coronary thrombosis.

The favourable effects of linoleic acid seem to be reserved for the main coronary supply and the arteries of the limbs.

XIV. China

We have little information about China. Considering the vast geographical area of this country, one should ask if it is possible to speak of China as an homogeneous entity or if it would not be more correct to consider the various topics according to the locality studied. Nevertheless, here is a summary of the main published papers.

The diet according to Wu[121] and Liu[64] consists of about 2626 calories a day and is rich in meat; previously it used to be mainly fish, Huang K'o-wei et al.,[45] 1960. The lipids came from pork fat, which according to Moses contains 36 per cent linoleic acid but particularly from natural vegetable oils, which represent about 85 per cent of the total fat. The authors emphasize the fact that eggs only represent a very small part of the diet and there is practically no milk.

The serum cholesterol level is on average 136 mg/100 ml and in the man who has had an infarction about 190 mg/100 ml. The β-lipoproteins undergo a similar change.

From the opinions of doctors, Oppenheim[74] estimates that the frequency of symptoms is about 13–16 per cent but medical examinations do not include electrocardiogram results so that the latent or slight forms are not detected.

At autopsy Huang K'o-wei et al.[45] observed coronary lesions in 5·4 per cent of cases and lesions of cerebral sclerosis in 3·5 per cent.

In conclusion it seems evident that after an adaptation of many centuries and a certain type of diet, particularly deprived of saturated fats, the serum cholesterol is low in normal subjects and is hardly increased in the confirmed atherosclerosis case. This helps to identify its cause rather as of hereditary than of dietary origin.

XV. Japan

Japan in the last 50 years has gone through periods of prosperity and great difficulty. During the last 20 years the population has increased very rapidly. There is actually a population of 90 million tending towards the 100 million mark. The population of one of the islands, Hokkaido, is given as 230 inhabitants per km^2 but in fact the real figure is much higher than this.

The diet is, however, generally frugal, being composed of rice, fish, soya and some vegetables.

Coronaries are rare (Keys,[56] Okinaka[73]). The restrictions of war reduced coronaries but lately they have slowly crept back to their normal level. The trend became redressed, particularly since 1925 at the time when there was an increase in the amount of dietary fat (Watanabe et al.[116]).

The serum cholesterol is low in the normal subject (Yoneyama et al.[122]). It increases progressively with age, being 170 mg/100 ml at 20 and rising to 234 mg/100 ml at 65 to 69, then slowly falling. It stays for the most part below the serum cholesterol of Americans of the same age and approaches that of the Neapolitans.

Toriyama[109] observed 0·18 per cent of infarctions in more than 7500 autopsies from 1901 to 1950. Otsu[75] has noticed a slight increase since 1945. Gore et al. in 1962[33] compared the results of autopsies done at Boston and

Kyushu on 350 subjects selected at random in each town. The authors found that the extent and importance of atherosclerotic lesions is about half as great in Japan as in Boston. The same authors report that the symptoms of infarc- tion are seven times less frequent at Kyushu than at Boston.

One experiment of Hilkier et al.[43] carried out at Honolulu showed that the Japanese type of diet (rice, fish, soya, vegetables), given to rats, lowered the serum cholesterol and weight but raised the arterial pressure.

The simplicity of these results is, however, lessened by the fact that certain authors (Kusukana,[60]) point out the different meanings that Japanese doctors sometimes give to the term atherosclerosis. In particular, they think that coronary attacks have been repeatedly classified as cerebral, when death was very rapid. Goredal et al.[34] remarked that atherosclerosis of the aorta was more severe in the Japanese than that of the coronaries. In general it does not seem to be a phenomenon of ethnic origin, since the Japanese in Hawaii or Los Angeles present more coronary symptoms. The authors Keys et al.[56] suppose that the modifications of the diet and the greater utilization of lipids is at the basis of this change.

In summary, the Japanese supply an argument in favour of a poor diet in general, containing little lipid and using above all lipids from vegetables and fish.

XVI. India

The studies on Hindu subjects are most often disappointing. The rarity of electrocardiogram records in the disease limits the more interesting results to those obtained at autopsy and therefore it is a matter of the hospital environ- ment. These autopsies themselves are few in number, due to religious prejudice which is very often opposed to their being carried out. Therefore it is hard to know what significance to give to the published figures. Finally it is a country with very different climates, depending whether one studies the north, placed at a high altitude, or the south with a hot climate.

The average percentages of atherosclerosis cardiopathies are as follows:

Bombay studied by Vakil[111]	13·5
Madras studied by Sanjivi[91]	13
Calcutta studied by Gupta[39]	14·4
Delhi studied by Padmavati[76]	11·3
Amritsar studied by Malhotra[65]	23
Simla (Himalaya) studied by Devichand[26]	6

When Padmavati[76] declares "India has the lowest incidence of coronary heart disease in the world" he is not followed by the majority of his colleagues.

Sex plays its usual part, Vakil[1(10)] on 4277 coronaries counted a ratio of about three men for each woman. The age which appears most affected is between 40 and 60.

U.F.A.—10

The diet presents several difficulties since it varies with region, race and religion. Here, according to Vakil, is the distribution with age, from more than 15,000 heart cases, of 4277 coronaries:

Type of heart disease	No. of cases	Age groups (in years)									
		0–10	11–20	21–30	31–40	41–50	51–60	61–70	71–80	81–90	91–100
Coronary	4277	0·05	0·5	2	17·8	31·9	22	14·3	9·7	1·2	0·4

At New Delhi, Wig et al.[118] have described the diet of the inhabitants:

> The diet of an average Punjabi is about 2,000 to 2,500 calories of which fats contribute approximately 20 per cent. Chapatties made from wheat, "atta", along with pulses and cooked vegetables constitute the main items. The non-vegetarian eats mutton, but usually not more than once a week or so. On the other hand, milk and curds are consumed in plenty, especially by people in rural areas. Practically all the cooking is done in "ghee" (clarified butter).

He distinguishes between vegetarians and non-vegetarians and gives the following table:

TABLE LXI. ATHEROSCLEROSIS AND DIET

	No. of cases	Positive cases	
		No.	%
Vegetarian	35	15	43
Non-vegetarian	80	41	51

Vakil[111] studying the effect of race, gives the following figures with reference to death from all causes: Hindus 70 per cent, Moslems 15 per cent, Others 12 per cent. But he concludes, however: "Communal differences in India are mainly based on religious beliefs and involve different dietetic habits and social customs. While the majority of Hindus are vegetarians, the great majority of non-Hindus are non-vegetarians."

Under-nutrition undoubtedly plays its part and it is just as well. Wijesekara[119] points out that "infarction was less frequently met with in patients who ate well," whereas the condition was apt to develop in those who consumed a minimum of eggs, meat and fatty foods. The lowest number of infarctions were seen among the Moslems who "are known to consume more animal foods than the Sinhalese or Tamils".

One can see how complex the question of atherosclerosis is in India. Diet certainly plays its part, but so large a number of other factors interfere, that it is difficult to say what exactly is the role of nutrition.

The results often underline the effect of under-nutrition and we emphasize the need for a balanced diet.

References

1. ABRAHAM, S. and MILLER, D. C., Serum cholesterol levels in American Indians. *Public Health Reports*, 1959, **74**, 392–8.
2. ADAMSON, L. F., Serum cholesterol concentrations of various ethnic groups in Hawaii. *J. Nutrit.*, 1960, **71**, 27–36.
3. ALVAREZ, W. C., The eskimos will be studied. *Geriatrics*, 1958, **13**, 769.
4. ANDERSON, M., WALKER, A. R. P., HIGGINSON, J. and LUTZ, W., Chemical and pathological studies on aortic atherosclerosis. *Arch. Path.*, 1959, **68**, 380–91.
5. ANTONIS, A., *Report of 4th International Conference on Biochemical Problems of Lipids.* Oxford University Press, London and New York, 1957.
6. ANTONIS, A. and BERSOHN, J., Serum triglycerides in South African Europeans and Bantu, and ischaemic heart disease. *Lancet*, 1960, **1**, 998–1002.
7. ANTONIS, A. and BERSOHN, I., The influence of diet on serum lipids in South African White and Bantu prisoners. *Amer. J. Clin. Nutrit.*, 1962, **10** (6), 484–99.
8. AZZOLINI, G. and MAZZONI, L., La cholestérolémie des vieillards. Etude sur 682 sujets de la population Bolognaise suivant l'âge et le sexe. *Minerva Med.*, 1960, **51**, 1258–64.
9. BARROW, J. G., QUINLAU, C. B., COOPER, G. R., WHITNER, V. S. and GOODLOE, M. H. R., Studies in atherosclerosis. III. An epidemiologic study of atherosclerosis in Trappist and Benedictine monks: a preliminary report. *Ann. Intern. Med.*, 1960, **52**, 368–77.
10. BARROW, J. G., QUINLAU, C. B., EDMANDS, R. E. and RODILOSSO, P. T., Prevalence of atherosclerosis complications in Trappist and Benedictine Monks. *Circulation*, 1961, **24**, 881–2.
11. BECKER, B. J. P., Cardiovascular disease in the Bantu and coloured races of South Africa. I. Incidence, pathology and general features. IV. Atheromatosis. *S. Afr. J. Med. Sci.*, 1946, **11**, 1–14 and 97–105.
12. BERSOHN, I. and WAYBURNE, J., *Amer. J. Clin. Nutrit.*, 1956, **4**, 117.
13. BERSOHN, J. and OBELOFSE, P. J., *S. Afr. J. Med.*, 1957, **31**, 1172; in WALKER, *Hormones and Atherosclerosis*, Academic Press, New York, 1959, 385–97.
14. BLOOMBERG, B. M., MILLER, K., KEELEY, K. J. and HIGGINSON, J., Urinary oestrogens and neutral 17-oxosteroids in the South African Bantu with and without hepatic disease. *J. Endocr.*, 1958, **17**, 182–90.
15. BROCK, J. F., Nutrition and the clinician. *Lancet*, 1959, **276**, 923–6.
16. BROELL, K. M. and TRULSON, M. F., Some mortality statistics of specific nationality groups in Boston. *Fed. Proc.*, 1962, **21**, 97.
17. BRONTE-STEWART, B., KEYS, A. and BROCK, J. F., Serum cholesterol, diet and coronary heart disease. An interracial survey in the Cape peninsula. *Lancet*, 1955, **269**, 1103–7.
18. BRUNNER, D. and LOEBE, K., Serum cholesterol, electrophoretic lipid pattern, diet and coronary artery disease: a study in coronary patients and in healthy men of different origin and occupations in Israel. *Ann. Intern. Med.*, 1958, **49**, 732–50.
19. BRUNNER, D., MANELIS, G. and LOEBE, K., Influence of age and race on lipid levels in Israel. *Lancet*, 1959, **276**, 1071–3.
20. BRUNNER, D., Atherosclerosis other vascular complications and lipid pattern in diabetic Yemenite Jews. *Circulation*, 1961, **24**, 895–6.

21. BRUNNER, D., Lipid pattern in Yemenite Jews and in middle-aged coronary patients without increased total serum cholesterol. *Circulation*, 1961, **24**, 896.

21a. BRUNNER, D., ALTMAN, S., LOEBE, K. and SCHWARTZ, S., Taux de cholestérol chez des sujets coronairiens ayant des taux augmentés de cholestérol sérique total ou non et chez des témoins bien portants. *J. Atheroscler. Res.*, 1962, **2**, 424.

22. CASLEY-SMITH, J., *Austr. J. Exp. Biol. Med. Sci.*, 1958, **7**, 47.

23. CHARTERS, A. D., Mortality from coronary heart-disease in Indian populations. *Lancet*, 1961, **1**, 773.

24. CORCORAN, A. C. and RABINOWITCH, J. M., A study of the blood lipids and blood protein in Canadian eastern arctic eskimos. *Biochem. J.*, 1937, **31**, 343–8.

25. CORCORAN, A. C., Serum cholesterol levels and blood pressure of Alaskan eskimo men. *Lancet*, 1958, 1122.

26. DEVICHAND, Aetiology and incidence of heart disease in India. *Indian Heart J.*, 1959, **11**, 117.

27. DEVICHAND, Heart disease in the Punjab. *Proc. A. Physicians India*, 1946, cited by MATHUR, K. S. in Problem of heart disease in India, *Amer. J. Cardiol.*, 1960, **5**, 60.

28. FERNEX, M., Note préliminaire sur la pathologie artérielle en milieu africain à Dakar. *Bull. Soc. Med. Afrique Noire de Langue Française*, 1960, **5**, 43–6.

29. FERNEX, M., Nombre de mastocytes dans leur relation avec l'athérosclérose. *Med. Hyg.*, 1961, **19**, 419.

30. GILLMAN, T., NAIDOO, J. J. and HATHORN, M., Fat, fibrinolysis and atherosclerosis in Africans. *Lancet*, 1957, 696–7.

31. GOFMAN, J. W., HANIG, M., JONES, H. B., LAUFFER, M. A., LAWRY, E. Y., LEWIS, A., MANN, G. V., MOORE, F. F., OLMSTED, F., YEAGER, F. G., ANDRUS, E. C., BORACH, J. H., BEAMS, J. W., FERTIG, J. W., PAGE, J., SHANNON, J. A., STARE, F. J. and WHITE, P. D., Evaluation of serum lipoprotein and cholesterol measurements as predictors of clinical complications of atherosclerosis. Report of a co-operative study of lipoproteins and atherosclerosis. *Circulation*, 1956, **14**, 691–741.

32. GORE, J., ROBERTSON, W. B., HIRST, A. E., HADLEY, G. G. and KOSEKI, Y., Geographic differences in the severity of aortic and coronary atherosclerosis. *Amer. J. Path.*, 1960, **36**, 559–74.

33. GORE, I., NAKASHIMA, T., IMAI, T. and WHITE, P. D., Coronary atherosclerosis and myocardial infarction in Kyushu, Japan and Boston Massachussetts. *Amer. J. Cardiol.*, 1962, **10**, 400–6.

34. GOREDAL, J., ROBERTSON, J., HURST, W. B., HADLEY, A. E. and KOSEKI, Y., Geographic difference in the severity of coronary atherosclerosis. *Amer. J. Path.*, 1960, **36**, 559.

35. GOUMENAKIS, G. and LENEGRE, J., Considérations sur une statistique de 12,670 consultants ou hospitalisés dans un service de cardiologie. *Arch. Mal. Cœur Vaisseaux*, 1950, 649–56.

36. GROEN, J. J., The effect of diet on the serum lipids of Trappist and Benedictine monks *Essential Fatty Acids* (Ed., SINCLAIR), Butterworths, London, 1958, 147–9.

37. GROEN, J. J., TIJONG, K. B., KOSTER, M., WILLEBRANDS, A. F., VERDONCK, C. and PIERLOOT, M., The influence of nutrition and ways of life on blood cholesterol and the prevalence of hypertension and coronary heart disease among Trappist and Benedictine monks. *Amer. J. Cin. Nutrit.*, 1962, **10** (6), 456–70.

38. GUIDRY, M. A., Comparison of serum lipids between young North Americans and Guatemalians. *Fed. Proc.*, 1962, **21** (2), 98.

39. GUPTA, cited by BARNEJA, J. C., Incidence of coronary heart disease in India. *Indian Heart J.*, 1960, **12**, 171.

40. HANNAH, J. B., Civilisation, race and coronary atheroma with particular reference to its incidence and severity in Copper Belt Africans. *Centr. Afric. J. Med.*, 1958, **4**, 1–5.

41. HEINBECKER, P., Studies on the metabolism of Eskimos. *J. Biol. Chem.*, 1928, **80**, 461–75.

42. HIGGINSON, J., GROBBELAAR, B. G. and WALKER, A. R. P., Hepatic fibrinosis and cirrhosis in man in relation to malnutrition. *Amer. J. Path.*, 1957, **33**, 29–44.

43. HILKER, D. M., WENKAM, N. S. and LICHTON, I. J., Cardiovascular effects of a Japanese diet in rats. *Fed. Proc.*, 1963, **22** (2), part L, 503.

44. HOAREAU, E. and DELANOE, G., Les cardiopathies par athérosclérose et la cholestérolémie en milieu marocain musulman. *Arch. Mal. Cœur Vaisseaux*, 1960, **53**, 333–54.

44a. HOWELL, M., La comparaison de la fibrinolyse et de la coagulation chez des hommes nigériens et européens. *J. Atheroscler. Res.*, 1965, **5**, 80.

45. HUANG K'O-WEI and HANG CHEN-PIAO. La rareté de l'athérosclérose chez les chinois et ses rapports avec les habitudes alimentaires. *Chinese Med. J.*, 1960, **80**, no. 5, 455.

46. JANKELSON, O. M., STEFANIK, P. A. and STARE, F. J., Serum lipids and apparent health of Italian-American factory workers in a Boston area. A four-year follow up. *Amer. J. Clin. Nutrit.*, 1962, **11** (2), 134–41.

47. JOUBERT, F., VAN BERGEN, A., BERSOHN, J. and WALKER, A. R. P. (In press).

48. KALLNER, G., Epidemiology of arteriosclerosis in Israel. *Lancet*, 1958, **274**, 1155–6.

49. KATZ, L. B., RHODES, G. J., GEORGE, R. S. and MOSES, C., Total serum cholesterol-lipid phosphorus ratio and S_f 12–20 concentration in hypertension diabetes and coronary artery diseases. *Amer. J. Med. Sci.*, 1953, **225**, 120–8.

50. KEYS, A., The physiology of the individual as an approach to a more quantitative biology of man. *Fed. Proc.*, 1949, **8**, 523–9.

51. KEYS, A., FIDANZA, F., SCARDI, V. and BERGANI, G., The trend of serum cholesterol levels with age. *Lancet*, 1952, **263**, 209–10.

52. KEYS, A., FIDANZA, F., SCARDI, V., BERGANI, G., KEYS, M. H. and DI LORENZO, F., Studies on serum cholesterol and other characteristics on clinically healthy men in Naples. *Arch. Intern. Med.*, 1954, **93**, 328–36.

53. KEYS, A., ANDERSON, J. T., FIDANZA, F., KEYS, M. H. and SWAHN, B., Effects of diet on blood lipids in man. *Clin. Chem.*, 1955, **1**, 34–52.

54. KEYS, A., FIDANZA, F. and KEYS, M. H., Further studies on serum cholesterol of clinically healthy men in Italy. *Voeding*, 1955, **16**, 492–8.

55. KEYS, A., ANDERSON, J. T., BIORCK, M. A. G., BROCK, J. F., BRONTE-STEWART, B., FIDANZA, F., KEYS, M. H., MALMROS, H., POPPI, A., POSTELI, T., SWAHN, B. and VECCHIO, A., Physical activity and diet in populations differing in serum cholesterol. *J. Clin. Invest.*, 1956, **35**, 1173–81.

56. KEYS, A., KUSUKAWA, A., BRONTE-STEWART, B., LARSEN, N. and KEYS, M. H., Lessons from cholesterol studies in Japan, Hawaii and Los Angeles. *Ann. Int. Med.*, 1958, **48**, 83.

57. KINNEAR, A. A., *S. Afr. J. Lab. Clin. Med.*, 1956, **2**, 263; in WALKER, *Hormones and Atherosclerosis*, Academic Press, New York, 1959, 385–97.

58. KORNERUP, V., Concentrations of cholesterol, total fat and phospholipids in serum of normal man. *Arch. Intern. Med.*, 1950, **85**, 398–415.

59. KOSITCHEK, R. J., WURM, M. and STRAUS, R., Biochemical studies in full-blooded Navajo Indians. II. Lipids and lipoproteins. *Circulation*, 1961, **23**, 219.

60. KUSUKAWA, A., Statistical findings of coronary heart diseases in Japan. *World Trends in Cardiology*, Keys and White, N.Y., Heber-Harper, 1951, p. 159.

61. LAURIE, W., WOODS, J. D. and ROACH, G., Coronary heart disease in the South African Bantu. *Amer. J. Cardiol.*, 1960, **5**, 48–59.

62. LEE, K. T. et al., Geographic study of arteriosclerosis. *Arch. Environment. Health*, 1962, **4**, 4.

63. LEWIS. B., Composition of plasma cholesterol ester in relation to coronary disease and dietary fat. *Lancet*, 1958, **275**, 71–3.

64. LIU, C. K., Cardiovascular diseases in China. *Amer. J. Cardiol.*, 1962, **10**, no. 3, 367–9.

65. MALHOTRA, R. P. and PATHANIA, O., cited by PADMAVATI, S., Five year survey of heart disease in Delhi. *Indian Heart J.*, 1958, **10**, 33.

66. MALMROS, H. and WIGAND, G., Atherosclerosis and deficiency of essential fatty acids. *Lancet*, 1959, 749–51.

67. MANN, G. V., NICOL, B. M. and STARE, F. J., The β-lipoprotein and cholesterol concentration in sera of Nigerians. *Brit. Med. J.*, 1955 (2), 1008–10.

68. MERSKEY, C., GORDON, H., LACKNER, H., SCHRIRE, V., KAPLAN, B. J., SONGINMIBASHAN, R., NOSSEL, H. L. and MOODIE, A., Blood coagulation and fibrinolysis in relation to

coronary heart disease. A comparative study of normal white men, white men with coronary heart disease and normal Bantu men. *Brit. Med. J.*, 1960, 219–27.

69. MILLER, D. C., TRULSON, M. F., MacCANN, M. B., WHITE, P. D. and STARE, F. J., Diet, blood lipids and health of Italian men in Boston. *Ann. Intern. Med.*, 1958, **49**, 1178–1200.

70. MOIA, B., L'athérosclérose coronarienne en Argentine. *Acta Cardiol.*, 1959, suppl. VIII.

71. MOSES, C., *Atherosclerosis: Mechanism as a Guide to Prevention*, Lea & Febiger, Philadelphia, 1963, 1 vol., 239 pp.

72. NIGRO, G., D'NDREA, L. and ORIENTE, P., Cardiopathies et facteurs dyslipidémiques dans une groupe homogène de pécheurs napolitains. *Minerva Med.*, 1960, **51**, 1868–72.

73. OKINAKA, S., Committee on the Coronary Circulation: The statistics review of cases with clinically diagnosed myocardial infarction and with anginal pains in several districts in Japan. *Jap. Circulation J.*, 1957, **21**, 78.

74. OPPENHEIM, F., Review of 100 autopsies of Shangaï Chinese. *China Med. J.*, 1925, **39**, 1067.

75. OTSU, S., SCHOZAWA, T., YAMADA, K , INOUE, K., ISHIYAMA, A., KAKEFUDA, K., SEKI, S., MURACHI, T., KAMEYAMA, M., FUJII, J., TSUKAKUSHI, H., KURAMOITO, K., TAKEDA, Y. and MURATA, K., Morphological and statistical studies on coronary sclerosis. *Kokyu to Junkan* (*Respiration & Circulation*), 1959, **7**, 61.

76. PADMAVATI, S., Five year survey of heart disease in Delhi. *Indian Heart J.*, 1958, **10**, 33.

77. PAGE, I. H., KIRK, E., LEWIS, W. H., THOMPSON, W. R. and VAN SLYKE, D. D., Plasma lipids of normal men at different ages. *J. Biol. Chem.*, 1935, **11**, 613–39.

78. PAYET, M., SANKALE, D., FERNEX, M. and BOURGEADE, A., La pathologie coronarienne chez l'Africain à Dakar. *Bull. Soc. Med. Afrique Noire de Langue Française*, 1960, **5**, 145–55.

79. PAYET, M., PILLE, G., SANKALE, M., PENE, P. and TRELLU, M., Le contexte humoral lipidique au cours de l'athérosclérose du Noir africain (à propos de 160 cas observés à Dakar). *Path. Biol.*, 1961, **9**, 1093–1100.

80. PAYET, M., SANKALE, M., PILLE, G. and N'DOYE, T., La ration lipidique du Sénégalais; sa place parmi les facteurs d'athérosclérose. *Ann. Nutrit. Aliment.*, 1961, **15**, 21–31.

81. PETT, L. B. and LUPIEN, P. J., Cholesterol levels of Canadians. *Fed. Proc.*, 1958, **17**, 488.

82. PICCHIO, E. and ROTTINI, E., Alimentazione é colesterolemia. *Minerva Med.*, 1958, **49**, 783–6.

83. QUINLAU, C. B., BARROW, J. G., COOPER, G. R., WHITNER, V. J. and GOODLOE, M. H. R., Variations of serum lipids in vegetarian and non-vegetarian males. *Amer. Heart Ass. in Circulation*, 1959, **20**, 753.

84. REEF, H. and ISAACSON, C., Atherosclerosis in the Bantu. The distribution of atheromatous lesions in Africans over 50 years of age. *Circulation*, 1962, **25**, 66–72.

85. ROELS, O. A., LEURQUIN, P. and TROUT, M., Serum polyunsaturated fatty acids in groups of Africans with low and high fat intake. *J. Nutrit.*, 1959, **69**, 195–201.

86. ROELS, O. A., ROELS-BROADHURST, D. M. and TROUT, M., Serum lipids and diet: a comparison between three population groups with low, medium and high fat intake. *J. Nutrit.*, 1963, **79** (2), 211–19.

87. ROLLEN, A., VASSAL, P., BIRMAN, R. and DURAND, C., Etude comparative du cholestérol sanguin chez l'Européen et le Nord-Africain en fonction du sexe, de l'âge, du poids et de la tension artérielle minimale. *C.R. Acad. Sci.* (*Paris*), 1959, **248**, 494–6.

88. ROSENMAN, R. H., FRIEDMAN, M. and BOASBERG, S., Lack of correlation of serum cholesterol and habitual diet of male and female adults. 34th Scientific Sessions of American Heart Association (Bal Harbour, 20–22 October 1961). *Circulation*, 1961, **24** (4, part II), 1024–5.

89. RUSKIN, H., COHN, T. D., BLOOMBERG, B. M. and GREENBLATT, J., Studies on the β-lipoproteins of the South African Bantu. *Amer. J. Med. Sci.*, 1958, **235**, 138–42.

90. SACKS, M. J., Aortic and coronary atherosclerosis in three racial groups in Cape Town. *Circulation*, 1960, **12**, 96–109.

91. SANJIVI, K. S., Heart disease in South India, *Proc. Ann. Conf. A. Physicians India*, 1946, cited by MATHUR, K. S., Problem of heart disease in India. *Amer. J. Cardiol.*, 1960, **5**, 60.

92. SCHAEFFER, L. E., ADLERSBERG, D. and STEINBERG, A. G., Heredity, environment and serum cholesterol. A study of 201 healthy families. *Circulation*, 1958, **17**, 537–42.
93. SCHRIRE, V., The racial incidence of heart disease at Groote Schuur Hospital, Cape Town. III. The less common forms of heart disease. *Amer. Heart J.*, 1960, **59**, 835–44.
94. SCHWARTZ, C. J. and CARSEY SMITH, J. R., *Austr. J. Exp. Biol. Med. Sci.*, 1958, **36**, 117.
95. SCOTT, E. M., GRIFFITH, J. V., HOSKINS, D. D. and WHALEY, R. D., Serum cholesterol levels and blood pressure of Alaskan Eskimo men. *Lancet*, 1958, **275**, 667–8.
96. SCOTT, R. F., DAOUD, A. S., FLORENTIN, R. A., DAVIES, J. N. P. and COLES, R. M., Comparison of the amount of coronary arteriosclerosis in autopsied East Africans and New-Yorkers. *Amer. J. Cardiol.*, 1961, **8**, 165–72.
97. SHAPER, A. G. and JONES, K. W., Cardiovascular disease in East Africa. Conference on Cardiovascular disease, 14–16 Jan., 1959. *Lancet*, 1959, 465.
98. SHAPER, A. G. and JONES, K. W., Serum cholesterol, diet and coronary heart disease. *Lancet*, 1959, 534–7.
99. SHAPER, A. G. *et al.*, Plasma lipids in an African tribe living on a diet of milk and meat. *Lancet*, 1961, **2**, 1324.
100. SHRIRE, V., The comparative racial prevalence of ischemic heart disease in Cape Town. *Amer. J. of Card.*, 1961, **8** (2), 173–7.
101. SINCLAIR, R. G., BROWN, G. M. and CRONK, L. B., Serum lipids of Eskimos. Effect of a high fat diet, (pemmican) and of fasting. *Fed. Proc.*, 1949, **8**, 251.
102. SOUTHWOOD, A. R., Aspect of preventive cardiology. I. The elaboration of public health. II. The rise of biochemistry. *Lancet*, 1959, 377–82, 435–41.
103. STAMLER, J., Cardiovascular diseases in the United States. *Amer. J. Cardiol.*, 1962, **10**, 319.
104. STRONG, J. P., WAINWRIGHT, J., MACGILL, H. C., GEER, J. C. and HOLMAN, R. L., Atherosclerosis in Bantu. *Circulation*, 1959, **20**, 1118–27; *Fed. Proc.*, 1959, **18**, 509.
105. STUART, K. L., SCHNECKLOTH, R. E., LEWIS, L. A., MOORE, F. E., CORCORAN, A. C., Diet, serum cholesterol, protein, blood haemoglobin and glycosuria in a West Indian community (St. Kitts. W.I.). *British Med. J.*, 1962, 17 Nov., 1283.
106. SVANBORG, A. and SVENNERHOLM, L., Plasma total lipid, cholesterol, triglycerides, phospholipids and free fatty acids in a healthy Scandinavian Population. *Acta Med. Scand.*, 1961, **169** (1), 43–9.
107. TOOR, M., Serum lipids and atherosclerosis. *J. Amer. Med. Ass.*, 1958, **166**, 817.
108. TOOR, M., BORN-BORNSTEIN, R., SCHADEL, M. and AGMON, J., Atherosclerosis in aged Yemenite and European immigrants to Israel. *Geriatrics*, 1962, **17** (3), 126–31.
109. TORIYAMA, K., HARUYAMA, T., SUZUE, J. and HATA, M., Statistical study on the autopsied cases with myocardial infarction, myocardial scar and coronary artery sclerosis. *Nihon-Taishitsugaku-Zasshi (Jap. J. Const. Med.)*, 1956, **5**, 21.
110. VAKIL, R. J., Cardiovascular diseases in India. *Amer. J. Cardiol.*, 1962, **10**, 380.
111. VAKIL, R. J., A study of rheumatic heart disease in Bombay province (India). *Indian Heart J.*, 1949, **1**, 15.
112. VANDEPUTTE, M., L'athérosclérose coronarienne chez les Congolais: Etude anatomo-pathologique. *Ann. Soc. Belge. Méd. Trop.*, 1958, **38**, 211.
113. WAINWRIGHT, J., Atheroma in the African (Bantu) in Natal. *Lancet*, 1961, 366–8.
114. WALKER, A. R. P. and ARVIDSON, U. B., Fat intake, serum cholesterol concentration and atherosclerosis in the South African Bantu. I. Low fat intake and the age trend of serum cholesterol concentration in the South African Bantu. *J. Clin. Invest.*, 1954, **33**, 1358–65.
115. WALKER, A. R. P., Some aspects of the endocrinological picture of the South African Bantu. A population relatively free from mortality from coronary disease. *Hormones and Atherosclerosis*, Academic Press, New York, 1959, pp. 385–402.
116. WATANABE, G. and UEMATSU, M., Epidemiology of coronary disease in Japan. *Nisshin-Igaku (New Med.)*, 1957, **44**, 347.
117. WHITE, P. D., *Acta Cardiol.*, 1959, suppl. VIII.
118. WIG, K. L., MALHOTRA, R. P., CHITKARA, N. L. and GUPTA, S. P., Prevalence of coronary atherosclerosis in Northern India. *British Med. J.*, 1962, 24 Feb., 510.

119. WIJESEKARA, J. G., Myocardial infarction based on a study of 100 cases. *Ceylon M. J.* 1954, **2,** 149.
120. WOLFE, DE M. J. and WHITE, H. M., *Austr. Ass. Med.*, 1958, **7,** 47.
121. WU, T. C., Relative incidence of various types of heart disease in Chengtu. An analysis of 840 cases. *Chinese J. Int. Med.*, 1958, **6,** 33.
122. YONEYAMA, Y., KITAMURA, M. and YOSHIRAWA, H., Normal values of total serum cholesterol in healthy Tokyo citizens. *Clin. Chim. Acta*, 1962, **7,** 529–36.

CHAPTER 15

The Effect of Hormones

WE WILL examine first the steroid oestrogens.

A. *The Steroids*

We shall include a rapid examination of analogous structural effects in our consideration of the oestrogens.

Oestrogens are found in every part of the body, including the aortic wall. Labelled oestradiol (6-7 ³H) has been found in the aortic wall.[57] Local action is, therefore, possible. The facts would appear to be as follows:

I. Ovariectomy in women under 45 years of age appears to have a definitely beneficial effect on coronary involvement[100] and on hyperlipaemia.[79]

II. Oestradiol has been the subject of a large number of investigations.

(a) In the hen. Most authors have observed that its administration was followed by increase of the serum cholesterol and lipid phosphorus[40, 91, 125, 126] with, in the experiments of Pick *et al.*[92] and Drill *et al.*,[29] reduction in the cholesterol/phospholipid ratio.[92] (Infante *et al.*, 1963;[50] Whiteside *et al.*, 1965.[123]) *In vitro* it increased the activity of a monophosphoesterase of the aorta.

(b) In the rat. Oestradiol interfered with the biogenesis of cholesterol.[72, 95] Blood cholesterol was increased,[77] but in moderate degree.[55] (Borden, T. A. *et al.*, 1964.[15]

(c) In man. Certain authors have failed to note any change in serum lipids.[46,100]

(d) Study of experimentally produced aortic lesions revealed aggravation in fowls.[87] Conversely, coronary lesions appeared to be reduced.[30, 87, 90, 91] They were also reduced in the investigations of Malinow *et al.*,[57] but these authors added an injection of dextran before administration of the oestradiol.

III. Oestrone has been less extensively studied. Spain *et al.*[105] administered oestrone to rabbits and noted more rapid disappearance of cholesterol implanted by means of gelatin sponges. They failed to note any change in blood cholesterol.

In the adult rat the serum cholesterol level is under the influence of oestrone and is decreased in February and the autumn and increased in the winter and spring (Edgren, 1963[35]).

IV. Various synthetic derivatives have been studied.

(a) Quite a number of authors have noted reduction of blood cholesterol and β-lipoproteins following administration of ethinyl oestradiol.[5, 16, 34, 60] whereas Berezin et al.[8] observed opposite effects in man, namely increase of total lipids and of cholesterol in most cases.

(b) In birds 17-α-methyl, 17-OH, 5-(10)-estrene, 3-one increased cholesterol and, to a less extent, phospholipids, increased β-lipoproteins and reduced α-lipoproteins.[27, 34]

(c) In birds 16-chlorestrone-3-methyl ester reduced blood cholesterol and the β-lipoprotein fraction,[34] and it reduced the lesions both in men[97] and in birds.[29]

(d) The following substances:

$R_1 =$ H, Me, Et.

$R_2 =$ OH, OMe.

had no effect on blood cholesterol or increased it, as they did the phospholipids, but the cholesterol/phospholipid ratio was reduced. Sometimes the blood cholesterol was even slightly reduced.[25] Regression of lesions has, however, been noted.[29]

(e) The substances having the structure:

R = OH, Me, Et, ethionyl.

had little effect on cholesterol and left lesions unchanged.[29]

V. *Male hormones.* Male hormones would appear to have little or no effect on the various manifestations of atherosclerosis.

A. *Testosterone esters.* Testosterone propionates are inactive in fowls,[30, 92, 124] in rats[13, 71] and in rabbits.[56]

They were active only when there was serious alimentary overloading, in the non-castrated rabbit[22] and after abnormal intake of cholesterol.[56]

B. *Methyltestosterone.* Methyltestosterone did not reduce the blood cholesterol of dogs on diets poor in cholesterol.[1] It increased the cholesterol if the diet was rich in cholesterol and lipids. It increased lipid anomalies in man.[5]

C. *Androstenedione.* Androstenedione had no effect on the lipids of the dog.

D. *F.S.H. and L.H.* In chickens injections of F.S.H. and L.H. increased the blood cholesterol but aortic lesions were inhibited.[14]

E. *Cortisone.* The responses varied greatly:

(1) Cortisone had no effect or only a weak effect on the blood cholesterol of rats[48, 112] and rabbits.[45]

(2) It increased the blood cholesterol of rabbits[2, 3, 32, 116, 122] and in man.[2]

(3) It nevertheless reduced cholesterol deposits in animals.[3, 48, 96, 116, 122]

The rate of transfer of the serum cholesterol in the aortic wall, when compared with that observed in normal rabbits, was shown to be 14 times higher in the stationary phase of atherosclerosis. In the regressive phase there was no significant difference between the controls and the atherosclerotic animals. The administration of cortisone to normal rabbits and L-thyroxine to the atherosclerotic rabbits did not significantly affect the process of cholesterol transfer. The rate of transfer between the serum and the aortic wall was essentially the same in all the groups. This does not indicate any change in permeability to serum cholesterol, in the endothelial wall of the aorta. The increase of transfer of serum cholesterol in the atheromatous aortas is considered to arise as a consequence of the hypercholesterolaemia (Felt *et al.,* 1963[38]).

B. *The Effect of Compounds from the Thyroid Gland*

I. *Thyroid insufficiency, blood cholesterol and atherosclerotic lesions.* The investigations were concerned with spontaneous and induced myxoedema.

(1) Spontaneous myxoedema. In 1953 Malmros *et al.*[58] investigated the various serum lipids: total lipids, cholesterol, phospholipids and β-lipoproteins were increased.

(2) Study of thyroid function in atherosclerotics by means of radioactive iodine revealed dysfunction in one-third of the cases. The blood cholesterol could, however, be normal even in subjects with slight hypothyroidism and atherosclerosis.[47] Nikkila *et al.*[75] observed a slight degree of hypothyroidism in 20 per cent of twenty individuals with coronary involvement. Goitre was no more frequent in these patients than in normal subjects.

(3) Thyroidectomy increased the blood cholesterol. This effect was minimal (16–18 per cent) when the animal was receiving nothing but its ordinary food. These facts were established for rabbits[103, 119] and for rats.[17]

The effect was more pronounced when the rabbit was given cholesterol. The effect of thyroidectomy was seen to be quite definite when comparison was made with controls merely given the atherosclerogenic diet.[21, 117] The aortic deposits were more extensive.[118]

In the dog thyroidectomy resulted in appreciable increase of blood cholesterol, phospholipids and in the cholesterol/phospholipid ratio, but it either produced only a moderate increase or failed to produce any change in the β-lipoproteins.[60]

When thyroidectomy was associated with the administration of cholesterol, the same changes occurred but they were very much greater, and the β-lipoproteins were also involved in the general rise.[60]

(4) In the rat the ingestion of thiouracil precipitated hypothyroidism and was accompanied by a pronounced increase of blood cholesterol (34 per cent).[17]

In addition, the aorta was thickened and there were cholesterol deposits sometimes in small quantities.[62] When a supply of cholesterol was provided at the same time, there were plaques with lipophages and cellular reactions even in the rat, which is generally very resistant to atherosclerosis.[39]

In the dog the ingestion of thiouracil alone raised the blood cholesterol, phospholipids, the cholesterol/phospholipid ratio and the β-lipoproteins of the serum. When a considerable quantity of cholesterol was supplied in the diet, the increases were much greater. There was not, however, the exceptionally marked activity of thiouracil seen in the rat.[60]

(5) Destruction of the thyroid with ^{131}I. Although the rat's oxygen metabolism was observed to decline when ^{131}I was injected intraperitoneally, there was only a relatively slight increase of blood cholesterol (18 per cent).[17]

II. *Administration of thyroid extracts.* There have been investigations on hens and man.

(1) *The hen.* The results are often fairly difficult to explain and, at first sight, frequently appear to be contradictory. It would, in fact, appear that numerous factors can intervene and that the responses depend greatly on the quantity of extract administered.

(a) Blood cholesterol. These investigations were on fowls receiving an atherosclerogenic diet. Michel *et al.*[66] observed reduction of blood cholesterol which was quite definite but did not persist after treatment ceased. Reduction was also observed in the investigations of Stamler *et al.*[106–110] In this case it was considerable (33 per cent).

Blood phosphatides were also reduced.

(b) Aortic lesions were not modified by the administration of thyroid extract.[106, 110] Coronary lesions were less frequent but were of equal severity.

(c) When an atherosclerotic condition was produced by the administration of cholesterol and the cholesterol was then withdrawn, there was regression of the signs in the serum or arteries. When thyroxine was given during this return to the normal state, the changes were somewhat paradoxical. After two weeks the blood cholesterol was only slightly below that of the control group.

The aortic lesions were much more severe in the group which had received thyroid extracts. The coronary lesions were also more severe and more frequent.

Generally, therefore, thyroxine retarded the return to normal. It may be, as we shall see later, that the thyroxine damaged the wall as it was given in large dosage. Such lesions favour the deposit of lipids.

(2) *Man.* The effects can only be studied in the serum. Reductions have been observed in the blood cholesterol,[4, 69, 79, 88, 114-15] in S_f 0–12 and S_f 12–20 serum lipoproteins,[113-15] in the total cholesterol/phospholipid ratio[104] and in the β-lipoproteins.[69]

On the other hand, the non-esterified fatty acids were increased. It is thought that this was evidence of increased metabolism.

If dried thyroid is given to rabbits who had previously received labelled cholesterol ($4\text{-}^{14}C$), the radio-activity found in the aorta decreases when compared with rabbits who had not been given dried thyroid.

III. *Administration of thyroxine.* The results with thyroxine were comparable to those with the complete extract.

(1) It had quite a definite effect on the various forms of lipidaemia.

(a) In myxoedematous subjects blood cholesterol was reduced even with a dose which had no effect on basal metabolism or on the electro-cardiogram.[111]

(b) Thyroxine neutralized the hypercholesterolaemia produced by trini-trotoluene in thyroidectomized rats.[64]

(c) It reduced blood cholesterol in chickens which were on an atheros-clerogenic diet.[109]

(d) The reduction of the blood cholesterol was very slight in the normal rat and more marked in the rat receiving cholesterol.[17]

(e) A dose of 4–6 mg daily definitely reduced blood cholesterol in human subjects with high blood cholesterol, clinical evidence of atherosclerosis but normally functioning thyroids.[52, 114-15]

(f) Strisower *et al.*[114-115] also noted reduction in the S_f 0–12 and S_f 12–20 dliporoteins.

(2) On the other hand, the arterial lesion seen in the chicken on an athero-sclerogenic diet was unchanged.[109]

D-thyroxine administered to hypercholesterolaemic men lowers the cholesterolaemia but to be effective it requires to be given in progressively larger doses (Brosius, 1962[20]).

This same D-thyroxine reduces the coagulability (Bernheim *et al.*, 1963[10]).

IV. *Administration of iodine-containing precursors of thyroxine.* Here again one finds the same effects.

(1) Effect on blood cholesterol.

(a) In the hen. Two lots of chickens receiving cholesterol both showed increase of blood cholesterol. The increase was less in one group when it was given tri-iodothyronine or di-iodothyronine.[17, 66, 109] Michel et al.[66] observed the same effect with 3-5-5'-tri-iodothyronine but it was of shorter duration.

(b) In the rat. Michel et al.[68] injected trinitrotoluene (W.R. 1339) (para-iso-octyl-poly-oxyethylene-phenol) and produced a hypercholesterolemia in excess of 400 mg/100 ml within two days. The administration of thyroid hormone partly neutralized this excess. The inhibitory effect was proportional to the dose ingested; the following were the activities of the various iodine compounds:

3-5-3'-tri-iodothyronine	1100
3-3'-5'-tri-iodothyronine	19
3-3'-di-iodothyronine	54
3-3'-5-5'-tetra-iodothyronine	100

Best et al.[11, 12] also noted favourable effects on blood cholesterol.

(c) In man. Reductions of about 15 per cent have been observed.[28, 89] 3-3'-5'-tri-iodothyronine has sometimes failed to produce any change in the blood cholesterol,[93] but this result would appear to be analogous with the low figures reported by Michel et al.[68]

(2) An effect on arterial lesions was noted in the experiments of Stamler et al.[109]

V. *Synthetic analogues of thyroxine.* The synthetic analogues of thyroxine are numerous; they are acids:

3-5-3'-	tri-iodothyroacetic (triac)
3-5-5'-5'-	tetra-iodothyroacetic (tetrac)
3-5-3'-	tri-iodothyropropionic (triprop)
3-5-3'-5-	tetra-iodothyropropionic (tetprop)
3-5-3'-5'-	tetra-iodothyroformic

Most authors state that they reduce blood cholesterol.[6, 17, 18, 41, 49, 53, 64–66, 70, 78, 101, 121]

Flynn et al.[41] also noted that total lipids and the phospholipids in the blood were reduced.

Pitt-Rivers et al.[94] failed to note any change in rabbits given triac and an atherosclerogenic diet.

Eades et al.[33] published a simplified *in vitro* technique with a view to looking at the inhibitors of cholesterol biosynthesis. This technique uses acetate labelled with ^{14}C and rat liver homogenate as the source of the enzymes. Among the various compounds tested *in vitro* were thyropropionic acid (To P) and several of its iodinated analogues. These compounds inhibited the incorporation of labelled acetate into the non-saponifiable lipid fraction by about 60 per cent. The compounds tri-iodinated at 3, 3′, and 5′ only caused an inhibition of about 35 per cent, whereas the tetra-iodinated molecule seemed to stimulate the incorporation of acetate. These results indicate that in the compounds tested, the number and position of the iodine on the *p*-hydroxy-phenoxy-phenol, has an effect on the incorporation of acetate into cholesterol by rat liver homogenate.

Hypophysectomy as far as lipid metabolism and atherosclerosis is concerned acts in the same way as the antithyroid compounds (Patek *et al.*[86]).

C. *Nicotinic Acid* (pyridine-*β*-carboxylic acid)

The formula of nicotinic acid is:

It is a heterocyclic compound with conjugated ethylenic bonds (i.e. it exhibits resonance, which gives an additional energy level).

(1) This acid reduced induced cholesterolaemia in the hen,[45] the rabbit[23, 63, 82] and in the dog.[26, 54]

(2) It reduced the blood cholesterol, normal or increased, in man. [7, 9, 19, 24, 36, 43, 74, 80–2, 102]

(3) It also reduced the various other forms of lipidaemia in the dog[54] and in man.[43, 83]

(4) It was found, however, to have no effect generally on the blood cholesterol of the rat.[31, 44] It had no effect in certain experiments on the dog,[76] on the rabbit[42] and finally, on man.[59]

(5) The aortic deposits were reduced in induced atherosclerosis in the rabbit.[82]

D. *Pyridoxine* (2-methyl-3-hydroxy-4,5-di(hydroxymethyl) pyridine)

The formula (on following page) for pyridoxine shows that it is also a cyclic system with resonance.

(1) It reduced blood cholesterol slightly but significantly in man.[37]

(2) It was, however, inactive in the normal rabbit and in the rabbit given an atherosclerogenic diet.[61]

$$CH_2OH$$

(structure diagram with ring positions labeled (1)–(6), showing CH$_2$OH at (4), HO—C at (3), C—CH$_2$OH at (5), H$_3$C—C at (2), CH at (6), N at (1))

E. *Derivatives from Arachidonic Acid*

Von Euler on the one hand and Bergstrom on the other showed that the effects on the fats are brought about by compounds derived from arachidonic acid; they gave them the name of prostaglandin.

F. *The Role of Adrenaline*

Ever since the beginning of research into experimental atherosclerosis, adrenaline has been known to be capable of giving rise to lesions of the aortic wall, which usually have only a remote connection to those of atherosclerosis. Jagannathan *et al.*[51] showed that eight out of eleven monkeys receiving adrenaline presented some local changes of the intima, characterized by the accumulation of neutral fats and acid mucopolysaccharides.

The monkeys which received large doses of adrenaline showed a substantial decrease of serum cholesterol at the end of 2 weeks and this drop was maintained. In the monkeys which had received distilled water, the change of serum cholesterol was not significant.

References

1. ABELLE, L. L., MOSBACH, E. H. and KENDALL, F. E., Cholesterol metabolism in methyl testosterone-treated dogs. *Circulation*, 1959, **20**, 970.
2. ADLERSBERG, D., DRACHMAN, S. R. and SCHAEFER, L. E., Effects of cortisone and ACTH on serum lipids in animals: possible relationship to experimental atherosclerosis. *Circulation*, 1951, **4**, 475.
3. ADLERSBERG, D., SCHAEFER, L. E. and WANG, C. I., Adrenal cortex, lipid metabolism and atherosclerosis: experimental studies in the rabbit. *Science*, 1954, **120**, 319–20.
3a. ADLERSBERG, D., Adrenocortical hormones and experimental atherosclerosis. *Hormones and Atherosclerosis*, Academic Press, New York, 1959, 197–204.
4. BARNES, B. O., Prophylaxis of ischaemic heart disease by thyroid therapy. *Lancet*, 1959, 149–52.
5. BARR, D. P., RUSS, E. M. and EDER, H. A., Influence of estrogens on lipoproteins in atherosclerosis. *Trans. Ass. Amer. Phys.*, 1952, **65**, 102–12.
6. BAUER, H. G., MACGAVACK, T. H. and SWELL, L., Depression of the serum cholesterol level by triiodothyropropionic acid. *J. Endocr.*, 1959, **19**, 490.
7. BELLE, M. S. and HALPERN, M. M., Oral nicotinic acid for hyperlipemia. With emphasis on side effects. *Amer. J. Cardiol.*, 1958, **11**, 449–52.

8. BEREZIN, D. and VON STUDNITZ, W., The effect of the administration of sex hormones on serum lipids and lipoproteins in women. *Acta Endocr.*, 1957, **25**, 427–44.
9. BERGE, K. Y., ACHOR, R. W. P., CHRISTENSEN, N. A., POWER, M. H. and BARKER, N. W., Hypercholesterolemia and nicotinic acid: long-term study. *Circulation*, 1959, **20**, 671.
10. BERNHEIM, C., FORSTER, G., LUTHY, E. and VON PLANTA, Traitement de l'hypercholestérolémie, de l'hyperlipémie et de la xanthomatose tubéreuse par la D-thyroxine. *Schweiz. Med. Wschr.*, 1963, **93** (6), 238–42.
11. BEST, M. M. and DUNCAN, C. H., Thyroid hormones and cholesterol metabolism: effects of side-chain substitutions. *Circulation*, 1959, **20**, 981.
12. BEST, M. M. and DUNCAN, C. H., Effect of tetraiodothyroformic acid on oxygen consumption of the cholesterol-thiouracil-fed rat. *Amer. J. Physiol.*, 1959, **196**, 857–8.
13. BLANPIN, O. and ASCHKENASY, A., Action du propionate de testostérone sur les protéines sériques ainsi que sur le cholestérol et les phospholipides sériques et erythrocytaires chez des rats carencés en protéines. *C.R. Soc. Biol.*, 1959, **153**, 997–9.
14. BOLENE-WILLIAMS, C., ROBBARD, S. and KATZ, L. N., Effect of FSH and LH on cholesteremia and atherogenesis. *Amer. J. Physiol.*, 1951, **167**, 769.
15. BORDEN, T. A., WISLER, R. W. and HUGHES, R. H., Etude physicochimique du système lipo-protéinique chez le rat mâle normal et celui traité avec oestrogène par rapport à l'athérosclérose. *J. Atheroscler. Res.*, 1964, **4**, 477–96.
16. BOSSAC, E., FELDMAN, CHUNI WANG and ADLERSBERG, D., Effect of prolonged use of oestrogens on circulating lipids in patients with idiopathic hyperlipemia or idiopathic hypercholesterolemia. *Circulation*, 1959, **10**, 234–42.
17. BOYD, G. S., Thyroid function, thyroxine analogs and cholesterol metabolism in rats and rabbits. *Hormones and Atherosclerosis*, Academic Press, New York, 1959, pp. 49–62.
18. BOYD, G. S. and OLIVER, M. F., Thyroid hormones and plasma lipids. *Brit. Med. Bull.*, 1960, **16**, 138–42.
19. BRAND, V. VON and SEITZ, W., Hemmung der Synthese von Fettsaüren und Cholesterin in der Leber *in vitro* und Senkung des Cholesterin-Gehaltes des menschlichen Serums durch Nicotin-Säurenamid. *Med. Klin.*, 1960, **55**, 723–5.
20. BROSIUS, F. C., Jr., Dextro-thyroxine and cholesterol: dextrothyroxine therapy in patients with hypercholesterolemia and arteriosclerotic heart disease. *J. Kansas Med. Soc.*, 1962, **63**, 461.
21. BROWN, H. B. and PAGE, I. H., The effect of graded dosages of iodide on plasma and liver cholesterol of normal, cholesterol-fed and thyroidectomized rabbits. *Amer. Heart J.*, 1949, **38**, 479–80.
22. BRUGER, M., WRIGHT, I. S. and WILAND, J., Experimental atherosclerosis. V. Effect of testosterone propionate and estradiol dipropionate on the cholesterol content of the blood and the aorta in castrate female rabbits. *Arch. Path.*, 1943, **36**, 612.
23. CAVA, B. E., ACHOR, R. W. P., BERGE, K. G., WAKIN, K. G., EDWARDS, J. E., MAC-KENSIE, B. F. and BARKER, N. W., Effect of nicotinic acid on experimental atherosclerosis of rabbits. *Proc. Mayo Clin.*, 1959, **34**, 502–10.
24. CHAZIN, B. J., Effect of nicotinic acid on blood cholesterol. *Geriatrics*, 1960, **15**, 423–9.
25. COHEN, L., Serum phospholipids in coronary artery disease. *J. Lab. Clin. Med.*, 1959, **54**, 352–6.
26. COMESANA, F., NAVA, E., FISHLEDER, B. L. and SODI PALLARES, D., The hypocholesterolemic effect of nicotinic acid, phenyl ethyl acetic acid and a combination of both in dogs. Preliminary communication. *Amer. Heart J.*, 1958, **55**, 476–80.
27. COOK, D. L., EDGREN, R. A. and SAUNDERS, F. J., Lipid-shifting properties of 17 α-methyl-17-hydroxy-5(10)-oestren-3-one, a steroid in both estrogenic and androgenic activities. *Endocrinology*, 1958, **62**, 798–803.
28. DELMEZ, J. P. and ENGEL, E., Essai de traitement de l'hypercholestérolémie par la l-triiodothyronine. *J. Suisse Med.*, 1957, **6**, 133.
29. DRILL, V. A., COOK, D. L. and EDGREN, R. A., Effect of new steroids on blood lipids. *Hormones and Atherosclerosis*, Academic Press, New York, 1959, 247–64.

30. DRILL, V. A., EDGREN, R. A. and COOK, D. L., Production of estrogenic side effects of steroids in man. *Hormones and Atherosclerosis*, Academic Press, New York, 1959, 371–6.
31. DUCAN, L. E., BUCK, K. and LYNCH, A., A quantitative analysis of the development of experimental canine atherosclerosis. *Fed. Proc.*, 1960, **19**, 16.
32. DURY, A., SWELL, L., Cortisone effect on exogenous cholesterol metabolism: isotope observations in cholesterol-fed rabbits. *Proc. Soc. Exp. Biol.*, 1959, **100**, 850–2.
33. EADES, C. H. and PHILLIPS, G. E., Effect of thyropropionic acid T_0 P and its iodinated analogues on incorporation of acetate-1-C^{14} into cholesterol by rat's liver homogenates. *Endocrinology, U.S.A.*, 1963, **72** (4), 514–17.
34. EDER, H. A., The effects of sex hormones on serum lipids and lipoproteins. *Hormones and Atherosclerosis*, Academic Press, New York, 1959, 335–48.
35. EDGREN, R. A., Variations saisonnières dans la teneur du sang en cholestérol chez le rat et sa réponse à l'oestrone. *J. Atheroscler. Res.*, 1963, **3**, 206.
36. ELLERSEN, P. and HOBLOTH, N., Traitement de l'hypercholestérolémie par l'acide nicotinique. *Ugeskr. Laeg.*, 1959, **121**, 205–8.
37. FAILEY, R. B., Effect in man of large doses of pyridoxine on serum cholesterol. *Circ. Res.*, 1958, **6**, 203–6.
38. FELT, V., ROHLING, S., HLADOVEC, J. and VOHNOUT, S., Transfer rate of serum cholesterol into the rabbit aortic wall in various phases of atherosclerosis and after application of cortisone CR thyroxine. *J. Atheroscler. Res., Pays-Bas*, 1963, **3** (4), 301–8.
39. FILLIOS, L. C., ANDRUS, S. B., AMNN, G. V. and STARE, F. J., Experimental production of gross atherosclerosis in the rat. *J. Exp. Med.*, 1956, **104**, 539–54.
40. FLEISCHMANN, W. and FRIED, I. A., Studies on the hypercholesterolemia and hypercalcemia induced by estrogen in immature chicks. *Endocrinology*, 1945, **36**, 406.
41. FLYNN, P. F., SPLITTER, S., BALCH, H. and KINSELL, L. W., Effect of tri-iodothyropropionic acid on blood lipids. *Circulation*, 1959, **20**, 984.
42. FRIEDMAN, M. and BYERS, S., Evaluation of nicotinic acid as an hypocholesteremic and anti-atherogenic substance. *J. Clin. Invest.*, 1959, **38**, 1328–33.
43. GALBRAITH, P. A., PERRY, W. F. and BEAMISH, R. E., Effect of nicotinic acid on serumlipids in normal and atherosclerotic subjects. *Lancet*, 1959, 222–3.
44. GAYLOR, J. L., HARDY, R. W. F. and BAUMANN, C. A., Effects of nicotinic acid and related compounds on sterol metabolism in the chick and rat. *J. Nutrit.*, 1960, **70**, 293–301.
45. GELLER, J. H., FISHER, E. R. and TAPPER, E., Aortic QO^2 of normal, cholesterol-fed, hypertensive and cortisone treated rabbits. *Fed. Proc.*, 1960, **19**, 14.
46. GLASS, S. J., ENGELBERG, H., MARCUS, R., JONES, H. B. and GOFMAN, J., Lack of effect of administered estrogen on the serum lipids and lipoproteins of male and female patients. *Metab. Clin. Exp.*, 1953, **2**, 133.
47. GOLDEBERG, G. G. and LEONOV, P. M., La funzione tiroidea nell'arteriosclerosi. *Minerva Med.*, 1959, **50**, 325.
48. GORDON, D., KOBERNICK, S. D., MACMILLAN, G. C. and DUFF, G. L., The effect of cortisone on the serum lipids and on the development of experimental cholesterol atherosclerosis in the rabbit. *J. Exp. Med.*, 1954, **99**, 371–86.
49. HILL, S. R., BARKER, S. B., MACNEIL, J. H., TINGLEY, J. O. and HIBBETT, L. L., The metabolic effect of the acetic and propionic acid analogs of thyroxine and triiodothyronine. *J. Clin. Invest.*, 1960, **39**, 523–33.
50. INFANTE, R. and POLONOVSKI, J., Biosynthèse des lipides dans l'hyperlipémie par oestrogènes chez le poulet. *J. Atheroscler. Res.*, 1963, **3**, 309.
51. JAGANNATHAN, S. N., MADHAVAN, T. V. and GOPALAN, C., L'effet de l'adrénaline sur la structure de l'aorte et sur le cholestérol sérique chez les singes. *J. Atheroscler. Res.*, 1964, **4**, 335.
52. JONES, R. J., Serum cholesterol reduction with D-thyroxine. *Circulation*, 1959, **20**, 979.
53. JOUAN, P., HAZARD, C., PAILHERET, J. and BARRE, F., Action de l'acide 3.5.3'-triiodothyroacétique sur les taux du cholestérol sanguin. *Ann. Endocr. (Paris)*, 1958, **19**, 473–7.

54. KRAUPP, O. and SCHNETZ, E., Der Einfluss des Heparins auf die hypocholesterin-
    ämische Wirkung der Nicotinsäure. *Arch. Exp. Path. Pharmak.*, 1959, **235**, 103–12.
55. LOEB, H. G., Effet du benzoate d'oestradiol sur les lipides du sérum de rats soumis à
    un régime riche en graisses. *Proc. Soc. Exp. Biol.*, 1942, **49**, 340–2.
56. LUDDEN, J. B., BRUGGER, M. and WRIGHT, I. S., Effect of testosterone propionate and
    estradiol dipropionate on the cholesterol content of the blood and aorta of rabbits.
    Endocrinology, 1941, **28**, 999–1001.
57. MALINOW, M. R., Distribution of oestradiol–6–7–³H in the arteries of normal and
    cholesterol fed rabbits. *Acta Endocr.*, 1959, **31**, 500–4.
58. MALMROS, H. and SHAHN, R., Lipid metabolism in myxedema. *Acta Med. Scand.*, 1953,
    145, 361–5.
59. MANCINI, M. and LAVITOLA, G., Acido nicotinico e livello del colesterolo totale nel
    siero e nelle frazioni α e β lipoproteiche. *Osped. Psichiat.*, 1956, **24**, 153; *Zbl. Ges.
    Neurol. Psychiat.*, 1958, **144**, 317.
60. MARMORSTON, J., ROSENFELD, S. and MELH, J., Experimental atherosclerosis in dogs.
    Hormones and Atherosclerosis, Academic Press, New York, 1959, 213–28.
61. MARTENS, F. W. and HOSKINS, D. W., Failure of parenterally administered pyridoxine
    to influence serum cholesterol levels and development of atherosclerosis in cholesterol
    fed rabbits. *Circ. Res.*, 1958, **6**, 159–62.
62. MARX, W. and MARX, L., Thyroid activity and tissue cholesterol distribution. *Amer.
    Heart J.*, 1949, **38**, 473–4.
63. MERRIL, J. M., BURKHALTER, J., KEITH, B. and EARLEY, W., Comparative effects of
    glycocyamine and nicotinic acid on experimental cholesterol atherosclerosis in rabbits.
    Circulation, 1959, **20**, 987–8.
64. MICHEL, R. and TRUCHOT, R., Effets de l'acide 3.5.3'-triiodothyroacétique sur le
    cholestérol et le coenzyme A du rat thyroïdectomisé. *C.R. Soc. Biol.*, 1958, **152**, 1071–3.
65. MICHEL, R. and TRUCHOT, R., Dégradation hépatique du cholestérol et thyroxine.
    C.R. Soc. Biol., 1959, **153**, 210–12.
66. MICHEL, R., TRUCHOT, R. and CABANNE, F., Influence de la 3.5.3'-triiodothyronine et
    de l'acide 3.5.3'-triiodothyroacétique sur la cholestérolémie du poulet radio-
    thyroïdectomisé. *C.R. Soc. Biol.*, 1959, **153**, 540–3.
67. MICHEL, R. and TRUCHOT, R., Sur la concentration hépatique du cholestérol chez le
    rat traité par la thyroxine. *C.R. Soc. Biol.*, 1959, **153**, 572–4.
68. MICHEL, R., TRUCHOT, R. and PETITMENGIN, M., Dosage biologique de l'effet anti-
    cholestérol de divers produits hormonaux thyroïdiens. *Bull. Soc. Chim. Biol.*, 1959, **41**,
    842–5.
69. MOSES, C., DANOWSKI, T. S. and SWITKES, H. I., Alterations in cholesterol and
    lipoprotein partition in euthyroid adults by replacement doses of dessicated thyroid.
    Circulation, 1958, **18**, 761.
70. MOSES, C. and DANOWSKI, T. S., Hormonal factors in the partition of lipoprotein
    cholesterol in healthy subjects. *Circulation*, 1959, **20**, 988.
71. MOSKOWITZ, M. S., MOSKOWITZ, A. A., BRADFORD, W. L. and WISSLER, R. W.,
    Changes in serum lipids and coronary arteries of the rat in response to estrogens.
    Arch. Path., 1956, **61**, 245–63.
72. MUKHERJEE, S. and ALFIN-SLATER, A., Effect of gonadectomy on biosynthesis of
    cholesterol from (¹⁴C) acetate in rat liver slices. *IVᵉ Congrès Chimie Biologique, Vienne*,
    1958, p. 204.
73. MYASNIKOV, A. L., MYASNIKOV, L. A. and ZAITZEV, V. F., The influence of thyroid
    hormones on cholesterol metabolism in experimental atherosclerosis in rabbits.
    J. Atheroscler. Res., Pays-Bas, 1963, **3** (4), 295–300.
74. NAVA, A., COMESANA, F., LOZANO, E., FISHLEDER, B. L. and SODI PALLARES, D., The
    effect of nicotinic acid, phenyl-ethylacetamide and a combination of both drugs on
    hypercholesterolaemic dogs and human beings. *Amer. Heart J.*, 1958, **56**, 598–606.
75. NIKKILA, E. A. and KARLSSON, K., Thyroid function and clinical coronary heart
    disease. *Acta Med. Scand.*, 1960, **166**, 195–203.

76. NORCIA, L. N., BROWN, H. J. and FURMAN, R. H., Non-hypocholesterolaemic action of nicotinic acid in dogs. *Lancet*, 1959, 1255.

77. OKEY, R. and LYMAN, M. M., Food intake and estrogenic hormone effects on serum and tissue cholesterol. *J. Nutrit.*, 1956, **60**, 65–74.

78. OLIVER, M. F. and BOYD, G. S., The influence of triiodothyroactic acid on the circulating lipids and lipoproteins in euthyroid men with coronary disease. *Lancet*, 1957, 124–8.

79. OLIVER, M. F. and BOYD, G. S., Effect of bilateral ovariectomy on coronary artery disease and serum lipid levels. *Lancet*, 1959, **2**, 690–4.

80. O'REILLY, P. O., DEMAY, M. and KOTLOWSKY, K., Cholesterolemia and nicotinic acid. *Amer. Arch. Intern. Med.*, 1957, **100**, 797–801.

81. O'REILLY, P. O., CALLBECK, M. J. and HOFFER, A., Sustained-release nicotinic acid (nicospan). *Canad. Med. Ass. J.*, 1959, **80**, 359–62.

82. PARSONS, W. B. and FLINN, J. H., Alterations in serum cholesterol and lipoprotein cholesterol by nicotinic acid. *Circulation*, 1958, **18**, 785.

83. PARSONS, W. B., Reduction in serum cholesterol level and other metabolic effects of large doses of nicotinic acid. *Circulation*, 1959, **20**, 747.

84. PARSONS, W. B., Experiences with *in vivo* production of fibrinolysis following parenteral administration if nicotinic acid in humans. *Circulation*, 1959, **20**, 989.

85. PARSONS, W. B. and FLINN, J. H., Reduction of cholesterol levels and β-lipoprotein cholesterol levels by nicotinic acid. *Arch. Intern. Med.*, 1959, **103**, 783–90.

86. PATEK, P. R., BERNICK, S., ERSHOFF, B. H. and WELLS, A., Induction of atherosclerosis by cholesterol feeding in the hypophysectomized rat. *Amer. J. Pathology*, 1963, **42**, 137–50.

87. PECK, W., WOODS, W. and RADAKOVICH, M., The effect of estrogen-like compounds on atherosclerosis in cholesterol fed cockerels. *Fed. Proc.*, 1960, **19**, 17.

88. PETERS, J. P. and AMN, E. B., The interrelations of serum lipids in patients with thyroid disease. *J. Clin. Invest.*, 1943, **22**, 715.

89. PEZOLD, F. A. and DROEGE, R., Untersuchungen an gesunden und klinisch manifesten Arteriosklerotikern über den Einfluss oraler Gaben von Triiodthyroin auf den Serum-Lipid-Konzentrationen, *Ärztl. Forsch.*, 1959, **9**, 561–7.

90. PICK, R., Estrogen-induced regression of coronary atherosclerosis in cholesterol-fed chicks. *Fed. Proc.*, 1952, **11**, 122–3.

91. PICK, R., STAMLER, J. and KATZ, L. N., Influence of estrogens on lipids and atherosclerosis in experimental animals. *Hormones and Atherosclerosis*, Academic Press, New York, 1959, pp. 229–46.

92. PICK, R., STAMLER, J., ROBBARD, S. and KATZ, L. N., Effects of testosterone and castration on cholesterolemia and atherogenesis in chicks on high fat, high cholesterol diets. *Circulation*, 1959, **7**, 202–4.

93. PITTMAN, J. A., TINGLEY, J. O., NICKERSON, J. F. and HILL, S. R., Antimetabolic activity of 3,3′,5-triiodo-DL-thyronine (T′3) in man. *Metabolism*, 1960, **9**, 293.

94. PITT-RIVERS, R. and TROTTER, W. R., Effect of triac on the reabsorption of cholesterol from atheromatous lesions in the aorta of the rabbit. *Brit. J. Exp. Path.*, 1957, **38**, 97–9.

95. PLAGGE, J. C., MARASSO, F. J. and ZIMMERMAN, H. J., Inhibition par oestrogènes du foie gras d'origine alimentaire. *Met. Clin. Exp.*, 1958, **7**, 154–61.

96. PRIOR, J. T., ROHNER, R. F., CAMP, F. A. and RUSTAD, H., The effects of cortisone upon aortic intimal repair in the hypercholesterolemic rabbit. *Arch. Path.*, 1959, **67**, 159.

97. RIVIN, A. U., Sc 8246, a new oestrogen analogue: lipoprotein effects with minimal feminization. *Metabolism*, 1959, **8**, 704–8.

98. RIVIN, A. U., Jaundice occurring during nicotinic acid therapy for hypercholesterolemia. *J. Amer. Med. Ass.*, 1959, **170**, 2088–9.

99. ROBINSON, R. W., COHEN, W. D. and HIGANO, N., Estrogen replacement therapy in women with coronary atherosclerosis. *Ann. Intern. Med.*, 1958, **48**, 95–101; *Canad. Med. Ass. J.*, 1958, **78**, 734.

100. ROBINSON, R. W., HIGANO, N. and COHEN, W. D., Effects of estradiol-17α in males with coronary heart disease. *Circulation*, 1959, **20**, 990.

101. RUEGAMER, W. R., ALPERT, M. and SILVERMAN, F. R., Thyroxine analogues and the control of plasma and liver cholesterol concentration. *Fed. Proc.*, 1959, **18**, 313.

102. RUTTER, N. and MYELER, L., Modifications cutanées après traitement par acide nicotinique en fortes doses. *Ned. T. Geneesk.*, 1960, **23**, 1114.

103. SHAPIRO, S., Influence of thyroidectomy, splenectomy, gonadectomy and suprarenalectomy upon the development of experimental atherosclerosis in the rabbit. *J. Exp. Med.*, 1927, **45**, 595–607.

104. SOFFER, A., YU, P. N. G., EPSTEIN, M. A. and OLSAN, E. S., Serum lipids studies in euthyroid subjects following the administration of thyroid. *Amer. J. Med. Sci.*, 1951, **222**, 426–35.

105. SPAIN, D. M., ARISTIZABAL, N. and ORES, R., Effect of oestrogens on resolution of local cholesterol implants. *Arch. Path.*, 1959, **68**, 30–3.

106. STAMLER, J., BOLENE, C., LEVINSON, E. and DUDLEY, M., The lipotropic action of dessicated thyroid in the cholesterol-fed chick. *Endocrinology*, 1950, **46**, 382–6.

107. STAMLER, J., BOLENE, C., KATZ, L. N., HARRIS, R., SILBER, E. N., MILLER, A. J. and AKMAN, L., Studies on spontaneous and cholesterol-induced atherosclerosis and lipid metabolism in the chick. The effects of some lipotropic and hormonal factors. *Amer. Heart J.*, 1949, **38**, 466.

108. STAMLER, J., SILBER, E. N., MILLER, A. J., AKMAN, L., BOLENE, C. and KATZ, L. N., The effect of thyroid and of dinitrophenol-induced hypermetabolism on plasma and tissue lipids and atherosclerosis in the cholesterol-fed chick. *J. Lab. Clin. Med.*, 1950, **35**, 351–61.

109. STAMLER, J., PICK, R. and KATZ, L. N., Further observations on the effect of thyroid hormone preparations on cholesterolemia and atherogenesis in cholesterol-fed cockerels. *Circulation Res.*, 1958, **6**, 825–9.

110. STAMLER, J., PICK, R. and KATZ, L. N., Influences of thyroid, pancreatic and adrenal hormones on lipid metabolism and atherosclerosis in experimental animals. *Hormones and Atherosclerosis*, Academic Press, New York, 1959, pp. 173–95.

111. STARR, P., Depression of the serum cholesterol level in myxedematous patients by an oral dosage of sodium dextrothyroxine which has no effect on the basal metabolic rate or electrocardiogram. *J. Clin. Endocr.*, 1960, **20**, 116–19.

112. STENGER, E. G., Der Cholesteringehalt verschiedener Rattenorgane unter dem Einfluss antiphlogistischwirkender Pharmaka. *Arch. Intern. Pharmacodyn.*, 1955, **102**, 403–18.

113. STRISOWER, B., GOFMAN, J. W., GALIONI, E. F., RUBINGER, J. H., POUTEAU, J. and GUZVICH, P., Long-term effect of dried thyroid on serum-lipoprotein and serum-cholesterol levels. *Lancet*, 1957, 120–3.

114. STRISOWER, B., ELMINGER, P., GOFMAN, J. W. and DE LALLA, O., The effect of L-thyroxine on serum lipoprotein and cholesterol concentrations. *J. Clin. Endocr.*, 1959, **19**, 117–26.

115. STRISOWER, E. H., Effect of desiccated thyroid substance and thyroid congeners upon serum lipoproteins and serum cholesterol levels. *Hormones and Atherosclerosis*, Academic Press, New York, 1959, pp. 315–33.

116. STUMPF, H. H. and WILENS, S. L., Inhibitory effect of cortisone hyperlipemia on arterial lipid deposition in cholesterol-fed rabbits. *Proc. Soc. Exp. Biol.*, 1954, **86**, 219–23.

117. TURNER, K. B. and KAYAT, G. B., Studies on the prevention of cholesterol atherosclerosis in rabbits. II. The influence of thyroidectomy upon the protective action of potassium iodide. *J. Exp. Med.*, 1933, **58**, 127–35.

118. TURNER, K. B. and BIDWELL, E. H., Further observations on the blood cholesterol of rabbits in relation to atherosclerosis. *J. Exp. Med.*, 1935, **62**, 721–32.

119. TURNER, K. B., PRESENT, C. H. and BIDWELL, E. H., The role of the thyroid in the regulation of the blood cholesterol of rabbits. *J. Exp. Med.*, 1938, **67**, 111–27.

120. TURNER, K. B. and DELAMATER, A., Effect of thyrotropic hormone on blood cholesterol of thyroidectomized rabbits. *Proc. Soc. Exp. Biol.*, 1942, **49**, 150–2.

121. Weston, R. E., The effects of 3.5.3' triiodothyropropionic acid on serum lipids of hypercholesterolemic euthyroid and hypothyroid subjects. *J. Clin. Invest.*, 1959, **38**, 1054.
122. Wang, C. I., Schaefer, L. E. and Adlersberg, D., Experimental studies on the relations between adrenal cortex, plasma lipids and atherosclerosis. *Endocrinology*, 1955, **56**, 628–38.
123. Whiteside, C. H., Fluckiger, H. B., Longenecker, J. B., Barboriak, J. and Sarett, H. P., L'hypercholestérolémie chez le poussin ayant reçu une injection de β-oestradiol. *J. Atheroscler. Res.*, 1965, **5**, 1–8.
124. Wong, H. Y. C., Anderson, J. E., Kimura, T. and Johnson, F. B., Changes in blood cholesterol and atherogenesis in roosters by exercise and androgen on plain mash after an "atherogenic diet". *Circulation*, 1958, **18**, 801.
125. Wong, H. Y. C., Johnson, F. B., Liu, B. and Shim, R., Comparative actions of female and male sex hormones on aortic atherosclerosis of cockerels fed a cholesterol sugar diet. *Circulation*, 1959, **20**, 993.
126. Zondek, B. and Mark, L., The induction of lipemia and calcemia in the cock by means of oestrogenic hormone. *Arch. Int. Pharmacodyn.*, 1959, **61**, 77–91.

CHAPTER 16

Conclusions

Theoretical Conclusions

NOBODY today can claim to have a theory for the physico-chemical or chemical mechanism of atherosclerosis.

To clear up a pathogenesis which appears singularly complex, more than in any other subject one is forced to use animal experiments to add to the chemical observations. But the analogies between the identity of the provoked lesion and the spontaneous lesion are poor indeed. "In biology phenomena are complicated by their inter-relationship to such an extent that the principles represented by the theories which we have been able to produce, are only provisional and to such an extent hypothetical that our deductions, although very logical, are completely uncertain and in any case cannot be experimentally verified", said Claude Bernard in his *Experimental Medicine*. And meanwhile, the experiment, following the expression of Goethe, "Becomes the only mediator between the object, the objective and the subjective". But here there is no lack of hypotheses. The mechanism that we are looking for comes from a number of causes which can be looked at with some experiments, but one should isolate them from each other which then reduces their significance. One can, however, use some of the experiments but one must distinguish between those capable of discovering the primary cause, those which demonstrate the illness and the additional causes which sometimes become the principal trouble but which are really only secondary.

I. What are the causes of the probable sensitive spots found in the arteries? Why is it that when subjects are placed under the same conditions of climate, diet, emotion, etc., one does not show any symptoms, while another subject similar in all ways, develops parietal lesions, often giving rise to thrombosis?

Certainly ageing which alters the cellular components, especially proteins and slows down their normal replacement, may be the principal cause but there are young atherosclerosis cases as is shown by early coronaries.

Should heredity be incriminated or to use a more chemical term, should one imagine an abnormal arrangement of the DNA? Our knowledge of the nucleoproteins and their anabolism has grown considerably during the last few years. But this is in the normal subject, it is not the same in atherosclerosis and unfortunately we will perhaps have to wait a long time to answer the questions posed by this class of compounds.

The deposits of fibrin in spontaneous lesions and of cholesterol in the experimental forms may asphyxiate the wall underlying the intima to produce the primary lesion. But it is not a matter of one hypothesis only. Some changes in the permeability of the cell have also been envisaged as well as osmotic properties but these are problematical and in fact ignore the origin of the lesion.

II. The formation of the deposits. Cholesterol is quantitatively the major compound in the atherosclerotic plaques. A small number of these cholesterol deposits are of external origin; in the majority of cases, the steroids are of internal origin formed in the organism, where their synthesis depends on the saturated fatty acids as well as sucrose. The triglycerides can constitute an important element by their presence and their action attracts more and more the attention of those who study these questions. Proteins by their hypertrophy dominate in the formation of pure sclerosis. The cause of such an anomaly is beyond us. On the contrary they more often slow down the rate of development of the illness.

All these remarks ought to lead to some practical conclusions.

III. The exchanges between the lipoproteins of the blood and those of the surrounding cells. Alterations of protein fractions can falsify these exchanges.

Dietary Conclusions

The diet which is required in atherosclerosis involves two distinct points. Firstly, a quantitative consideration. The meals which ought to be taken in moderate quantity so as not to strain the already tired heart should also be defined by their total calorific value. One should not get any fattening of the sick person, so that weighing each day will be most useful. If possible, it is desirable to recover the same weight as at the age of 20 and one can say that achieving this is difficult if not impossible.

Bread will do to control the weight, a reduction of bread very often leads to a very rapid fall of weight and on the contrary if the weight tends to fall too rapidly, then bread taken in more or less greater quantities can re-establish the equilibrium. Finally, it ought to be remembered that an excessive reduction of weight in the elderly person should not be countenanced.

Let us now examine the qualitative conditions and see what foods can be harmful in increasing the deposits at the level of the atheroma, cholesterol being one of the principal constituents of these deposits.

Cholesterol has two origins, firstly it can be preformed. This is a case which ought to be considered although it certainly does not represent the most important or frequent form. Firstly, certain products ought to be eliminated for they contain very large quantities of preformed cholesterol: brains and crustacea which contain 2 per cent of cholesterol will be eliminated. Around the kidney there are found fats which very often contain fragments of the adrenals, which themselves contain from 2 to 10 per cent cholesterol. Consequently it will be wise to do without kidneys which are always surrounded by perirenal fat. This fat becomes forgotten in the diet and is thus introduced surreptitiously and in a way that is often ignored by the patient.

The greater part of cholesterol that is found in the body arises from biosynthesis, that is to say that cholesterol is built up from acetyl coenzyme A which comes from either saturated fatty acids or carbohydrates. One should thus eliminate saturated fatty acids from the diet in atherosclerosis, which is not always easy. It is necessary first to define them. To simplify, we say that the saturated fatty acids are solid at room temperature, that is to say around 20°C, whereas the unsaturated fatty acids on the contrary are liquid. The saturated fatty acids are the major constituents of butter and also milk where they are found in suspension and not in solution. They are already solid in cream which is less dangerous than butter since it contains only half the fat by weight, but generally cooks use twice the amount that one can take.

Finally, one will eliminate solid margarine and the vegetable fats which starts off as a liquid containing excellent fats but which becomes altered by saturation at the double bonds and ends up with the same consistency as butter. The fats have been submitted to a reduction which removes all their dietetic qualities. Finally we have seen that animal fats also contain large quantities of saturated fatty acids and that among them the most important were those from mutton.

To sum up, we eliminate butter and milk products in general, margarine and also meat fat. One can eat meat, however, and it is important that in atherosclerosis meat is eaten and particularly by the elderly. But it is easy to get rid of fats, the visible fats with a knife and the intercellular fats by warming. The latter are removed by preparing the meat in the form of a grill. Obviously there remains the intracellular fats. It is difficult to get rid of all of them; on heating the cells burst and a certain amount escapes, but actually it does not all disappear. This is a necessary drawback that we do not know how to deal with. A meat soup contains as much fat as the meat so it is the grill which represents the essential element of the diet in atherosclerosis.

We have seen that eggs and particularly egg yolks contribute fatty acids of which a relatively large quantity is made up of the saturated fatty acids. Another disadvantage which is not at first apparent arises from the fact that these compounds are present in a colloidal form. During digestion the colloidal structure should be destroyed but a certain amount always remains. Now colloids have a tendency to fasten on to the walls of the vessels they encounter and consequently eggs can be dangerous from this point of view. Without being too strict it is advisable not to give an egg ration of more than one or two a week at the most.

Fish, on the other hand, are rich in polyunsaturated fatty acids with long carbon chains which can only be considered as beneficial to the recovery of these patients. They will then be recommended as often as possible. (Certain fish such as sardines, mackerel or cod are very moderately priced.) Vegetables and fruit are obviously one of the basic requirements of the diet and, in general less rich in saturated fats. They can be prepared in many different ways. It is the same for potatoes and pasta, while in the last two cases it is advisable to avoid making the patient more obese, as potatoes cause a very rapid increase in weight, pasta seem to be better tolerated, although the reason for this cannot easily be explained. In Italy, for example, where pasta is frequently used, and is a customary part of every meal, the Italians are, surprisingly, slim and do not appear affected by this kind of diet.

To make palatable a diet which would otherwise be diffcult to accept because of its limitations, it follows that certain seasonings should be added to the dishes concerned. Although salad made with olive oil would appear the most suitable method of presentation, large or small quantities of maize oil can be added according to the seriousness of the illness. Maize oil has a less savoury and not quite so delicate taste as olive oil and gives the impression of a watery and not too pleasant liquid. However, it can be tolerated when mixed with olive oil in various quantities according to the circumstances. To complete it, a certain number of sauces could be added, sauces which are ready manufactured, but liquid, and in particular tomato sauces, which everybody is familiar with. Fresh fruit could be replaced by stewed fruit, served in different ways, but it is necessary in all cases to avoid putting in too large a quantity of sugar, to agree with the latest ideas expressed against sucrose. Although from this list can be made up some very acceptable menus, we only need, for example, what makes up the basic diet of some families in the south of France, in particular Provence, where oil has replaced butter which is never used, and cookery is nevertheless often delicious.

Index